Notes for Cellists

NOTES FOR PERFORMERS

Kyle Dzapo, Series Editor

Notes for Flutists
Kyle Dzapo

Notes for Clarinetists
Albert R. Rice

Notes for Violists
David M. Bynog

Notes for Cellists
Miranda Wilson

Notes for Cellists

A Guide to the Repertoire

MIRANDA WILSON

Oxford University Press is a department of the University of Oxford.
It furthers the University's objective of excellence in research, scholarship,
and education by publishing worldwide. Oxford is a registered trade mark of
Oxford University Press in the UK and in certain other countries.

Published in the United States of America by Oxford University Press
198 Madison Avenue, New York, NY 10016, United States of America.

© Oxford University Press 2024

All rights reserved. No part of this publication may be reproduced, stored in a retrieval system,
or transmitted, in any form or by any means, without the prior permission in writing of Oxford
University Press, or as expressly permitted by law, by license or under terms agreed with the
appropriate reprographics rights organization. Inquiries concerning reproduction outside the scope
of the above should be sent to the Rights Department, Oxford University Press, at the address above.

You must not circulate this work in any other form
and you must impose this same condition on any acquirer

CIP data is on file at the Library of Congress

ISBN 9780197623749 (pbk.)
ISBN 9780197623732 (hbk.)

DOI: 10.1093/9780197623770.001.0001

The manufacturer's authorised representative in the EU for product safety is
Oxford University Press España S.A. of El Parque Empresarial San Fernando
de Henares, Avenida de Castilla, 2 – 28830 Madrid (www.oup.es/en or
product.safety@oup.com). OUP España S.A. also acts as importer into Spain
of products made by the manufacturer.

*This book is dedicated to my dear father,
Roger Wilson, who taught me how to write about music.*

Contents

From the Series Editor — xi
Preface — xiii

1 THE DAWN OF AN ERA

1.1 Domenico Gabrielli (1651/1659–1690):
Ricercar No. 2 in A Minor (1689) — 3

1.2 Johann Sebastian Bach (1685–1750): Suite No. 3 in
C Major, BWV 1009 — 6

1.3 Antonio Vivaldi (1678–1741): Sonata in B♭ Major,
RV 46 (also known as Op. 14, No. 6) — 10

1.4 Jean-Baptiste Barrière (1707–1747): Sonata IV in
G Major from *Livre IV* (ca. 1739) — 14

2 CLASSICAL VIRTUOSI

2.1 Luigi Boccherini (1743–1805): Sonata in A Major,
G. 4 (ca. 1770s) — 21

2.2 (Franz) Joseph Haydn (1732–1809): Concerto in
C Major, Hob. VIIb:1 (ca. 1762/1765) — 26

2.3 Ludwig van Beethoven (1770–1827): Sonata in A Major for
Piano and Cello, Op. 69 (ca. 1808) — 32

3 A MARRIAGE OF TRUE MINDS: THE ROMANTIC CELLO-PIANO SONATA

3.1 Fanny Hensel, born Fanny Mendelssohn-Bartholdy
(1805–1847): *Sonata o Fantasia* H-U 238 and
Capriccio H-U 247 for cello and piano (1829) — 39

3.2 Felix Mendelssohn-Bartholdy (1809–1847): Sonata No. 2
in D Major for Cello and Piano, Op. 58 (1843) — 43

3.3 Frédéric Chopin (1810–1849): Sonata in G Minor,
     Op. 65 (1845–47)   49

3.4 Louise Farrenc (1804–1875): Sonata in B♭ Major,
     Op. 46 (1858)   53

3.5 Johannes Brahms (1833–1897): Sonata No. 1 in E Minor,
     Op. 38 (1862–65)   58

3.6 Ethel Smyth (1858–1944): Sonata No. 2 in A Minor,
     Op. 5 (1887)   62

4 PATHWAYS TO IMPRESSIONISM

4.1 Camille Saint-Saëns (1835–1921): Cello Concerto No. 1 in
     A Minor, Op. 33 (1872)   69

4.2 Édouard Lalo (1823–1892): Cello Concerto in
     D Minor (1877)   73

4.3 Gabriel Fauré (1845–1924): *Élégie* for Cello and Piano,
     Op. 24 (1880)   78

4.4 Claude Debussy (1862–1918): Sonata in D Minor (1915)   81

5 THE GREAT CONCERTOS

5.1 Robert Schumann (1810–1856): Concerto in A Minor for
     Cello and Orchestra, Op. 129 (1850–54)   89

5.2 Pyotr Ilich Tchaikovsky (1840–1893): *Variations on a
     Rococo Theme* for Cello and Orchestra, Op. 33 (1876–77)   96

5.3 Antonín Dvořák (1841–1904): Concerto in B Minor
     for Cello and Orchestra, Op. 104 (1894–95)   101

5.4 Ernest Bloch (1880–1959): *Schelomo:
     Rhapsodie Hébraïque* (1915–16)   110

5.5 Edward Elgar (1857–1934): Concerto in E Minor for
     Cello and Orchestra, Op. 85 (1919)   117

5.6 Dmitri Dmitriyevich Shostakovich (1906–1975):
     Cello Concerto No. 1 in E♭ Major, Op. 107 (1959)   123

6 BEYOND ROMANTICISM: NEW DIRECTIONS IN THE SONATA

6.1 Serge Rachmaninoff (1873–1943): Sonata in G Minor, Op. 19 (1901) — 133

6.2 Samuel Barber (1910–1981): Sonata in C Minor, Op. 6 (1932) — 139

6.3 Sergei Prokofiev (1891–1953): Sonata for Cello and Piano, Op. 119 (1949) — 144

7 SOLOS FROM EASTERN EUROPE

7.1 Zoltán Kodály (1882–1967): Sonata for Solo Cello, Op. 8 (1915) — 151

7.2 György Ligeti (1923–2006): Sonata for Cello Solo (1948/1953) — 155

7.3 Sofia Gubaidulina (b. 1931): *Ten Preludes* for Solo Cello (1974) — 159

8 HOLY MINIMALISM

8.1 Arvo Pärt (b. 1935): *Spiegel im Spiegel* for Cello and Piano (1978) — 165

8.2 Sir John Tavener (1944–2013): *The Protecting Veil* for Cello and String Orchestra (1988) — 169

9 THE NEW VIRTUOSITY

9.1 Benjamin Britten (1913–1976): Suite for Cello No. 1, Op. 72 (1964) — 175

9.2 Coleridge-Taylor Perkinson (1932–2004): *Lamentations: Black/Folk Song Suite* (1973) — 179

9.3 Bright Sheng (b. 1955): *Seven Tunes Heard in China* (1995) — 183

9.4 Giovanni Sollima (b. 1962): *Alone* for Solo Cello (1998) — 188

10 AMERICAN VOICES

10.1 Dorothy Rudd Moore (1940–2022): *Dirge and Deliverance* for Cello and Piano (1971) — 193

10.2 Mark Summer (b. 1958): *Variations: Lo, How a Rose E'er Blooming* (1995) — 197

10.3 Adolphus Hailstork (b. 1941): *Theme and Variations on "Draw the Sacred Circle Closer"* for Solo Cello (2014) — 200

10.4 Reena Esmail (b. 1983): *Varsha* (2019) — 204

Bibliography — 207
Index — 217

From the Series Editor

"Notes for Performers" is a series born of my desire to help musicians connect performance studies with pertinent aspects of scholarship. My favorite theory professor, John Buccheri (Northwestern University), used to say that to know a piece intuitively, technically, and intellectually is to *really* know a piece. While some may argue that one should simply "play from the heart," knowledge can be a powerful tool in strengthening or refining a performer's instincts. Additionally, when musicians are armed with knowledge, they can enhance their audiences' understanding of compositions. Having served as a pre-concert lecturer for the Chicago Symphony Orchestra for more than twenty years, I have had the satisfaction of helping audiences engage more fully with the music they are about to hear. I hope this series will encourage performers to offer written or spoken commentary to enhance their audiences' listening experiences.

While all musicians will gain insights from the books in the series, the writing is intended for undergraduate students, perhaps with a bit of professorial guidance. The selection of pieces is admittedly subjective. Each author is asked to identify the best-known compositions written for the instrument. It is my hope that instrumentalists will view each volume as a starting point for connecting performance studies with scholarship and that it will encourage them to explore other works in a similar fashion. Many more works are worthy of inclusion in each volume and, in time, perhaps second volumes may be added with additional compositions, including more recent works that have stood the test of time and become part of a given instrument's core repertoire.

There have long been helpful resources available to performers for learning about chamber, orchestral, and operatic works, but similar in-depth information to guide one's understanding of a given orchestral instrument's solo repertoire has thus far been noticeably absent from bookshelves. The goal of this series is to fill that open space on the shelf, and my goal as Oxford's "Notes for Performers" editor is to contribute to the intellectual understanding necessary, as Dr. Buccheri would suggest, for a musician to *really* know a piece.

Kyle Dzapo
Professor of Music
Bradley University

Preface

I have always felt that the disciplines of music performance, history, and theory should inform and enrich each other. During my student years, I was astonished at the artificial separation of the practical and academic aspects of music-making in some university music departments. Would it not make more sense, I wondered, to integrate them? Early in my career, the teachers who helped and inspired me the most were those whose own careers combined more than one discipline. Two of my dearest mentors, Edward Dusinberre and the late Alexander Ivashkin, proved that it was possible to succeed in both performing and writing about music. I try to follow their example in my work as a professor of cello and music history.

When Kyle Dzapo, the series editor of Notes for Performers, approached me about creating this book, I was overjoyed. (I may or may not have shouted "Yes!" before she even finished her sentence.) Writing about the core cello repertoire for Oxford University Press was a dream come true. It was also a daunting challenge, given the vast amount of music composers have written for our instrument. Who was I to decide what was core and what wasn't?

Some of this anxiety went away after I stumbled across *Well-Known Violoncello Solos and How to Play Them with Understanding, Expression and Effect* (1923) by the German cello historian Edmund van der Straeten. It was both surprising and comforting to see that van der Straeten's repertoire list contained a few warhorse compositions alongside many others that are now forgotten. The core repertoire seemed to have changed a lot over the course of a century, and it was liberating to realize that it did not have to be an immutable monument to the past. Our repertoire lives, grows, and evolves as cellists assimilate new pieces by living composers, discover unjustly neglected ones from earlier eras, and set aside those that no longer appeal to us. We cannot predict how fashions will change any more than the erudite van der Straeten could a hundred years ago.

This realization didn't solve the problem of choosing pieces. When I started a spreadsheet to list important compositions for solo cello, cello and piano, and cello and orchestra, the rows ran into the hundreds, then thousands. From a cellist's point of view, this was a good problem to have—what could be better than having a lot of music to play? For the author of a book on core repertoire, however, it required difficult choices. Because of the constraints of word limits, I decided to limit my selections to one piece per composer (with an exception for Hensel, whose two single-movement cello pieces often appear side by side in concert programs). This was not easy, since picking just one Bach suite or Beethoven sonata felt like having to pick a favorite child. After much back-and-forth with cellist friends, I settled on pieces that we felt were the most approachable for undergraduate players. This is why I chose, for example, Haydn's C major concerto over the much more demanding one in D major, and Brahms's E minor sonata over the F major. I was also eager to include works by living composers and composers from historically underrepresented groups, so it was enlightening to learn what other cello professors in the United States and around the world were assigning to their students. My sincere thanks go to Karla Hamelin, Brian Hodges, Rachel Johnston, George Kennaway, Michelle Kesler, Julia Cory Slovarp, and Ka-Wai Yu for their thoughtful answers to pedagogy- and repertoire-related questions.

Notes for Cellists is a book for players of ages and levels—pre-college students, undergraduate and graduate students, private teachers, school orchestra directors, university professors, professional players, and amateurs. I hope it will serve as a guide for listening and reference, a resource for program notes, and a point of departure for further research in music history or analysis. As I was writing, I thought of my own students, many of whom understand something of harmony and form but have not yet attempted to analyze a Bach prelude, Romantic sonata, or non-diatonic piece. There were many existing analyses on the "blockbuster" repertoire in this book, but for some pieces, I had to make my own from scratch. Doing so enhanced my enjoyment of music I had played for years, and I hope it will enhance yours too.

I am eternally grateful to Zara Cannon-Mohammed and the editorial team at Oxford University Press for believing in this project, and to Kyle Dzapo for her help with my book proposal. I could not have completed *Notes for Cellists* without the help of the faculty and staff of the University of Idaho Library, who sleuthed out hard-to-find materials, delivered dozens of articles, and patiently answered my research questions. My fellow performer-writers at the University of Idaho Lionel Hampton School of Music, especially Barry Bilderback, Leonard Garrison, and Diane Worthey, offered valuable advice on research and writing.

Finally, I would like to thank my family. How I wish that my mother, Gillian Bibby, had lived to see the publication of this book. She knew it was in the works, though, and I like to think she's still cheering me on. My most heartfelt thanks go to my father, Roger Wilson, my brother, Charles Wilson, my husband, Sean Butterfield, and our daughter, Eliana, for their love and support.

1
THE DAWN OF AN ERA

1.1

Domenico Gabrielli (1651/1659–1690)

Ricercar No. 2 in A Minor (1689)

The Baroque era originated in Italy, as did the instruments of the violin family. By the mid-seventeenth century, instrument builders had codified the proportions and acoustics of the violin, but not the cello.[1] The youngest member of the violin family was still in an experimental stage and could come in many shapes, sizes, and string tunings. Even its name was in dispute, with various historical sources describing it as a "bass violin," "tenor viola," or *violoncino*, as well as the more familiar *violoncello*.[2] In ensembles, it typically took the accompanying *basso continuo* role. A solo repertoire did not yet exist, probably because of problems with size and tone quality in the early instruments. In Cremona, the Amati family was building large-model cellos with a back length of seventy-nine centimeters. Their sound was resonant enough, but their size made them unwieldy for players. Violinmakers in the city of Brescia, thirty-five miles from Cremona, favored a smaller model with a back length of seventy-one centimeters. While these came with built-in advantages for ease of playing, the thick gut strings of the time could only produce a weak, muffled tone.

In the northern Italian city of Bologna, instrument builders came up with a solution to this problem by creating silver-wound gut strings, whose higher tension allowed for crisper articulation and tone production on a seventy-one-centimeter instrument.[3] At a stroke, smaller cellos were now both practical and acoustically viable. It is therefore no accident that the first solo cello repertoire originated in Bologna.

A flourishing center for music and especially for string playing, Bologna was home to the world's oldest university and two major music institutions,

---

[1] John Dilworth, "The Cello: Origins and Evolution," *The Cambridge Companion to the Cello*, ed. Robin Stowell (Cambridge: Cambridge University Press, 1999), 1.

[2] Stephen Bonta, *Studies in Italian Sacred and Instrumental Music in the Seventeenth Century* (Aldershot: Ashgate, 2003), 5–43.

[3] Stephen Bonta, "From Violone to Violoncello: A Question of Strings," *Journal of the American Musical Instrument Society* 3 (1977), 64–97.

the Accademia Filarmonica and the Basilica di San Petronio. The latter boasted special associations with cello playing, in part because of an acoustic that favored low-pitched instruments.[4] When Maurizio Cazzati (1616–1678) became the music director of San Petronio in 1657, he hired a bassline-heavy group of instrumentalists to complement the existing vocal ensemble, including several cellists. San Petronio's lineage of distinguished cellist-composers began with Giovanni Battista Vitali (1632–1692), Petronio Franceschini (1651–1680),[5] and Domenico Gabrielli.

Nicknamed "Mingéin dal viulunzel" ("Little Domenico of the cello" in the Bolognese dialect) for his virtuoso playing, Gabrielli also excelled at composition. Following studies with Franceschini and the composer Giovanni Legrenzi, he won a position at the Accademia Filarmonica and later succeeded Franceschini at San Petronio. He wrote many oratorios and cantatas for the church, and operas for the secular audiences of Venice, Modena, and Turin. As his career grew, Gabrielli often left Bologna on tour. The San Petronio authorities tolerated his frequent absences until 1687, when they fired him for failing to show up to an important feast day. Gabrielli immediately found a new position in Modena, which seems to have provoked his former employers to regret their decision, since they hastily invited him back. Gabrielli returned to San Petronio and remained there for the rest of his life.[6]

The lively charm of Gabrielli's compositions would have won over the most irritable employer. As well as large-scale works, Gabrielli composed several pieces for his own instrument. These included cello sonatas with basso continuo accompaniment, a canon for two cellos, and seven *Ricercare* for unaccompanied cello. The title reveals something of Gabrielli's motivation for composing them, since the Italian word means "search" or "research." Each *Ricercar* comprises a rhapsodic, improvisatory collection of musical ideas.[7] While Gabrielli may have been familiar with the organ *Ricercare* of predecessors such as Claudio Merulo (1533–1604) and Girolamo Frescobaldi (1583–1643), there was no blueprint for a cello version in this or any other genre. Gabrielli's *Ricercare* were entirely experimental, each markedly different in length, structure, and character. All make a feature of

---

[4] Anne Schnoebelen, "Performance Practices at San Petronio in the Baroque," *Acta Musicologica* 41 (January–June 1969), 44.

[5] Schnoebelen, 47.

[6] John Suess and Marc Vanscheeuwijk, "Gabrielli, Domenico," *Grove Music Online*, ed. Deane Root. http://oxfordmusiconline.com.

[7] John Caldwell, "Ricercare," *Grove Music Online*, ed. Deane Root, http://oxfordmusiconline.com.

Gabrielli's virtuosity as a cellist in their brilliant passagework, double stops, and chords.

The longest and arguably most interesting of the set is *Ricercar* No. 2 in A minor. Unlike the single-movement structures of most of the others, it falls clearly into four through-composed sections. The first three end on the dominant harmony, indicating that they are to be performed without a break. Though Gabrielli gives no instructions for tempo or mood, the meter changes between sections signal contrasting speeds and characters. The first section is in common time and the second in 3/2, suggesting a more relaxed tempo. For the third section, Gabrielli returns to common time before switching to 12/8 for the fourth. The sections are all in A minor, and none stray far from this key. While there are a handful of tonicizations and trips through the circle of fifths, the only modulations are to C, the relative major. This comparatively static harmonic plan allows Gabrielli the freedom to play with chains of syncopations, rhythmic contrasts, and other rhetorical flourishes. Rapid sequential passagework and "echo" effects in the second section anticipate Antonio Vivaldi's use of such devices. In the fourth section, the compound meter suggests a pastoral character, or perhaps a *giga* like the ones that conclude each of Bach's Six Cello Suites.

It is unclear whether Bach knew Gabrielli's compositions, but we may still consider the *Ricercare* the indirect predecessors of Bach's works for solo cello. Both Gabrielli and Bach discovered idiomatic ways to create both melody and harmonic accompaniment on a single bowed instrument. In his *Ricercare*, Gabrielli sought and found a new voice for the cello—that of a solo instrument.

Table 1.1.1 Gabrielli, *Ricercar* No. 2, analysis

Section	1	2	3	4
Measures	1–51	52–153	154–205	206–227
Thematic material	Common time, rhythmic character with syncopated sections and sequential melodic patterns	3/2 meter, implied slower pulse, repetitive passagework, echo effects	Return to common time and the opening character, large leaps	Compound time, pastoral dance-like character
Key(s)	A minor	A minor with sequential circle of fifths progressions	A minor with sequential circle of fifths progressions	A minor

1.2

Johann Sebastian Bach (1685–1750)

Suite No. 3 in C Major, BWV 1009

I. Prelude   II. Allemande   III. Courante   IV. Sarabande
V. Bourrée I–Bourrée II–Bourrée I da capo   VI. Gigue

Bach wrote his Six Cello Suites between 1717 and 1723 during his tenure as Capellmeister at the court of Prince Leopold of Anhalt-Cöthen. He would later recall this as a happy time in his professional life, with colleagues who were among the finest musicians in Germany and a generous, music-loving employer. Bach's brief was to create secular music for the court's entertainment, and it was during these years that he composed some of his most celebrated instrumental works: the six Brandenburg Concertos, the first book of the *Well-Tempered Clavier*, the Violin Sonatas and Partitas, and the Cello Suites.

At this point in the early eighteenth century, the repertoire for unaccompanied cello was still in its infancy. The scope and substance of Bach's Cello Suites outweighed that of his predecessors, including Domenico Gabrielli, Giovanni Battista Vitali, Domenico Galli, and Giuseppe Colombi. The idea of composing several multi-movement works for a self-harmonizing solo instrument, while not new in the violin and viola da gamba literature, was unprecedented for the cello. It is possible that with this composition, Bach sought to elevate the cello to the standing of the violin as a solo instrument. Because he never explained his motivations, we can only speculate on what they were.

No autograph manuscript of Bach's Cello Suites survives, and the works remained unpublished until a century after their composition. Once the cellist-editors of the nineteenth-century Bach Revival brought them into the concert hall, however, they became central to the cello repertoire. Today there are dozens of editions and hundreds of recordings of the Cello Suites, and they stand among the best-known compositions for the cello.

All six of Bach's Cello Suites have a six-movement plan composed of an opening Prelude and five movements in binary forms: Allemande,

Courante, Sarabande, a pair of *galanterie* dances (Menuets in the First and Second Suites, Bourrées in the Third and Fourth Suites, and Gavottes in the Fifth and Sixth Suites), Gigue. The French titles refer to dance movements, though Bach did not intend these compositions for literal dancing. French culture was in vogue all over Europe and dancing was a vital component of a nobleman's education. In writing stylized dance movements as purely musical forms, Baroque composers conjured up the idea, if not the reality, of dancing.

A Prelude, literally a piece that precedes other compositions, was a common way to begin an instrumental suite. Organists of the German Baroque, including Bach, prided themselves on their skill at *Präludieren*, "preluding," before church services. In the Cello Suites, Bach's Preludes elaborately introduce the harmonies and characters of each composition. We could even regard their melodic styles as a form of written-out improvisation. All but one of Bach's Cello Suites open with a "pattern prelude," a procedure Bach had used before in his Prelude in C Major from *The Well-Tempered Clavier*. Pattern preludes work through a series of harmonic progressions using repetitive broken-chord shapes. Bach's Prelude to the Third Cello Suite begins with the opening gesture of a descending C major scale and falls into clear, pattern-based sections. The first introduces the key and the dashing character of the movement in scalar motion, and subsequent sections work toward modulations to the second key area, G major, and the third key area, A minor. The middle section features an outpouring of arpeggiated chordal progressions on a dominant pedal. Interestingly Bach appears to have imported this progression from a similar passage in the second movement of Arcangelo Corelli's Trio Sonata, Op. 5, No. 3.[1] After this, a protracted section in dominant harmony begins the journey back to the home key. Once Bach has achieved this harmonic preparation, he prolongs the return to C major in virtuoso displays of scalar material and chords. A coda adds a final bravura flourish of a double trill that leads into a final restatement of the opening gesture, followed by a triumphant concluding chord.

By Bach's time, the Allemande—a French word meaning "German"—was no longer danced in the ballroom. The instrumental Allemande was now a serious, substantial musical form, second only in substance to the Prelude. Melodic material in the Allemande of the Third Cello Suite, like that in the

---

[1] David Watkin, "Corelli's Op. 5 Sonatas: Violino e Violone *o* Cembalo?" *Early Music* 24, no. 4 (November 1996): 660.

Prelude, begins with a descending C major scale gesture. The melody here is more circuitous and rhythmically varied, however, and contains features such as chains of double stops that did not occur in the Prelude. Like all the binary dance movements in the Third Suite except the second Bourrée, the Allemande modulates to G major in the first section and back to C major in the second.

All of Bach's Courantes for cello, except for that of the Fifth Suite, are not true French Courantes but Italian Correntes—Bach often used the terms interchangeably. Both forms are in triple time, but the Corrente has a faster tempo. The Courante of Bach's Third Cello Suite, in contrast to the scalar melodies of the Prelude and Allemande, takes its melodic material mostly from arpeggiated triads. Its melodic shapes remarkably resemble those in the bassline of the aria "Phoebus hurries with swift horses" from Bach's Wedding Cantata BWV 202,[2] another work in C major from his Cöthen period.

By Bach's time, the danced Sarabande was an elegant affair, having shed its disreputable associations with an earlier choreography from the New World. As a musical form, the Sarabande had a stately tempo in slow triple meter with an emphasis on the second beat. Some Sarabandes, like that of the Third Cello Suite, add extra elegance through dotted rhythms. Here, Bach uses the descending C major scale to underpin the harmonic structure of the Sarabande, creating a sense of unity with the Prelude and Allemande.[3] It is a reflective, serious movement with a brief and surprising tonicization of D minor that may allude to the Sarabande of the Second Cello Suite.[4]

Unlike the aristocratic Allemande and Courante, the Bourrée had its origins as a folk dance. In a quick duple meter with an anacrusis, it typically featured simple, balanced melodic lines. While some of Bach's pairs of *galanterie* dances—the Menuets in the Second Cello Suite, for example—are in stark contrast with each other, the two Bourrées in the Third Suite are thematically related. Therefore, even though the second Bourrée is in the parallel minor mode, this does not dramatically alter the easygoing pastoral mood.

In another instance of Bach's interchangeably using French and Italian terms, the concluding Gigue is more properly termed a Giga[5]—an Italian

---

[2] Mark M. Smith, "The Drama of Bach's Life in the Court of Cöthen, as Reflected in His Cello Suites," *Stringendo* 22, no. 1 (2000): 33.

[3] Heinrich Schenker, "The Sarabande of J. S. Bach's Suite No. 3 for Unaccompanied Violoncello," trans. Hedi Siegel, *The Music Forum* 2, ed. William J. Mitchell and Felix Salzer (1970): 274–282.

[4] Smith, 33.

[5] Meredith Little and Natalie Jenne, *Dance and the Music of J. S. Bach*, 2nd ed. (Bloomington and Indianapolis: Indiana University Press, 2001), 157.

instrumental form that may or may not have accompanied physical dancing. In both sections of the Gigue of the Third Suite, Bach's melodic line begins without self-generated accompaniment, then progresses into a two-voice *bariolage* and double stopping, bringing the Suite to an optimistic, bravura conclusion.

Table 1.2.1 Bach, Suite No. 3 in C Major, Prelude, analysis

Section	Opening gesture	Modulating episode	Modulating episode	Cadential section	Sequential section
Measures	1–7	7–18	18–21	21–27	27–37
Thematic material	Descending scalar gesture. Further scalar material in ascending and descending motion	Sequential question-answer phrases, scalar material	Mixture of chordal and scalar material		Sequential broken chords and scalar progressions
Key(s)	C major	C major to G major	Tonicizations of A major, D minor, E major, A minor	To A minor	A minor with tonicizations of G major, C major, F major, C major

Section	Modulating episode	Dominant pedal section	Prolonged dominant section	Cadential section	Coda
Measures	37–44	45–61	61–71	77–82	82–88
Thematic material	Sequential broken chords	Sequential broken chords on a harmonic progression from Corelli	Scalar material	Chordal material	Sequential material, double trill, final statement of descending C major scale gesture
Key(s)	C major with tonicizations of A minor, D minor, B minor, E minor, C major, F major, D minor	G major	To C major	C major	C major

1.3

Antonio Vivaldi (1678–1741)

Sonata in B♭ Major, RV 46 (also known as Op. 14, No. 6)

I. Largo (Preludio)   II. Allegro (Allemanda)   III. Largo
IV. Allegro (Corrente)

By Vivaldi's lifetime, the cello was an established solo instrument. After the early innovations of the Bolognese cellist-composers, the cello caught on among composers and performers throughout Italy. Bologna continued to boast excellent cellists such as Gabrielli's student Giuseppe Jacchini (1667–1727), and Modena produced the cello-playing Bononcini brothers Giovanni (1670–1747) and Antonio Maria (1677–1726). In Naples and Rome, Francesco "Francischello" Arborea (1691–1739) pioneered *capotasto* (thumb position), an important advancement in technique.

Venice, too, had its share of famous cellists. Vivaldi, who spent a large part of his career there, would likely have had the chance to hear Gabrielli's student Antonio Caldara (1671–1736) at the Basilica di San Marco. Another top player was Antonio Vandini (ca. 1690–1778), who worked briefly under Vivaldi at the Ospedale della Pietà. Vandini's virtuoso playing, which drew praise from the music historian Charles Burney,[1] may well have inspired some of Vivaldi's compositions for solo cello.

This large output included at least twenty-seven cello concertos and ten sonatas for cello and continuo. The collection of six sonatas known as Vivaldi's Op. 14 dates to the 1720s or earlier.[2] Though no autograph manuscript of the compositions has survived, the musicologist Eleanor Selfridge-Field has shown that there is little reason to doubt their authenticity.[3] Two eighteenth-century copies survive; one, by an anonymous Italian copyist of

---

[1] Charles Burney, *The Present State of Music in France and Italy* (London: T. Becket, 1771), 135–136. Burney observed that Vandini played with an "old-fashioned" viola da gamba-style underhand bow hold.

[2] The sonatas in this collection are now labeled RV 47, 41, 43, 45, 40, and 46 in the Ryom-Verzeichnis catalogue.

[3] Eleanor Selfridge-Field, "Vivaldi's Cello Sonatas," *Vivaldi, Vero e Falso*, ed. L. S. Olschki (Venice: Istituto Italiano Antonio Vivaldi, 1992), 127–147.

the mid-1720s,⁴ is the likely source of the first printed edition (1740) by the Parisian firm Le Clerc.⁵

All six of the Op. 14 sonatas follow the slow-fast-slow-fast four-movement plan pioneered by Arcangelo Corelli (1653–1713). All movements are in rounded binary form, some with repeats of the two sections. Vivaldi's signature style features—driving rhythms, syncopation, sequences, scalar and arpeggiated passagework—abound throughout. Though there is no evidence that Vivaldi himself played the cello, he understood how to compose idiomatically for the instrument. Vivaldi's compositions for cello contain fewer technical demands than those for the violin, his own instrument, but they signal how far cello technique had developed since the early days in Bologna. The first cello solos had a relatively narrow range of pitches, whereas the ambitus in Vivaldi's cello sonatas is wide enough that he had to use the tenor clef for the upper range. Vivaldi's choice of keys is also more adventurous: of the six sonatas in his Op. 14, three are in B♭ major, a less intuitive key for cellists than the "open-string" keys. Vivaldi casts the cello in the role of melodic soloist, taking full advantage of the instrument's capacity for lyricism.

For the musicologists André Micheletti and William Teixeira da Silva, the opening *Largo* of RV 46 recalls the *messa di voce* of Vivaldi's operatic arias.⁶ This term, whose literal meaning is "placing of the voice," refers to "the singing or playing of a long note so that it begins quietly, swells to full volume, and then diminishes to the original quiet tone."⁷ The long slur markings in both of the eighteenth-century manuscripts suggest a *cantabile* tone, though there are also staccato marks, some of which have slurs above them in the manner of Italian Baroque vocal performance practices.⁸

If the first movement is songful, the second is more dancelike. (The second eighteenth-century manuscript, housed in the Musikbibliothek des Grafen von Schönborn-Wiesentheid in Germany, gives the second and fourth movements the dance titles *Allemanda* and *Corrente*. We have no way of knowing whether this was Vivaldi's idea or an editorial embellishment.) The cello part dashes vigorously through syncopated rhythms and running sixteenth notes against the relatively stable rhythms of the bassline.

---

⁴ Now housed at the Bibliothèque Nationale in Paris.
⁵ Due to the increased popularity of the cello in France, Le Clerc published no fewer than twenty-six collections of cello sonatas between the late 1730s and 1750s.
⁶ André Luis Giovanini Micheletti and William Teixeira da Silva, "Cello Development from Gabrielli to Vivaldi," *Revista Música Hodie, Goiânia* 14, no. 2 (2014): 26–27.
⁷ Ellen T. Harris, "Messa di voce," *Grove Music Online*, ed. Deane Root, http://www.oxfordmusiconline.com.
⁸ Micheletti and Silva, 27.

Table 1.3.1 Vivaldi, Sonata in B♭, *I. Largo (Preludio)*, analysis

Section	A	B	A	
Measures	1–8	9–18	18–28	29–33
Thematic material	Introduction of main theme	Sequential theme on circle of fifths progressions	Reprise of main theme	Cadential material
Key(s)	B♭ major	Tonicizations of C minor, F minor, B♭ major, E♭ major, A♭ major	G minor to B♭ major	B♭ major

Table 1.3.2 Vivaldi, Sonata in B♭, *II. Allegro (Allemanda)*, analysis

Section	A		B		
Measures	1–5	6–12	13–14	15–22	23–34
Thematic material	Introduction of main theme	Sequential patterns	Variant of main theme	Circle of fifths progressions	Reprise of opening material
Key(s)	B♭ major	F major	F major	D minor, G minor, C minor	B♭ major

In contrast, the continuo becomes more of an equal partner to the melodic line in the third movement. The only movement in the sonata in a key other than B♭, this *Largo* in G minor moves through chains of syncopated suspensions and resolutions over a chromatic bassline. Vivaldi's use of the harmonic minor scale in the cello part creates a sense of dissonance and anguish that is absent from the three other movements.

Optimism returns in the *Allegro* finale, where the playful juxtaposition of triplet and duplet rhythms and rapid-fire intervallic leaps lead the sonata, and the Op. 14 collection, to an energetic final cadence.

Table 1.3.3 Vivaldi, Sonata in B♭, III. Largo, analysis

Section	Opening section	Repetition of opening section	Continuation	Modulating section	Reprise
Measures	1–3	4–5	6–9	9–15	15–20
Thematic material	Introduction of main theme, descending chromatic bassline	Reversal of cello and continuo lines	Continuation and modulation	Main theme material	Return of opening material
Key(s)	G minor	G minor	To C minor	C minor, G minor, D minor, G minor	G minor

Table 1.3.4 Vivaldi, Sonata in B♭, IV. Allegro (Corrente), analysis

Section	A			B		
Measures	1–8	9–13	14–27	28–31	35–39	40–57
Thematic material	First thematic group, triplet and duplet rhythms	Second thematic group, large leaps	Cadential section	First thematic group material	Continuation of first thematic group material	Reprise of first thematic group material
Key(s)	B♭ major	To F major	F major	D minor	D minor	B♭ major

1.4

Jean-Baptiste Barrière (1707–1747)

Sonata IV in G Major from *Livre IV* (ca. 1739)

I. Andante   II. Adagio   III. Allegro prestissimo

By the beginning of the eighteenth century, the cello had entirely superseded the viola da gamba in Italy as the low-voiced string instrument of choice. In France, however, the cello was a newcomer. Jean-Baptiste Barrière, one of the earliest French cellists, was born in 1707; Martin Berteau, the "founder of the French school of cello playing,"[1] a year later.

The cello's late arrival in France was due in part to the musical preferences of King Louis XIV (1638–1715), who sought to protect French culture from foreign influences. In all the arts, the king favored French rationality over Italian passion. In music, he preferred stylized French dance movements over the new Italian *concerto grosso* and trio sonata forms. There was also the matter of France's venerable tradition of virtuoso viola da gamba playing, as epitomized by the gambist-composers Marin Marais (1656–1728) and Antoine Forqueray (1672–1745). These favorites of the king exploited the viola da gamba's capacity for plangent tone and rich chordal playing to perfection. Their popularity among the nobility therefore kept the viola da gamba in fashion in France long after it became obsolete in Italy.

As the eighteenth century progressed, the attractions of Italian music and instruments became harder for French musicians to resist. In his 1724 collection *Les goûts réunis* ("The Reunited Tastes"), François Couperin (1668–1733) deliberately assimilated French and Italian styles, acknowledging the influence of the Italian violinist-composer Arcangelo Corelli (1653–1713). Visiting Italian virtuosi became celebrities in Paris, and in 1736 the *Concert spirituel* series featured its first solo cellist, the Neapolitan Salvatore Lanzetti (1710–1780). Lanzetti's cello sonatas—he wrote at least

---

[1] Mary Cyr, "Berteau [Berthault, Bertaud], Martin," *Grove Music Online*, ed. Deane Root, http://oxfordmusiconline.com.

twenty-four—contained high-pitched passages that showcased his skill in thumb position.

Barrière likely had the chance to observe Lanzetti's dazzling playing in Paris, since by then he was living in the city. All we know about his early years is that he was the son of a shoemaker from Bordeaux,[2] but in 1731, aged twenty-four, he shows up in the records of the Paris Opéra orchestra.[3] The cello was overtaking the viola da gamba in popularity, as evidenced by the demand for repertoire: between the 1730s and 1750s, Parisian publishers released dozens of volumes of cello sonatas.[4] Some were by the influential Italians Antonio Vivaldi (1678–1741) and Benedetto Marcello (1686–1739), others by French composers Joseph Bodin de Boismortier (1689–1755), Michel Corrette (1707–1795), and Barrière himself.

Not everyone was pleased about the rise of the cello. One viola da gamba enthusiast, Hubert Le Blanc, felt moved to author a polemical pamphlet, *Defense of the Bass Viol Against the Enterprises of the Violin and the Pretensions of the Cello* (1740).[5] Le Blanc saw the violin family as lower-class arrivistes and an affront to the aristocratic viol. The violin, he raged, was "a little runt and a pygmy," the cello "a cancer, hated, a miserable devil."[6] His effort was in vain, as even the great Forqueray admitted that "the viol, despite its advantages, has fallen into a kind of oblivion."[7]

For a time, some musicians played both gamba and cello as the occasion demanded. In his treatise of 1741, Michel Corrette included a section for gambists wishing to make the switch, confidently assuring the nervous student that "Nothing is so simple as the fingerboard of the cello."[8] Barrière himself appears to have played the *pardessus de viole* as a second instrument and wrote a fifth volume of sonatas to this high-pitched member of the viol family.[9] Corrette's contemporary Berteau started his career on viola da gamba before a performance by the Italian cellist Francesco "Francischello" Alborea inspired

---

[2] Mary Cyr, *Style and Performance for Bowed String Instruments in French Baroque Music* (Surrey: Ashgate, 2012), 190.
[3] Jérôme de La Gorce, "L'orchestre de l'Opéra et son évolution de Campra à Rameau," *Revue de Musicologie* 76, no. 1 (1990), 40.
[4] Eleanor Selfridge-Field, "Vivaldi's Cello Sonatas," *Vivaldi, Vero e Falso*, ed. L. S. Olschki (Venice: Istituto Italiano Antonio Vivaldi, 1992), 127–147.
[5] Hubert Le Blanc, *Défense de la basse de viole contre les entreprises du violon et les prétentions du violoncel* (Paris: Pierre Mortier, 1740).
[6] Le Blanc, 30, translation mine.
[7] Antoine Forqueray, *Pièces de Viole avec la Bass Continuë* (Paris: Leclair, 1747), dedication page.
[8] Michel Corrette, *Méthode théorique et pratique pour apprendre en peu de tems le violoncelle dans sa perfection* (Paris: Boivin, 1741), 43.
[9] A posthumous inventory of Barrière's belongings lists six cellos and six *pardessus de violes*. See Cyr, *Style and Performance*, 191.

him to take up the cello. Many biographers have repeated an unreliable story that Barrière, too, studied with Alborea in Italy during a three-year absence from Paris, but the dates do not line up with Alborea's travels during the period.[10]

The details of Barrière's trip may remain unknown, but we can deduce from changes to his compositional style that he absorbed many Italian influences. His pre-Italy compositions—*Livres I* and *II* of sonatas for cello and basso continuo—show characteristics inherited from the viola da gamba tradition, including a limited pitch range, ornaments, double stops, French forms such as the *rondeau*, a few movements with dance titles, and a "mannered" style.[11] In *Livres III* and *IV*, published after his return from Italy, Barrière includes more Italian features in his writing—virtuoso passagework, ornate runs, a broader range, and more complicated rhythms.[12] The movements in these later sonatas are typically in binary form and have Italian titles.

The fourth sonata in *Livre IV* reveals the full range of Barrière's mature style. Anomalously among Barrière's sonatas, its bassline is completely unfigured, suggesting that Barrière did not intend for a second continuo instrument (such as a harpsichord) to fill out the harmonies. The second cello part contains as many double stops as the first, making it less a bassline accompaniment than an equal partner in the texture. The overall mood of the sonata is lyrical, with plenty of Italian touches such as the dynamic indications of *forte* and *piano* and a virtuoso finale marked *prestissimo*. Rather than adopting the slow-fast-slow-fast four-movement plan of Corelli's trio sonatas, Barrière sticks to three movements—a nod, perhaps, to Lanzetti, who also used three-movement plans. The first movement, *Andante*, is in rounded binary form with repeats. The harmony is conservative, with just one modulation to D major in the first section and a return to G major in the second. Within these boundaries, Barrière includes Italian-style triplet divisions of the beat and Corellian devices such as chains of syncopated suspensions and resolutions. The second movement, *Adagio*, looks back to Barrière's earlier French style in its use of trills, grace notes, and rhetorical flourishes. The rapid final movement is a tour de force of competitive cello solos. The two cellists veer from homophonic sections in frantic *bariolage* to back-and-forth passages that sound less like a duet than a duel. Though the overall form is binary, Barrière interrupts the second section with a brief *Adagio* interlude, a moment of sorrow that seems to farewell the melancholy second movement once and for all before launching back into *prestissimo* at full tilt. This finale is the best-known of Barrière's compositions and a staple of the cello duo repertoire.

[10] Mary Cyr, "Barrière, Jean," *Grove Music Online*, ed. Deane Root, http://oxfordmusiconline.com.
[11] Sylvette Milliot, *Le violoncelle en France au XVIIIème siècle* (Paris: Champion Slatkin, 1985), 86–92.
[12] Milliot, 86–92.

Table 1.4.1 Barrière, Sonata IV, *I. Andante*, analysis

Section	A			B						A	
Measures	1–6	7–10	11–15	16–31	32–37	38–43	44–51	52–55	56–73		
Thematic material	First thematic group	Second thematic group, first cello in bassline role	Second thematic group, second cello in bassline role	Dominant pedal leading into cadential material derived from the first thematic group	First thematic group, additional double stops	First thematic group	Second thematic group, additional double stops	First thematic group, sequential suspensions and resolutions	Dominant pedal, synthesis of first and second thematic groups, cadential material		
Key(s)	G major	G major	To D major	Dominant of D major	D major	G major	C major, D major	To G major	G major		

Table 1.4.2 Barrière, Sonata IV, *II. Adagio*, analysis

Section	A	B		A	
Measures	1–4	5–9	10–12	13–15	16–18
Thematic material	First thematic group	Second thematic group	Third thematic group	Reprise of first thematic group	Coda
Key(s)	G minor to D major	B♭ major	G minor to D major	G minor	G minor

Table 1.4.3 Barrière, Sonata IV, III. Allegro prestissimo, analysis

Section	A				
Measures	1–5	6–11	12–14	15–22	23–37
Thematic material	Canon theme	Homophonic passagework and bariolage	Quasi-canon with syncopation	Dominant pedal	Closing section on material from the canon theme
Key(s)	G major	G major	G major	Dominant of D major	D major

Section	B							
Measures	28–32	33–38	39–47	48–50	51–55	56–66	67–69	70–77
Thematic material	Quasi-canon	Homophonic passagework and bariolage	Antiphonal theme	Homophonic passagework and bariolage	Adagio interlude	Reprise of material from 1–11	Quasi-canon with syncopation	Coda on fragments of material from 1–4
Key(s)	D major	D major	Tonicizations of G major and B minor	B minor	B minor	G major	G major	G major

2
CLASSICAL VIRTUOSI

2.1

Luigi Boccherini (1743–1805)

Sonata in A Major, G. 4 (ca. 1770s)

I. Adagio II. Allegro III. Affettuoso

Many virtuoso performer-composers write principally for their own instrument, but not Luigi Boccherini. Alongside a distinguished performing career as Europe's leading cellist, he composed twenty-seven symphonies, nearly a hundred string quartets, more than a hundred string quintets, and dozens of other chamber works.[1] He did, of course, write for the cello too, composing twelve cello concertos and up to forty-three sonatas for cello and continuo.[2]

Boccherini's cello playing amazed his contemporaries, not least because of his effortless technique in ultra-fast tempi and his predilection for the highest *tessitura*. Of Boccherini's performances, one journalist wrote, "he charmed us by the incomparable sonority and peculiarly expressive singing tone of his instrument."[3] The violinist Pierre Baillot described one of his concerts as "full of grace, freshness, and purity, and of such particular expression that one must cite it as a model for those who study the cello."[4]

Ridolfo Luigi Boccherini was born into an artistic family in Lucca, Italy in 1743. His father Leopoldo, a double bassist and cellist, was ambitious for his five children. He took them on extended trips around Italian and Austrian cities in search of career opportunities, and these efforts paid off. A concert review of 1758 describes the fifteen-year-old Luigi's successful performance of his own compositions, accompanied on the double bass by his proud papa. Three other Boccherini siblings became professional ballet dancers, another an opera singer.[5]

---

[1] Christian Speck and Stanley Sadie, "Boccherini, (Ridolfo) Luigi," *Grove Music Online*, ed. Deane Root, http://oxfordmusiconline.com.

[2] Christian Speck, "Boccherini as Cellist and His Music for Cello," *Early Music* 33, no. 2 (2005): 197.

[3] Germaine de Rothschild and Andreas Mayor, *Luigi Boccherini: His Life and Work* (London: Oxford University Press, 1965).

[4] Pierre Baillot, Jean-Henri Levasseur, Charles-Simon Catel, and Charles Baudiot, *Méthode de violoncelle* (Paris: Janet et Cotelle, 1805), 4.

[5] Daniel Heartz, "The Young Boccherini: Lucca, Vienna, and the Electoral Courts," *The Journal of Musicology* 13, no. 1 (Winter 1995): 103–116.

Accustomed to life on the road, Boccherini spent much of his early career touring Europe with his violinist friend Filippo Manfredi. In around 1770, he settled in Spain, having won a position at the court of the music-loving Infante Luis Antonio Jaime, younger brother of King Carlos III. Accompanying him was his young bride, an accomplished soprano named Clementina Pellicia. It was during this happy period that Boccherini published his Sonata in A Major for cello and continuo.[6]

This lively piece had romantic associations for the newlywed couple. The second movement bears a strong resemblance to another of Boccherini's compositions, a concert aria for soprano and orchestra titled "Se d'un amore tiranno" G. 557. The text of the aria came from a poem by Pietro Metastasio that describes a woman's conflicted passions for her lover: "If I thought I would triumph over the tyranny of love, leave me in this deception, let me flatter myself that I no longer love!"[7] A flamboyant obbligato for solo cello introduces and punctuates the verses of the aria, suggesting that Boccherini composed "Se d'un amore tiranno" as a vehicle for himself and his wife. The cello and soprano lines are remarkably similar, both displaying coloratura passagework and a wide ambitus of pitches (the cello part spans over five octaves).[8]

Though Boccherini scored the Sonata in A Major for cello and bassline, the absence of figured bass suggests that he intended for the accompanying instrument to be a second cello rather than a keyboard instrument.[9] All three movements are in the same key, as is typical of Boccherini's sonatas with slow-fast-fast movement plans.[10] While Boccherini's formal structures do not conform neatly to textbook descriptions, we can loosely analyze the opening movement as an ABA form. The title *Adagio*, with the literal meaning "at ease," implies a character of genial charm rather than a slow tempo. The melodic language in this movement echoes the operatic singing techniques of the time, introducing copious written-out ornaments, cadenza-like melismas, and other rhetorical flourishes. The central *Allegro*,

---

[6] Boccherini's Sonata in A Major was the sixth in a collection (G.13, G.6, G.5, G.10, G.1, and G.4) published in the 1770s by Bremner of London. Though Boccherini wrote many cello sonatas, these six were the only ones to appear in print during his lifetime.

[7] "Se d'un amor tiranno credei di trionfar, lasciami nell'inganno, lasciami lusingar che più non amo." Translation mine.

[8] See André Luís Giovanini Micheletti, "The Role of Luigi Boccherini in the Development of Cello Technique" (PhD diss., Indiana University, 2014), 87–93.

[9] Speck (198) concludes that Boccherini intended his sonatas as duets for two cellos.

[10] See Speck, 197. In Boccherini's sonatas with a fast-slow-fast movement plan, the middle movement is usually in a contrasting key.

in rounded binary form, develops themes from the aria into long passages of dashing bariolage, interrupting here and there with fragments of graceful, syncopated melody. The *Affettuoso*, another binary movement, returns to the agreeable mood of the first movement, this time in triple meter. Decorative filigree melodies bring the sonata to an elegant ending.

Boccherini's compositions for the cello extended the technique to new levels. His infinitely lyrical writing requires the cello to sing in every vocal range from *basso profundo* to high soprano.[11] By marrying earlier eighteenth-century harmonies and forms with the balanced phrase structures of Haydn and other contemporaries, his style seamlessly combines the Baroque and the Classical.

---

[11] Elisabeth Le Guin, *Boccherini's Body: An Essay in Carnal Musicology* (Berkeley and Los Angeles: University of California Press, 2006), 23.

Table 2.1.1 Boccherini, Sonata in A Major, II. *Allegro*, analysis

Section	A		B			A	
Measures	1-4	5-6	7-10	11-13		14-18	19-22
Thematic material	First thematic group	Transition	Second thematic group	Cadential section		First thematic group	Cadential section
Key(s)	A major	To E major	E major	E major		E major to A major	A major

Table 2.1.2

Section	A				
Measures	1-4	5-14	14-21	21-25	25-29	30-33
Thematic material	"Se d'un amore tiranno" theme	First thematic idea	Second thematic idea	Arpeggiated passagework	Second thematic idea	Closing theme
Key(s)	A major	A major to E major	E major	E major	E major	E major

Section	B						
Measures	34-37	38-45	45-64	65-71	71-75	75-79	80-83
Thematic material	First thematic idea	First thematic idea	Transitional passagework	Second thematic idea	Transitional arpeggiated passagework	Second thematic idea	Closing theme
Key(s)	Dominant of A major	A major/A minor	A major	A major	A major	A major	A major

Table 2.1.3

Section	A				B				
Measures	1–16	17–24	25–28	29–36	37–44	45–52	53–72	73–76	77–84
Thematic material	First thematic group	Second thematic group	Transitional passagework	Closing theme (derived from second thematic group)	Second thematic group	Transition with A major pedal	Second thematic group	Transitional passagework	Closing theme (derived from second thematic group)
Key(s)	A major	E major	E major	E major	E major	A major	E major to A major	A major	A major

2.2

(Franz) Joseph Haydn (1732–1809)

Concerto in C Major, Hob. VIIb:1 (ca. 1762/1765)

I. Moderato   II. Adagio   III. Finale: Allegro molto

In 1761, Joseph Haydn won the position of Vice-Kapellmeister to the noble Esterházy family. It was an impressive achievement for a musician not yet thirty. Haydn's duties at court included supervising the instrument collections, the sheet music archive, and a small orchestra of top European musicians.[1] Though Haydn's responsibilities included authority over the musicians' conduct, several of them also became firm friends.

Joseph Weigl (1740–1820), the sole cellist of the ensemble, was one such friend. The relationship must have been close, since Weigl asked Haydn to stand godfather to his son. Weigl also inspired Haydn's first piece for solo cello, the sparkling Concerto in C Major.

In composing this work, Haydn repurposed "a handful of motives" from an earlier cantata written in celebration of his princely employer's name-day in 1763. Like the cello concerto, *Destatevi o miei fidi*, Hob. XXIVa:2 is in C major, a key eighteenth-century music theorists associated with rejoicing.[2] Its second movement, a vocal duet with the flattering title "Gran d'eroe" ("Great hero"), supplied a dashing scalar figure and a military-sounding dotted-rhythm motive that reappear in the first and third movements of the cello concerto (see Figures 2.2.1 and 2.2.2). Another stylistic device from the cantata, a solo line that begins on a long-held pitch before blossoming into virtuoso melody, appears in the second and third movements of the concerto (Figure 2.2.3).

In contrast to Haydn's second cello concerto in D major (1783), a work of his artistic maturity, the concerto in C owes something to the *ritornello* structures of the Baroque *concerto grosso*. Though some scholars label

---

[1] Georg Feder and James Webster, "Haydn, (Franz) Joseph," *Grove Music Online*, ed. Deane Root, http://oxfordmusiconline.com.

[2] Judy Tarling, *Weapons of Rhetoric: A Guide for Musicians and Audiences*, 2nd ed. (Hertfordshire: Corda Music Publications, 2005), 77.

Figure 2.2.1 Haydn, *Destatevi o miei fidi* Hob. XXIVa:2, II. "Gran d'eroe", mm. 27–30

Figure 2.2.2 Haydn, Concerto in C Major, Hob. VIIb:1, *I. Moderato*, mm. 19–21

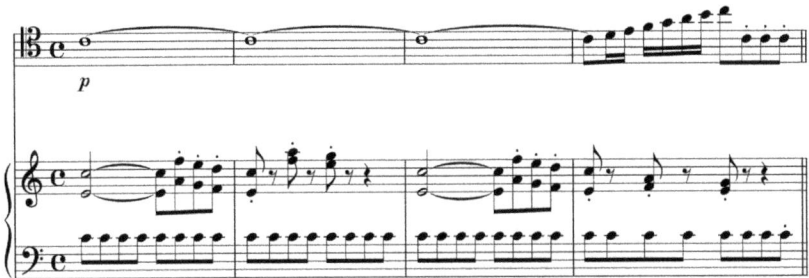

Figure 2.2.3 Haydn, Concerto in C Major, Hob. VIIb:1, *III. Finale: Allegro molto*, mm. 41–44

Haydn's structural plans for the outer movements as monothematic sonata-allegro forms,[3] this description seems inadequate given the abundance of melodic material. The first movement in particular features over a dozen short motives that appear in various keys and combinations over a broad three-part structure.[4] If Haydn's expositions, developments, and recapitulations do not correspond exactly to their textbook definitions, this may be because the textbooks themselves were far in the future.

The instrumentation is relatively light, which is unsurprising given the relatively small ensemble Haydn had at his disposal. The only wind instruments are two oboes and two horns in the first and third movements. Their usual role is to double string parts during *tutti* sections, then drop out during solo sections to avoid drowning out the cello. As the only cellist in the group, Weigl himself would have had to reinforce the bassline during *tutti* sections.[5] This made a busy evening's work for the cellist, since the solos demand stamina and brilliant technique. In the first movement, Haydn writes fleet-footed passages, often in the high tessitura. A difficult double-stopped passage in thumb position reappears several times at the ends of sections. New melodic material in the development section demands fluency through rapid key changes and even rapider string-crossings.

A more relaxed tempo in the second movement provides a break from fast playing, but not from virtuoso techniques. Here, the cellist must negotiate delicate filigree melodies in thumb position, sometimes with added double stops. In the *allegro molto* finale, brilliant scalar and arpeggiated passagework require a strong head for heights. Aside from a few episodes of *Sturm und Drang* in development sections, the mood throughout is one of irrepressible joy.

Weigl may have continued to perform Haydn's C major concerto, but the score apparently got lost and the work was never published. For almost two centuries, the only evidence it had ever existed was an incipit in Haydn's *Entwurf-Katalog*, a thematic listing of his compositions. In 1961, the musicologist Oldřich Pulkert made the discovery of a lifetime while moving a score collection from Radenín Castle in the former Czechoslovakia to the National Museum of Prague. Among the priceless treasures was a set of eighteenth-century parts for the lost Haydn concerto. Though they were not in Haydn's handwriting, scholars quickly established their authenticity. The work was published soon afterwards, and ever since has been one of the most popular works in the cello repertoire and a perennial favorite with audiences.

---

[3] Gerhard Anders, liner notes to *Haydn: Cello Concertos*, Naxos 8.555041, 2001.

[4] For a useful analysis of these motives, see Edward Niel Furse, "Perspectives on the Reception of Haydn's Cello Concerto in C, With Particular Reference to Musicological Writings in English on Haydn's Concertos and the Classical Concerto" (MMus thesis, University of Birmingham, 2009), 85–86.

[5] Sonja Gerlach, preface to Joseph Haydn, *Konzert in C für Violoncello und Orchester* (Kassel: Bärenreiter, 1988), v.

Table 2.2.1 Haydn, Concerto in C Major, I. Moderato, analysis

Exposition (orchestral introduction)

Measures	1–5	6–7	8–11	12–15 (beat 2)	15 (beat 3)–18	19	20–21
Motive	1	2	3	4	5	6	7
Key(s)	C major	G major	G major	C major	G major to C major	C major	C major

Exposition (solo)

Measures	22–26	27–32 (beat 2)	32 (beat 3)–34 (beat 2)	34 (beat 3)–36 (beat 2)	36 (beat 3)–39	40	41–42 (beat 2)	42 (beat 3)–45	46–47 (beat 2)
Motive	1	3	8	9	5	6	7	10	7
Key(s)	C major	C major to C major	G major	G major	G major	G major	G major	G major	G major

Development (orchestral introduction)

Measures	47 (beat 3)–48	49–50	51–52	53–55	56	57–58
Motive	1	11	12	4	6	7
Key(s)	G major	G major	G major	G major	G major	G major

(*continued*)

Table 2.2.1 Continued

Development (solo)

Measures	59–63	64–67 (beat 2)	67 (beat 3)–71 (beat 2)	71 (beat 3)–77 (beat 2)	77 (beat 3)–80	81–83 (beat 2)	83 (beat 3)–84 (beat 2)	84 (beat 3)–88 (beat 2)	88 (beat 3)–89 (beat 3)
Motive	1	3	13	14	5	15	6	10	16
Key(s)	G major	C major to A minor	A minor	A minor, D major, G major, C major, F major, dominant of A minor	A minor	A minor	A minor	A minor	A minor

Development closing section (orchestral)

Measures	89 (beat 3)–93	94–95 (beat 2)	95 (beat 3)–96
Motive	5	17	6
Key(s)	A major, D minor, G major, C major, dominant of D minor	Dominant of C major, dominant of G major	Dominant of C major

Recapitulation (solo)

Measures	97–101	102–104	105–106	107–110 (beat 2)	110 (beat 3)–113 (beat 2)	113 (beat 3)–116	117–121 (beat 2)	121 (beat 3)–122 (beat 2)	122 (beat 3)–126 (beat 2)	123 (beat 3)–126	127–128
Motive	1	3	8	18	19	20	5	6	7	10	7
Key(s)	C major	Dominant of C major	C major	C major	C major	C major	C major, F major, C major	C major	C major	C major	C major

Cadenza (solo)

Measures	-
Motive	-
Key(s)	-

Coda (orchestral)

Measures	129–130 (beat 2)	130 (beat 3)–133	134	135–136
Motive	1	5	6	7
Key(s)	C major	C major	C major	C major

2.3

Ludwig van Beethoven (1770–1827)

Sonata in A Major for Piano and Cello, Op. 69 (ca. 1808)

I. Allegro, ma non tanto   II. Scherzo   III. Adagio cantabile–Allegro vivace

The years 1802 through 1812 marked the beginning of Beethoven's artistic maturity as he moved further and further from the Mozart- and Haydn-influenced language of his early period. In new works like the "Eroica" Symphony (1803–04) and the three "Razumovsky" Quartets, Op. 59 (1806), Beethoven explored extremes of length, complexity, and emotional expression. Small wonder, therefore, that the publisher Breitkopf und Härtel suggested the title *Grande Sonate pour Pianoforte et Violoncelle*[1] for Beethoven's Op. 69, since it too was a more ambitious example of its genre than any predecessor.

It was 1808, a year that had already been extremely productive for Beethoven. By the time he set about completing Op. 69, he had already composed the Fifth and Sixth Symphonies, the Piano Trios, Op. 70, and the Choral Fantasy, Op. 80. Having previously composed two sonatas and three sets of variations for cello and piano, he was not new to the instrumental combination, but in Op. 69 he reimagined its possibilities. This landmark work would become the first composition for cello and piano to treat the instruments as equal partners in melody and harmony.

In doing so, Beethoven created what the cellist and scholar Lewis Lockwood describes as "the foundation of the nineteenth-century cello sonata repertoire."[2] It was no easy task, as Lockwood discovered when studying Beethoven's multiple sketches and revisions in the autograph of the first movement.[3] No composer had yet attempted what Beethoven was trying to achieve, so there was no map to follow. What emerged from the struggle

---

[1] Ludwig van Beethoven, *Grande Sonate pour Pianoforte et Violoncelle*, Op. 69 (Leipzig: Breitkopf und Härtel, 1809).
[2] Lewis Lockwood, *Beethoven: The Music and the Life* (New York: W. W. Norton, 2003), 305.
[3] Lewis Lockwood, *Beethoven: Studies in the Creative Process* (Cambridge, MA: Harvard University Press, 1992), 17–94.

Figure 2.3.1 Bach, *St. John Passion* BWV 245, XXX. "Es ist vollbracht," mm. 1–3

was a strikingly cohesive achievement in sonata form. In the introductory cello melody that opens the work—the rising perfect fifth from A to E, the falling perfect fourth from F♯ to C♯—Beethoven created more than a lyrical melody. These opening pitches also herald the principal modulations in the first movement: the exposition modulation to E major, then modulations to F♯ minor and C♯ minor in the development.[4]

In the short but turbulent development section of the first movement, Beethoven introduces a new theme that has intrigued musicians from the nineteenth century to the present day. Initially, the material appears to be derived from part of the opening cello solo, but it also bears a marked resemblance to an aria from Johann Sebastian Bach's *St. John Passion*. "Es ist vollbracht" ("It is finished"), an alto solo accompanied by an *obbligato* for viola da gamba, is a mournful meditation on the last hours of Christ's life (see Figure 2.3.1). For some commentators, the resemblance between Bach's theme and Beethoven's (Figure 2.3.2) is too strong to be coincidental.

No one has yet uncovered evidence that Beethoven knew the *St. John Passion*. Though unofficial copies of the work had circulated for years,[5] it would not be published until three years after Beethoven's death. In his exploration of the allusive history of "Es ist vollbracht," the musicologist Christopher Alan Reynolds observes: "If [Beethoven] did not know the Bach theme, then we must conclude that Beethoven and Bach created nearly identical forms of a theme that must be considered a musical topic for suffering."[6] Beethoven, who had already lost much of his hearing, was no stranger to suffering. It was only a few years since the Heiligenstadt Testament, Beethoven's anguished letter to his brothers in which he described his increasing deafness,

---

[4] For a detailed analysis, see Eytan Agmon, "The First Movement of Beethoven's Cello Sonata Op. 69: The Opening Solo as a Structural and Motivic Source," *The Journal of Musicology* 16, no. 3 (Summer 1998): 394–409.

[5] Christopher Alan Reynolds, *Motives for Allusion: Context and Content in Nineteenth-Century Music* (Cambridge, MA: Harvard University Press, 2003), 155.

[6] Reynolds, 148.

Figure 2.3.2 Beethoven, Sonata in A Major for Piano and Cello, Op. 69, I. *Allegro ma non tanto*, mm. 107–110

suicidal ideation, and resolution to live on for his art. If Beethoven had by chance glimpsed the score of the *St. John*, the despair of "Es ist vollbracht" would have resonated deeply.

Reynolds argues persuasively that versions of Bach's theme appear in dozens of eighteenth- and nineteenth-century compositions from Carl Philipp Emanuel Bach and Wolfgang Amadeus Mozart to Robert Schumann, Felix Mendelssohn, and Fanny Hensel.[7] (Even if Beethoven did not know "Es ist vollbracht," the Bach-loving siblings Hensel and Mendelssohn certainly did. They also knew Beethoven's works, including the Cello Sonata, Op. 69 and the Piano Sonata, Op. 110, in which the theme appears again. Schumann and the Mendelssohns used the "Es ist vollbracht" theme in various guises in their own compositions.[8])

After the emotional turmoil of the development section, Beethoven restores equanimity in the recapitulation. The opening theme returns, but this time both instruments are playing. Here, the piano embellishes the

---

[7] Reynolds, 148–161.
[8] Reynolds, 149.

theme with a delicate descant melody in triplets. One by one, Beethoven resolves all the thematic materials in the home key, though not without a few signature Beethovenian surprises such as sudden dynamic changes and virtuoso asides for both instruments.

The second movement is a substantial *scherzo* in the tradition of the first "Razumovsky" Quartet. Through rhythmic play and the large-scale structure, the second movement of Op. 69 subverts the menuet-trio movement of eighteenth-century sonata form into something altogether less well-mannered. Constant syncopations for the cello create a sense of rhythmic uncertainty, with both instruments chasing each other around as in a high-stakes game of leapfrog. Marc D. Moskovitz and R. Larry Todd characterize this movement as pastoral because of its drones, comparing it to "a rustic hurdy-gurdy."[9]

Considering the length of the *scherzo*, Beethoven's decision not to write a full slow movement seems logical. At only eighteen measures, the touching *Adagio cantabile* functions as an introduction to the sparkling finale rather than as a complete movement. The key center, E major, creates a sense of yearning for resolution into A major. When this finally arrives, the *Allegro vivace* finale begins with high speed and energy. Beethoven's first two cello sonatas end in light-hearted rondo movements, but the grandeur of Op. 69 calls for the counterbalance of a larger-scale finale. The *Allegro vivace* is in sonata-allegro form, but a less complicated one than that of the first movement. Over driving rhythms in the piano part, the cellist performs technically challenging passagework, often in thumb position and the upper register.

These demands would not have fazed Antonín Kraft, the first performer of the work. As one of the leading cellists of his time, his previous accomplishments included the premiere of Haydn's famously difficult D major cello concerto. Kraft first performed Op. 69 at a private recital in 1809, with Beethoven himself at the piano. A few weeks later, Kraft's son Nicolaus played the cello part at the first public performance with Beethoven's student Baroness Dorothea Ertmann. It has remained central to the cello repertoire ever since.

With his Op. 69, Beethoven established the cello as a credible counterpart to the piano and opened up new worlds of expressive potential for the cello-piano medium. This landmark composition became a prototype for Romantic-era cello-piano works by Hensel, Mendelssohn, Farrenc, Brahms, and various others.

---

[9] Marc D. Moskovitz and R. Larry Todd, *Beethoven's Cello: Five Revolutionary Sonatas and Their World* (Woodbridge, UK: The Boydell Press, 2017), 114.

Table 2.3.1 Beethoven, Sonata in A Major, Op. 69, I. *Allegro, ma non tanto*, analysis

Section	Exposition			
Measures	19–34	34–45	46–60	71–76b
Material	First theme	Transition	Second theme	Closing section
Key	A major	A major, E major	E major	Dominant of A

Section	Development		
Measures	77–89	89–103	104–111
Material	First theme, parallel minor mode	Material from exposition closing section. Cello introduces a descending scalar countertheme.	Transition to recapitulation
Key	A minor, modulating sequentially and chromatically to C major	C major, with tonicizations of F major	Modulating sequentially and chromatically to A major

Section	Recapitulation					
Measures	112–126	127–141	142–156	157–166	167–171	172–220
Material	First theme	Transition	Second theme	Closing section	Transition to coda	Coda
Key	A major	A major, cadences on dominant chord	Recapitulated in A major	A major	A major	A major

3
A MARRIAGE OF TRUE MINDS
The Romantic Cello-Piano Sonata

3.1

Fanny Hensel, born Fanny Mendelssohn-Bartholdy (1805–1847)

Sonata o Fantasia H-U 238 and *Capriccio* H-U 247 for cello and piano (1829)

1829 was an eventful year in the life of Fanny Mendelssohn-Bartholdy, soon to be Fanny Hensel. She and her brother Felix, both leading figures in the nineteenth-century Bach revival, were involved in ambitious plans to perform Bach's *St. Matthew Passion* for the first time in a century. A few months later, she would marry her longtime admirer, the artist Wilhelm Hensel. In an era when the husbands of women artists often expected them to give up their work after marriage, Wilhelm actively encouraged his wife's composition. This must have been a refreshing change from the railings of Hensel's father, Abraham Mendelssohn-Bartholdy, who once wrote to her: "Music will perhaps become [Felix's] profession, whilst for *you* it can and must only be an ornament, never the root of your being."[1]

In her compositions of that year, Hensel started trying out larger-scale forms than those of her signature genres, lieder and miniatures for the piano. Barely a year after the death of Beethoven, whose sonatas had revolutionized the genre, she explored sonata form in her *Ostersonate* (Easter Sonata). She further experimented with sonata-allegro structures in two single-movement pieces for her cellist brother Paul, the *Sonata o Fantasia* and *Capriccio* for cello and piano.

The Baroque movement titles Hensel chose, *fantasia* and *capriccio*, may stem from her lifelong love of and immersion in Bach's music. In Bach's time, the term *fantasia* implied improvisatory musical language[2] and the *capriccio*

---

[1] R. Larry Todd, *Fanny Hensel: The Other Mendelssohn* (New York: Oxford University Press, 2010), 48.
[2] Christopher D. S. Field, E. Eugene Helm, and William Drabkin, "Fantasia," *Grove Music Online*, ed. Deane Root, http://oxfordmusiconline.com.

a whimsical mood.³ By the nineteenth century, the meaning of the terms had evolved. For Beethoven and Schubert, the *fantasia* allowed for a more flexible, structurally freer approach to Classical sonata form. Well-known examples of this include Beethoven's "Moonlight" Sonata (subtitled *quasi una fantasia*) and Schubert's *Wanderer Fantasy*. These works, along with Beethoven's Cello Sonata, Op. 102, No. 1 and Schubert's *Fantasie*, D. 934 for violin and piano, may have served as models for Hensel's *Sonata o Fantasia*.⁴

The formal freedom in *Sonata o Fantasia* makes it difficult to analyze. We may regard it as a highly flexible take on the sonata-allegro: though it adheres to the Classical model of exposition-development-recapitulation, the recapitulation is disproportionately shorter than the concluding coda. Another interpretation might define it as a multi-movement composition in five linked sections, with a return of the opening material as a cyclical "reminiscence" in the fourth section. The first section (or introduction to the exposition) begins in G minor, with thematic material that strongly resembles the cello solo from the third movement of Beethoven's String Quartet, Op. 59 No. 1 ("Razumovsky"). Hensel switches the harmony to the parallel major mode as she begins the second section (or exposition). The short middle section (or development) goes through circle of fifths progressions, modulating back to G minor for a quick return (or recapitulation) of the opening material before progressing into a much longer coda in G major. Whichever way we interpret the form, there are four distinct but related themes; while their characters differ, they all feature descending phrase shapes and appoggiatura-like accented dissonances.

In the *Capriccio*, too, Hensel shows an experimental approach to form. It is harder to analyze the three-part form as a sonata-allegro plan, however, since the second section does not develop thematic material from the first in the manner of a traditional development section. Instead, the structure seems to create a thesis, antithesis, and synthesis of ideas. Hensel begins in A♭ major with a theme in compound meter whose *siciliano* rhythms echo the pastoral tropes of the Baroque. Though she briefly tonicizes B♭ minor, D♭ major, and F minor in this opening section, Hensel makes no outright modulations. It therefore comes as a surprise to the listener when the second section begins suddenly and rapidly in F minor and in common time. Even if this part of the *Capriccio* is not a "textbook" thematic development, Hensel's

---

³ Erich Schwandt, "Capriccio," *Grove Music Online*, ed. Deane Root, http://oxfordmusiconline.com.
⁴ Todd, 137.

Figure 3.1.1 Hensel, *Capriccio* H-U 247, mm. 108–110

chromaticism and modulations through D, G, C, and B♭ create the sense of harmonic upheaval associated with the idea of development. Adding to the turmoil is a melodic motive (beginning in m. 108) reminiscent of the aria "Es ist vollbracht" from Bach's *St. John Passion* (Figure 3.1.1). In quoting this material, Hensel alludes not only to Bach, but to the development theme in the first movement of Beethoven's Cello Sonata, Op. 69.[5]

The harmonic and melodic unrest of the middle section eventually dissipates through slowed harmonic rhythm and dominant pedals that hint at a modulation into B♭. At the last minute, Hensel uses the E♭ triad to pivot abruptly back to A♭ major and a quasi-recapitulation of the opening section. By integrating the melodic and harmonic material of the first section with the freer textural style of the second, Hensel creates a sense of resolution as the *Capriccio* concludes peacefully.

---

[5] Christopher Alan Reynolds, *Motives for Allusion: Context and Content in Nineteenth-Century Music* (Cambridge, MA: Harvard University Press, 2003), 149–150.

Table 3.1.1 Hensel, *Sonata o Fantasia* H-U 238, analysis

Section	*Andante doloroso* (introduction)	*Prestissimo* (main section of the exposition)	*Poco più lento* (development)	*Tempo del Andante ma in modo di fantasia* (recapitulation)	*Allegro molto moderato* (coda)
Measures	1–38	39–79	80–113	114–125	126–160
Thematic areas	1	2	3	1	4
Key(s)	G minor, C minor modulation, return to G minor	G major, circle of fifths progression, D major	D major, tonicizations of G major, B major, E minor, A minor, dominant harmony of G	G minor	G major, brief tonicization of C, return to G

Table 3.1.2 Hensel, *Capriccio* H-U 247, analysis

Section	A	B	A
Measures	1–27	28–140	141–175
Thematic material	First theme	Second theme ("Es ist vollbracht" allusion, 108–110)	First theme
Key(s)	A♭ major, tonicizations of B♭ minor, D♭ minor, B♭ minor, F major, A♭ cadence	F minor, tonicizations of D major, C major, F major, C major, A♭ major, E♭ minor, A♭ major, F minor, E♭ major, A♭ major	A♭ major

3.2

Felix Mendelssohn-Bartholdy (1809–1847)

Sonata No. 2 in D Major for Cello and Piano, Op. 58 (1843)

I. Allegro assai vivace   II. Allegretto scherzando   III. Adagio
IV. Molto allegro e vivace

Almost a quarter of a century separates Beethoven's last cello sonata (1815) and Felix Mendelssohn's first (1838). A handful of cello sonatas appeared in the intervening years, of which only Hensel's single-movement *Sonata o Fantasia* remains in the core repertoire. An 1819 sonata by Franz Xaver Wolfgang Mozart (1791–1844) owes less stylistically to the composer's contemporaries than to his long-dead father. Three sonatas from 1820 by George Onslow (1784–1853), the so-called "French Beethoven,"[1] are more modern in style but never gained much of a footing among cellists. Johann Nepomuk Hummel (1778–1837) may have enjoyed a reputation as one of Europe's greatest composers during his lifetime,[2] but his 1824 sonata is a light work containing little innovation.

Mendelssohn is therefore the first major composer since Beethoven to make large-scale contributions to the cello-piano sonata. His affinity with the cello likely began in the family home with his cellist brother Paul, to whom he dedicated the *Variations Concertantes*, Op. 17 (1829) and Sonata No. 1 in B♭ Major, Op. 45 (1838). Over the course of his career, Mendelssohn composed further works for the cello at the behest of Europe's leading cellists. For Alfredo Piatti (1822–1901), he sketched a now-lost cello concerto,[3] and

---

[1] Viviane Niaux, "George Onslow: le Beethoven français," *Les sources du romantisme français* (October 2009): 1–18

[2] Joel Sachs and Mark Kroll, "Hummel, Johann Nepomuk," *Grove Music Online*, ed. Deane Root, http://oxfordmusiconline.com.

[3] R. Larry Todd, *Mendelssohn: A Life in Music* (New York: Oxford University Press, 2003), 546.

for Lisa Cristiani (1827–1853), one of the earliest women virtuosi, he wrote the *Lied ohne Worte*, Op. 109. Two other salon pieces, *Assai tranquillo* (1835) and the "Mendelssohn-Merk" variations (1830), came out of Mendelssohn's respective collaborations with Julius Rietz (1812–1877) and Joseph Merk (1795–1852).[4] In 1843, Mendelssohn completed his most substantial piece for cello and piano, the Sonata No. 2 in D Major, Op. 58. The dedicatee was Count Mateusz Wielhorski (1794–1866), a founding figure in Russian cello playing and a student of Beethoven's friend Romberg.[5]

1843 also marked the completion of Mendelssohn's "Scottish" Symphony, Op. 56 and the incidental music to *A Midsummer Night's Dream*, Op. 61. Aged thirty-four, Mendelssohn was at the height of his artistic maturity and one of the most sought-after musicians in Europe. Many considered him the heir to Beethoven. This comparison certainly applies to Mendelssohn's compositions for cello which, like Beethoven's, treat cello-piano writing as a dialogue of equals. Though his compositional style looked back to Beethovenian tradition, it was also progressive in matters of form. In writing four full movements in Op. 58, Mendelssohn arguably went beyond Beethoven's achievements in the genre with his ambitious approach to sonata-allegro form in the first and last movements.

The opening *Allegro assai vivace* begins in a lively mood. The first theme starts with the motive of an ascending arpeggiated D major triad in the first inversion. Underneath this optimistic cello melody, rapid block chords for the piano create a racing "heartbeat" effect. The second theme does not contrast strongly with the first in emotion; the character throughout is one of energy and exuberance. At the end of the exposition, Mendelssohn does not call for a repeat, perhaps (as Douglass Seaton speculates) because "the main thematic material is almost constantly evolving."[6] The same is perhaps true of the *Allegretto scherzando* movement, whose form is almost but not quite a rondo. With a more reserved character than the famous *Scherzo* of Mendelssohn's *Midsummer Night's*

---

[4] These two compositions are unfinished fragments. R. Larry Todd has reconstructed performing editions of both. See Felix Mendelssohn-Bartholdy and R. Larry Todd, *Sämtliche Werke für Violoncello und Klavier* (Kassel: Bärenreiter Verlag), 2017.

[5] Geoffrey Norris, "Wielhorski, Count Mateusz," *Grove Music Online*, ed. Deane Root, http://oxfordmusiconline.com.

[6] Douglass Seaton, "Review of *Sämtliche Werke für Violoncello und Klavier*/Complete Works for Violoncello and Piano, ed. R. Larry Todd," *Nineteenth-Century Music Review* 15, no. 1 (2018): 147.

Dream music, it features two contrasting themes, one in spiky pizzicato and the other gently lyrical.

The third movement, *Adagio*, is formally and stylistically the most interesting of the four. It opens with a piano solo in richly arpeggiated chords in the style of a Lutheran chorale. Mendelssohn's use of chorales and chorale-like themes is not unusual in his other works, such as the "Reformation" Symphony, Op. 107, but in an abstract work like Op. 58 the stylistic departure is unexplained. Mendelssohn may have included it here as an implied statement of faith—Mendelssohn's formerly Jewish family had converted to Protestant Christianity during his childhood—or perhaps a nod to Bach, whose music he revered.

After this first theme concludes, the cello introduces the second theme, a gentle *arioso*. The following material seamlessly combines the two themes. The movement concludes with the piano in the melodic role, while the cellist sustains the tonic note with the bow for the last seven measures while simultaneously plucking the open G-string with the left hand on the first and third beats of each measure. The effect recalls the sound of the sustaining foot pedal on a church organ—an additional "sacred" touch.

The finale, which thematically resembles that Mendelssohn's Piano Concerto in D Minor, Op. 40, marks a return to the energetic mood of the first movement. Though it is roughly in sonata-allegro form, Mendelssohn does not work through traditional Classical procedures—an extended coda, for example, is far longer than the very short development section.

Though he was still a young man, Mendelssohn tragically died just four years after completing this work. On October 8, 1847, a diary entry by his friend Ignaz Moscheles[7] recalled spending the evening at Mendelssohn's home listening to the composer and Julius Rietz perform Op. 58 alongside Beethoven's two sonatas Op. 102. The day after this pleasant soirée, Mendelssohn suffered the first of the strokes that would kill him. He died on November 4.

---

[7] Felix Moscheles, ed., *Letters of Felix Mendelssohn to Ignaz and Charlotte Moscheles* (Boston, MA: Ticknor and Company, 1888), 290.

Table 3.2.1 Mendelssohn, Sonata in D Major, I. *Allegro assai vivace*, analysis

Section	Exposition				
Measures	1–40	40–66	67–105	106–121	122–153
Thematic material	First theme	Transition	Second theme	First theme	Closing theme
Key(s)	D major	A major	A major	A major	A major

Section	Development				
Measures	154–198	198–214	214–226	227–238	238–260
Thematic material	First theme	Second theme	First theme	Dominant pedal	Retransition
Key(s)	Tonicizations: A, B minor, E minor, F♯ minor, B minor, G major	C major	To D major	A major	Tonicization of E major, then descending chromatic bassline towards dominant harmony

Section	Recapitulation				
Measures	261–328	329–377	378–392	392–397	398–451
Thematic material	First theme; 279: second theme; 313: first theme	Closing section on material from first theme	First theme	First theme	Coda
Key(s)	D major	D major	E♭ major (part of a Neapolitan progression)	To dominant of D major	D major

Table 3.2.2 Mendelssohn, II. *Allegretto scherzando*, analysis

Section	A	B	A	B	A and B
Measures	1–51	51–88	93–133	134–153	154–183
Thematic material	First theme	Second theme	First theme developed	Second theme	Coda (material from both themes)
Key(s)	B minor	D major/G major	B minor	B major/E major	B major/B minor

Table 3.2.3 Mendelssohn, III. *Adagio*, analysis

Section	A	B	Synthesis of A and B	Coda
Measures	1–12	12–29	29–41	41–47
Thematic material	Chorale theme	*Arioso* theme	Chorale and *arioso* themes combined	Cadential material
Key(s)	G major	E minor; tonicization of A minor; dominant harmony of G major	G major	G major

Table 3.2.4 Mendelssohn, IV. Molto allegro e vivace, analysis

Section	Introduction and exposition				
Measures	1–20	20–56	56–88	89–100	101–119
Thematic material	Introduction theme	Exposition: first theme	Second theme	Closing theme	Coda based on introduction theme
Key(s)	D major	D major	A major	A major	A major

Section	Development	Recapitulation and codas			
Measures	120–148	149–163	164–177	177–212	
Thematic material	First theme	First theme	Second theme	Coda 1, first theme material	Coda 2, introduction and first theme material
Key(s)	D major	D major	D major	D major	D major

3.3
Frédéric Chopin (1810–1849)
Sonata in G Minor, Op. 65 (1845–47)

I. Allegro moderato   II. Scherzo   III. Largo   IV. Finale: Allegro

Almost all Frédéric Chopin's compositions are for his own instrument, the piano, but his friendships with cellists led him also to write a significant amount of music for the cello. Chopin's attraction to the instrument began early with the youthful Piano Trio, Op. 8 (1828–29). Not long after this, he met the cellist Josef Merk (1795–1852) during a long stay in Vienna. A leading cellist and friend to many composers, including Schubert, Merk inspired Chopin's *Introduction et Polonaise Brillante*, Op. 3. After he moved to Paris in 1831, Chopin made a lifelong friend in the Théâtre Italien cellist Auguste Franchomme (1808–84). Chopin and Franchomme became inseparable, socializing, performing, and even composing together. Their creative partnership included the co-composition of the *Grand Duo Concertant* (1832) on themes from Giacomo Meyerbeer's opera *Robert le diable*. The resulting work showcases the immense technical skill of both partners.

Unable to return to Poland because of political upheavals there, Chopin built a reputation in France as "one of the most radical and penetrating musical minds of the post-Beethoven era."[1] He began a nine-year love affair with the wealthy, cross-dressing novelist George Sand and moved in with her. On an ill-fated vacation to Mallorca with Sand and her children, he contracted the illness—probably tuberculosis—that would eventually kill him. Chopin's health, which had always been delicate, declined rapidly. So too did his relationship with Sand, especially after he took her adult daughter's side in a family quarrel. Heart and health broken, Chopin started work on another piece for Franchomme, the Cello Sonata, Op. 65.

---

[1] Jim Samson, "Chopin, Fryderyk Franciszek," *Grove Music Online*, ed. Deane Root, http://oxfordmusiconline.com.

The composition cost him a great deal of effort. He made over a hundred pages of sketches for Op. 65 before he could commit to making a complete draft.[2] It was not—as critics suggested—that Chopin could not handle the demands of sonata form, but that he wanted to transform and modernize it beyond Classical boundaries.[3] One such modernization was his ambitious expansion of sonata-allegro form in the first movement. At 234 measures, the *Allegro moderato* spends 114 of them on an exposition and 92 on a development, but only 28 on a "compressed"[4] recapitulation, with the length of the development making an extensive recapitulation unnecessary. It seems extraordinary today that Chopin's friends advised him and Franchomme to leave the first movement out of the premiere performance on February 16, 1848, because they felt it "contained too many ideas."[5] It is more likely they could not understand the broad scope of Chopin's innovations.

The themes in this opening movement are *cantabile* in character, demonstrating Chopin's lifelong love of *bel canto* singing. Also present in the first theme are hints of an allusion to "Gute Nacht," the first song in Schubert's *Winterreise*,[6] evidenced by the falling melodic line with a dotted-rhythm pattern on the last beat of the measure. Schubert's song cycle chronicles the lonely journey of a rejected lover, a role in which Chopin had recently found himself. The opening words by Wilhelm Müller—"I arrived a stranger, a stranger I depart"—must have spoken powerfully to his wounded feelings. This theme lasts for twenty-three measures and does not modulate away from G minor. A transitional section begins, but it too lingers in G minor as if reluctant to depart. A secondary key area of B♭ major finally arrives in time for the entry of the second theme; by the time he progresses towards a closing theme, Chopin has modulated to D minor. The unusually long development section grows out of variants of the first theme and transition theme from the exposition, traveling through tonicized keys on its way to an iteration of the second theme in G major. All the recapitulation needs to recapitulate is the closing theme material.

The key scheme of the first movement, G minor–B♭ major–D minor–G minor, mirrors the plan of principal keys for each of the movements. Chopin

---

[2] Janet Schmalfeldt, *In the Process of Becoming: Analytical and Philosophical Perspectives on Form in Early Nineteenth-Century Music* (New York: Oxford University Press, 2011), 216.

[3] See Anatole Leikin, "The Sonatas," *The Cambridge Companion to Chopin*, ed. Jim Samson (New York: Cambridge University Press, 1992), 161.

[4] Andrew I. Aziz, "The Evolution of Chopin's Sonata Forms: Excavating the Second Theme Group," *A Journal of the Society for Music Theory* 21, no. 4 (December 2015): 9.

[5] Frederick Niecks, *Frederick Chopin as Man and Musician*, 1902 edition (Urbana, IL: Project Gutenberg, 2009), 551.

[6] Leikin, 185.

has switched the second movement (D minor) and third (B♭ major), but this was not necessarily his original plan, as we can see in a manuscript copy of the cello part in Franchomme's hand where the second and third movements are reversed.[7] Chopin's decision to "frame" the slow movement between two quick movements is more effective, however, since the mercurial character of the second movement provides necessary contrast from the melancholy of the first. This *Scherzo*, with its Classical menuet-trio form, has the most traditional structure of the four movements. Following a lyrical middle section, a reprise of the *scherzo* is a shortened version of the original rather than the *da capo* that composers of the past might have used.

In the *Largo*, Chopin creates another unusual formal structure by using contrapuntal lines to "overlap" between thematic and harmonic sections.[8] Chopin uses the time signature 3/2, unusually for the period, and this creates opportunities for hemiola and other rhythmic and metrical nuances.[9] The texture has three distinct voices: the melodic voice, the broken chordal inner voice, and the bassline. Cello and piano exchange melodic and bass parts in irregular phrase patterns; cadences do not occur in tandem with phrase endings, meaning that it is difficult to divide the movement into formal sections. Only at the very end of the movement do the cello and piano simultaneously present melodic material, at last unifying the complicated melodic, harmonic, and rhythmic resources.

The final *Allegro* is a flexible essay in rondo form, with sharply contrasting thematic materials and considerable chromaticism. A *più mosso* coda ends in the parallel major key, resolving the turbulent emotions of this long and complicated work.

By the time Chopin and Franchomme performed Op. 65, Chopin was in painfully frail health. Charles Hallé, who attended the dress rehearsal of Op. 65, recalled that Chopin "went around the room bent like a half-opened penknife."[10] Faithful Franchomme was with Chopin until the last, playing the cello for his friend as he lay on his deathbed. We have him to thank for this composition that enriches both the cello repertoire and the evolution of sonata form.

---

[7] August Franchomme, *Partie de violoncelle de la Sonate pour Piano et Violoncelle de Chopin écrite sous sa dictée par moi Franchomme*, manuscript, 1847, housed at the Bibliothèque Nationale de France.

[8] See W. Dean Sutcliffe, "Chopin's Counterpoint: The *Largo* from the Cello Sonata, Opus 65," *The Musical Quarterly* 83, no. 1 (Spring 1999): 114–133.

[9] Schmalfeldt, 225.

[10] Niecks, 549.

Table 3.3.1 Chopin, Sonata in G Minor, Op. 65, I. Allegro moderato, analysis

Section	Exposition				
Measures	1–23	24–60	61–68	69–91	92–113
Thematic material	First theme	Transition	Introduction to second theme	Second theme	Closing theme
Key(s)	G minor	G minor	Dominant harmony of B♭ major	B♭ major	D minor

Section	Development			Recapitulation		
Measures	114–148	149–174	175–182	183–197	198–206	206–234
Thematic material	Variants on first theme and transition theme	Transition	Introduction to second theme	Second theme	Second part of second theme	Closing theme
Key(s)	G major, modulations, ends D minor	D minor, modulates, ends with dominant harmony of A minor	Dominant harmony of G major	G major	B♭ major	G minor

3.4

Louise Farrenc (1804–1875)

Sonata in B♭ Major, Op. 46 (1858)

I. Allegro moderato   II. Andante sostenuto   III. Finale: Allegro

Louise Farrenc was born Jeanne-Louise Dumont in an annex of the Sorbonne, where her father worked as a sculptor. She grew up surrounded by her bohemian parents' artistic friends and was a frequent performer at their community soirées. Though she considered a career in visual art, her talent for music was even greater.

This unconventional upbringing may explain why it never occurred to Farrenc to give up her career after marriage, as talented women of the era often did. While studying counterpoint, orchestration, and composition with Anton Reicha during her teens, she fell in love with a flutist-composer named Aristide Farrenc. A musician of average ability, Aristide was unfazed by the seventeen-year-old Louise's superior musicianship. Soon after their marriage, the young bride returned to her studies, and Aristide, realizing he had a better head for business than for composition, founded a music publishing company. The marriage was a happy partnership of equals. Aristide's company was successful, acquiring the rights to compositions by Beethoven and Johann Nepomuk Hummel—two composers who would significantly influence Farrenc's composition.

Farrenc's dual career as a pianist and composer went from strength to strength. In her compositions, she favored serious, Viennese-inspired Classicism over the sentimental salon pieces of the time. As well as compositions for her own instrument, Farrenc wrote large-scale chamber works and three symphonies. The unusual instrumentation of her two piano quintets—violin, viola, cello, double bass, and piano—owes less to the example of Schubert's "Trout" Quintet than to a work by her mentor, Hummel. Though Farrenc was reticent about self-promotion, critics praised her compositions.[1] No less a figure than Robert Schumann published a positive review of Farrenc's

---

[1] Bea Friedland, "Louise Farrenc, 1804–1875: Composer-Performer-Scholar" (PhD diss., City University of New York, 1975), 32.

Air russe varié, describing the variations as "so sure in outline, so logical in development—in a word, so finished—that one must fall under their charm... especially since a subtle aroma of romanticism hovers over them."[2]

In 1842, Farrenc became one of the first women professors at the Paris Conservatoire, and the only one with a full-time appointment. She remained there for three decades teaching piano to women students, since the rules of the Conservatoire dictated that women professors could not teach composition, nor could they teach men.[3] (These rules remained in place until well into the twentieth century.[4]) Farrenc never let such restrictions stop her. With the success of her nonet for woodwinds and strings (1849), she finally had the political capital she needed to confront the Conservatoire administration over the matter of her salary, which was lower than that of her male colleagues. Her arguments convinced her employers, and from then on she received equal pay. The Institut de France twice rewarded her achievements with an important award, the *Prix Chartier*, in 1861 and 1869.[5]

Farrenc composed her cello sonata in 1858 and published it three years later. While it postdates Frédéric Chopin's sonata by more than a decade, it does not share Chopin's ardently Romantic language. (Though they had a mutual friend in the cellist Auguste Franchomme, there is no evidence Farrenc and Chopin ever met.[6]) The three movements are essentially conservative in design: the outer movements are in Classical sonata-allegro form, and most of the phrases within them correspond to Mozartean period and sentence structures. The contour of the opening theme is so similar to that of a cello sonata in B♭ major by Bernhard Romberg (1867–1841) that it is possible Farrenc used it as a model for idiomatic cello writing. Cello passagework in the third movement suggests that Farrenc was also familiar with the second of Beethoven's Op. 5 sonatas, in which similar string-crossing patterns accompany melodic material in the piano part. The strongest influence, however, seems to have been yet another sonata B♭ major, Felix Mendelssohn's Op. 45. Farrenc's concept of form, like Mendelssohn's, drew upon past traditions;[7] her concessions to Romanticism were melodic lyricism

---

[2] Bea Friedland, "Louise Farrenc (1804–1875): Composer, Performer, Scholar," *Musical Quarterly* 60, no. 2 (April 1974): 264.
[3] Friedland, PhD diss., 68.
[4] Friedland, PhD diss., 309–310.
[5] Bea Friedland, "Farrenc Family," *Grove Music Online*, ed. Deane Root, http://oxfordmusiconline.com.
[6] Friedland, PhD diss., 206.
[7] Friedland, PhD diss., 288.

and a predilection for modulating to unexpected keys, often through mediant harmony.

Farrenc's dedicated her Op. 46 to her chamber music colleague Charles Lebouc (1822–1893),[8] a former student of Franchomme. Since she wrote it to perform herself, it comes as no surprise that the piano part is demanding; the cello part, too, demands agility in all registers of the instrument. Like Beethoven's sonatas "for piano and cello" (a word order Farrenc may have copied from him), Farrenc's writing for cello and piano treats the instruments as equal partners.

After a brief piano introduction composed of ascending arpeggiated chords over a bassline, the cellist introduces the expansive first theme. For now, apart from a couple of tonicizations in F major and G minor, the harmony does not stray far from the principal key of B♭ major. A transition modulates to the secondary key of F major, with a brief detour to the unexpected key of D♭ major along the way. The second theme begins in F major. While it is as lyrical as the first, its contour tends towards descending motion, in contrast to the predominantly ascending contour of the first theme. The harmony remains in F until the end of the exposition, with some characteristically colorful tonicizations of F minor, D♭ major, and B♭ minor.

The development section starts dramatically in G minor and rapidly begins a series of tonicizations and modulations to distant keys. E♭ major gives way to A♭, and through a clever enharmonic respelling of a C♭ into a B♮, the harmony arrives seamlessly in B major – about as far from the original key as possible. Here, some new thematic material begins. Farrenc navigates her way out of B major as deftly as she began, through another enharmonic respelling that eventually leads back to F major. This arrival signals a move back to B♭ for the recapitulation, introduced by a mini-cadenza for cello alone.

The recapitulation returns as expected to the first theme, but the piano harmony changes. Gone are the regular arpeggiated chords from the exposition, and in their place the pianist's right hand weaves a syncopated descant theme around the cello melody. A few excursions in mediant harmony aside, the transitional and second themes go through the expected resolutions, and an extended closing section reinforces B♭ major as it prepares for a coda in emphatic unison.

---

[8] Katharine Ellis, "Female Pianists and their Male Critics in Nineteenth-Century Paris," *Journal of the American Musicological Society* 50, nos. 2–3 (Summer–Autumn 1997): 358, 381.

Farrenc's second movement, *Andante sostenuto*, contains further harmonic surprises. The structure, ABCABCA, has something in common with rondo form, but the slow tempo (quarter note = 92) is incompatible with the definition. The compound meter suggests a pastoral topic, and the character is one of peaceful elegance. The home key is an E♭ major, and the A and B sections seldom venture beyond the tonic key or its dominant, B♭ major. The two C sections, however, use mediant harmony to pivot to the exotic keys of G♭ major and C♭ major. Each time, Farrenc uses a pivot chord to restore E♭.

The rapid finale features a thematic back-and-forth between piano and cello, with the instrumentalists constantly interrupting the other to take over the melodic part. Farrenc takes the harmony on another series of quick tonicizations, including a few trips around the circle of fifths. Beethovenian passagework for the cellist matches the intense virtuosity of the piano part. Just when it seems as if the piece will end quietly, a surprise *forte* three measures before the end leads to a lively final cadence.

Farrenc's compositions precede the renaissance in French musical life that began after the founding of the Third Republic in 1870.[9] Her Op. 46 is an important precursor to later nineteenth-century French cello sonatas by Camille Saint-Saëns, Marie Jaëll, and Léon Boëllmann. Though it fell from favor after her lifetime, the "Farrenc revival" of the twenty-first century has deservedly brought her work back into the concert hall.

---

[9] Stephen Sensbach, *French Cello Sonatas 1871–1939* (Dublin: The Lilliput Press, 2001), xiv.

Table 3.4.1 Farrenc, Sonata in B-flat Major, Op. 46, I. *Allegro moderato*, analysis

Section	Exposition					
Measures	1–3	3–26	26–52	53–74	75–98	99–111
Thematic material	Introduction (piano)	First theme	Transition	Second theme	Transition to closing section	Closing section
Key(s)	B♭ major	B♭ major; tonicizations of F major and G minor; cadence in B♭ major	B♭ major, modulation to F major, tonicization of D♭ major	F major	Chromatic harmony, tonicizations of F minor, D♭ major, B♭ minor	F major

Section	Development					
Measures	112–117	118–146	147–161	162–167	168–171	
Thematic material	Introduction (piano)	First theme	Development theme (derived from first and second theme material)	Contrapuntal variant of first theme	Mini-cadenza leading to recapitulation	
Key(s)	G minor to E♭ major	E♭ major to A♭ major, modulation to B major through enharmonic respellings	B major, tonicizations of E minor, F minor	Dominant of B♭ major	Dominant of B♭ major	

Section	Recapitulation					
Measure numbers	172–197	198–215	216–237	238–244	245–287	288–293
Thematic material	First theme with additional piano descant	Transition (same material as exposition)	Second theme	Transition to closing section	Closing section	Coda
Key(s)	B♭ major	E♭ major, tonicizations of C minor, G♭ major, F major	B♭ major	Interlude in D major, to B♭ major	B♭ major, tonicization of D minor, dominant pedal of B♭ major	B♭ major

3.5

Johannes Brahms (1833–1897)

Sonata No. 1 in E Minor, Op. 38 (1862–65)

I. Allegro non troppo   II. Allegretto quasi menuetto   III. Allegro

The years between 1859 and 1865 were a richly creative period in Brahms's career, especially for chamber music. Before he began the Cello Sonata, Op. 38, Brahms wrote the String Sextet No. 1, Op. 18 (1859–60), the first two Piano Quartets, Op. 25 and Op. 26 (1861), and the monumental Piano Quintet, Op. 36 (1861). During the three-year gestation of Op. 38, he began his String Sextet No. 2, Op. 36 (1864–65), and shortly afterwards completed the Horn Trio, Op. 40 (1865).

Brahms was familiar with cello technique and repertoire, having had lessons during his childhood. Though he is unlikely to have crossed paths with another Hamburg resident, the eminent cellist Bernhard Romberg (1767–1841), he knew Romberg's compositions well enough to repurpose several themes from them in Op. 38.[1] The five cello-piano sonatas of Beethoven were also influences, particularly the last, Beethoven's Op. 102, No. 2. Though Brahms's musical language throughout is turbulently Romantic, several aspects of Op. 38 look back to Baroque and Classical procedures such as Bach's fugues, menuet and trio form, and so on.

Brahms's contemporaries regarded him as the heir to Beethoven, a flattering comparison with the downside that they also measured his compositions against those of his predecessor. The knowledge of this must have caused Brahms considerable anxiety. Famously self-critical, he destroyed any material that did not meet his standards, including some of his plans for Op. 38. Brahms's early ideas for a slow movement did not make it past his ruthless self-censorship, therefore the work does not have one.[2]

---

[1] William Klenz, "Brahms, Opus 38: Piracy, Pillage, Plagiarism, or Parody?," *The Music Review* 34 (1973): 39–50.

[2] Margaret Notley posits that the "lost" slow movement of Op. 38 later ended up in Brahms's Cello Sonata No. 2, Op. 99. See Margaret Notley, "Brahms' Cello Sonata in F Major and Its Genesis: A Study in Half-Step Relations," *Brahms Studies*, ed. David Brodbeck (Lincoln: University of Nebraska Press, 1994), 1:139.

The opening movement of Op. 38, *Allegro non troppo*, begins darkly with a low-pitched theme for the cello to the accompaniment of austere piano chords on the off beats. The first phrase arpeggiates the E minor triad in ascending motion and reaches a high point on the lowered sixth scale degree. Intensity builds as Brahms's harmony moves toward unexpected tonicizations of C and F majors, though by the time the second theme arrives it is in the more expected key of B minor. The oscillating arpeggiations of a B minor triad in the second theme provide a vehicle for favorite Brahmsian rhythmic devices, such as syncopation and hemiola. The closing theme to the exposition, in contrast to the first theme, is mostly stepwise and in descending motion.

These thematic materials collide spectacularly in the development section. Brahms intensifies the stormy mood with a dramatic gesture of repeated two-octave leaps for the cellist. After this, a tight-knit recapitulation gathers the thematic and motivic material back together. Over the concluding chords, the cellist plays three whole notes on G-sharp, the mediant degree of the tonic parallel major triad. By ending on an imperfect authentic cadence in this manner, Brahms creates a sense of open-endedness that resolves only with the start of the second movement in A minor.

Here, Brahms unifies the menuet and trio sections by giving them thematically similar material. To create contrast, he varies their textures: the voice-leading in the menuet section is relatively straightforward, whereas the trio features undulating broken-octave figures that recall the pianistic writing of Robert Schumann.[3]

The concluding *Allegro* is an homage to both Beethoven and Bach. In form and character, Brahms appears to have taken the fugal finale of Beethoven's Op. 102, No. 2 as a model for his own last movement. The subject of the fugue, however, bears more of a resemblance to Bach's Contrapunctus XVII from *The Art of Fugue*, BWV 1080.[4]

This combination of fugal and sonata-allegro procedures creates an unusual hybrid form.[5] Even more unusual is the fact that the second theme is absent from a recapitulation that does not begin in the tonic key. That Brahms

---

[3] Daniel Gregory Mason compares this section to *Des Abends* from Schumann's *Fantasiestücke* Op. 12. See Mason, *The Chamber Music of Brahms* (New York: MacMillan, 1933), 71–72.

[4] Wilhelm Altmann, "Bach-Zitate in der Violoncello-Sonate op. 38 von Brahms," *Die Musik* 12 no. 2 (October 2, 1912): 84–85.

[5] Michael Musgrave, *The Music of Brahms* (London and Boston, MA: Routledge & Kegan Paul, 1985), 107.

Figure 3.5.1 Brahms, Sonata No. 1 in E Minor, Op. 38, *III. Allegro*, mm. 1–5

Figure 3.5.2 Bach, *The Art of Fugue* BWV 1080, Contrapunctus XVII, subject

could break the rules so persuasively is testimony to his assimilation of two centuries' worth of compositional techniques.

Brahms dedicated the Cello Sonata, Op. 38 to Josef Gänsbacher (1829–1911), a music educator and amateur cellist. Perhaps as a concession to Gänsbacher's lack of skill, Brahms placed most of the cello part in the low to middle registers of the instrument. The piano part is often in the same register as the cello, and this created balance problems for Gänsbacher at the first performance. According to a member of the audience, "Brahms played so loud that the worthy Josef complained that he could not hear his cello at all—'Lucky for you, too', growled Brahms, and let the piano rage on."[6]

Fortunately, many other cellists quickly and enthusiastically adopted Op. 38 into their concert programs. One was the soloist Robert Hausmann (1852–1909), who championed the work and brought it permanently into the repertoire. Two decades later, Brahms made Hausmann the dedicatee of his Sonata No. 2 in F Major, Op. 99.

---

[6] Henry S. Drinker, *The Chamber Music of Johannes Brahms* (Philadelphia, PA: Elkan-Vogel, 1932), 81.

Table 3.5.1 Brahms Sonata in E Minor, *III. Allegro*, analysis

Section	Exposition					
Measures	1–4	5–8	9–15	16–19	20–24	25–30
Thematic material	Fugue exposition				Fugue continuation	Fugue closing section
Cello	–	Subject	C.S. 1	C.S. 2	C.S. 1	–
Piano R.H.	–	–	Subject	C.S. 1	C.S. 2	–
Piano L.H.	Subject	Countersubject 1	C.S. 2	Subject	C.S. 2	Subject
Key(s)	E minor	Dominant of E	E minor	E minor	B major	

Section	Exposition (continued)		
Measures	31–43	44–52	53–75
Thematic material	Transition 1 (derived from fugue subject)	Transition 2 (derived from fugue subject)	Second theme (derived from fugue countersubject 1)
Key(s)	E minor to V 4/2 of G major	Dominant of G major	G major

Section	Development		
Measures	76–90	91–115	115–122
Thematic material	*Animato*, material derived from fugue subject	Material derived from fugue subject and countersubject	Retransition
Key(s)	G major to dominant of C	Tonicizations of D major, F-sharp major, C-sharp major, to dominant of E	B major

Section	Recapitulation			
Measures	123–131	132–174	158–174	175–198
Thematic material	Second theme reprised	Material derived from fugue subject and countersubjects	Transition, material derived from fugue subject	*Più presto* coda, material derived from fugue subject
Key(s)	B major	Dominant of E minor	E minor	E minor

3.6

Ethel Smyth (1858–1944)

Sonata No. 2 in A Minor, Op. 5 (1887)

I. Allegro moderato   *II. Adagio non troppo*   *III. Allegro vivace e grazioso*

Like her compatriot and contemporary Edward Elgar, Ethel Smyth cherished teenage ambitions of studying composition at the Leipzig Conservatorium. Unlike Elgar, she did not lack the funds to go, but first she had to overcome parental opposition. Her upper-class military father raged against her ambitions, shouting "I would sooner see you under the sod!",[1] but Smyth's will was stronger than his. Triumphant, the nineteen-year-old composer left England for Germany, where she would stay for many years.

Smyth's first composition lessons with Carl Reinecke (1824–1910) did not meet her expectations, and in later life she remembered him as "one of those composers who turn out music by the yard without effort or inspiration."[2] After a year, she left the Conservatorium for private instruction with the composer and Leipzig Bach-Verein conductor Heinrich von Herzogenberg. She became a close friend of Herzogenberg's family, through whom she met her idol, Johannes Brahms. The famously prickly composer gave Smyth some helpful advice on composition, though he did not hide his scorn for women composers.[3]

Brahms was not alone in his sexism, since many critics of the era did not believe women capable of creating great art. Smyth resorted to publishing her compositions under the gender-neutral pen-name "E. M. Smyth" to get a fairer hearing. Even then, she had to contend with critics such as George Bernard Shaw, who dismissed her work as "neat and dainty . . . but . . . not in its right place on great occasions."[4] On another occasion, Shaw expressed

---

[1] Ethel Smyth, *Impressions That Remained: Memoirs by Ethel Smyth* (London: Longmans, Green & Co., 1920), 1:124.
[2] Smyth, 1:164.
[3] Smyth, 1:264.
[4] George Bernard Shaw, *The Bodley Head Shaw: Shaw's Music*, ed. Dan H. Laurence (London: Max Rheinhardt, 1981), 2:54.

"stupefaction" that a "heroically brassy overture" of Smyth's could have been written by a woman.[5] Even when reviews were positive, their tone was patronizing. One praised Smyth's work for "virility" and the "absence of the qualities that are usually associated with feminine productions."[6]

Smyth did not let this, or anything else, stop her. Her compositions won the respect of many preeminent musicians, including Edvard Grieg, Clara Schumann, Sir Arthur Sullivan, and Pyotr Ilich Tchaikovsky. She disproved those who doubted women's ability to compose in large-scale forms by writing several operas, including *The Wreckers* (1902–04). A well-known suffragette, she contributed to the feminist cause by composing the rousing anthem *March for the Women*.

Smyth's Sonata, Op. 5 was not her first composition for cello and piano. An early attempt from around 1880, only recently published,[7] is highly derivative of Schubert's Arpeggione Sonata. Seven years later, Smyth had established herself in Leipzig's music scene and developed a more distinctive style. At a chamber music reading hosted by the composer Julius Röntgen, Smyth befriended his nephew, the cellist Julius Klengel (1859–1933). Inspired by Klengel's gifts, Smyth turned once more to the cello. Klengel became the dedicatee of Op. 5, though it is doubtful whether he ever performed it. He and Smyth may well have read through it privately, but the first known public performance did not take place until 1926.[8]

Smyth's Sonata, Op. 5 has three movements in the traditional Classical pattern of fast-slow-fast. The first movement begins with an ominous theme in A minor for the cello, against a background of dark, oscillating chords in the piano part. Modulation to C major brings in a more optimistic second theme. A stormy development ensues, but once Smyth reaches the recapitulation, the mood lightens. The persuasive charm of the return of the second theme banishes all earlier darkness, and the movement concludes in A major. (All three movements of Op. 5 begin in minor keys and end in their parallel majors, suggesting that this was a favorite device for Smyth.) Though the first movement is in sonata-allegro form, Smyth omits the customary exposition repeat, so the playing time is relatively short.

---

[5] Shaw, 2:558.
[6] J. A. Fuller Maitland, "Smyth, Ethel," *Grove's Dictionary of Music and Musicians*, ed J. Fuller Maitland (1910), 4:490. Quoted in Eugene Gates, "Damned If You Do, Damned If You Don't: Sexual Aesthetics and the Music of Dame Ethel Smyth," *Kapralova Society Journal* 4, no. 1 (Spring 2006): 3.
[7] Ethel Smyth, Cello Sonata No. 1 in C Minor (1880), ed. George Kennaway (Leeds: Magellan Publications, 2022).
[8] Amy Zigler, "Selected Works of Dame Ethel Smyth" (PhD diss., University of Florida, 2009), 223.

The second movement, an *Adagio* in ternary form, exploits the songful qualities of the cello's tenor register. Cellist and pianist take turns in melodic and accompanying roles in a dialogue of equals, often interjecting and finishing each other's phrases. This movement, too, ends in the parallel major mode, as does the last movement. In the tradition of Classical-era finales, Smyth's concluding *Allegro vivace* is in rondo form. The restless dance rhythms of its principal theme recall those in David Popper's *Tarantella*, Op. 33. Between iterations of the rondo, lyrical themes and meter changes create contrast.

Brahmsian gestures abound in Smyth's Sonata, Op. 5: spun-out melodic lines, syncopation, hemiola, cross-rhythms, and chromatic modulation. The overall style, however, displays Smyth's signature traits of vigorous energy and intense, changeable emotion. Smyth possibly realized—or Klengel told her—that the bass-heavy range and thick polyphony in Brahms's Sonata No. 1, Op. 38 could cause difficulties with balance in performance. Smyth avoided these pitfalls by placing the cello and piano in contrasting registers and by keeping the texture relatively sparse. As a result, her Sonata Op. 5 is highly idiomatic and sonorous for both instruments.

Table 3.6.1 Smyth, Sonata in A Minor, I. Allegro moderato, analysis

Section	Exposition				
Measures	1–16	17–26	27–41	42–49	50–61
Thematic material	First theme	Transition	Second theme	Transition	Closing section (first and second theme material)
Key(s)	A minor	Modulating to C major	C major (with chromatic progressions)	C major to A minor	A minor to E major

Section	Development				
Measures	62–73	74–77	78–87	88–97	
Thematic material	First theme	Transition	Second theme	Retransition	
Key(s)	E major to C♯ minor/major	E major to B major	B major	B minor to dominant of A minor	

Section	Recapitulation				
Measures	98–114	115–125	126–140	141–148	149–160
Thematic material	First theme	Transition	Second theme	Transition	Coda
Key(s)	A minor	Reaffirmation of A minor	A major	A minor, tonicization of D major	Tonicization of D minor, A minor

Table 3.6.2 Smyth, Sonata Op. 5, II. *Adagio non troppo*, analysis

Section	A		B	A			Coda
Measures	1–20	20–38	38–53	53–65	66–77	77–95	105–117	117–132
Material	First theme	Second theme	New material	Closing theme	First theme	"Development" theme	Closing theme from B section	Cadential material derived from the first theme
Key(s)	E minor	To D major	D major	Tonicizations of G minor and E minor	E minor	E minor	E minor	E minor, ending in E major

Table 3.6.3 Smyth, Sonata Op. 5, III. *Allegro vivace e grazioso*, analysis

Section	A	B	A	C	A	D
Measures	1–22	23–34	35–48	49–82	83–112	113–170
Thematic material	6/8 theme	3/4 theme	6/8 theme	2/4 theme	6/8 theme	2/4 theme
Key(s)	A minor	A minor	E minor to C major	C major	E minor	F major to A minor

Section	A	B	A	C	A	Coda (A, D)
Measures	171–192	193–204	206–218	219–264	265–284	285–300 and 301–311
Thematic material	6/8 theme	3/4 theme	6/8 theme	2/4 theme	6/8 theme	6/8 and 2/4 themes
Key(s)	A minor	A minor	A minor	A major	A minor	A minor to A major

4
PATHWAYS TO IMPRESSIONISM

4.1

Camille Saint-Saëns (1835–1921)

Cello Concerto No. 1 in A Minor, Op. 33 (1872)

I. Allegro non troppo   II. Allegretto con moto
III Un peu moins vite–Molto allegro

Over the course of his long life, Camille Saint-Saëns came to dominate the French music scene. He was a polymath who composed prolifically in every genre, made editions of French Baroque compositions by Charpentier, Lully, and Rameau, and even authored plays and scientific essays. Hector Berlioz quipped of the teenage Saint-Saëns: "He knows everything but lacks inexperience." Franz Liszt, hearing him improvise at the Église de la Madeleine in Paris, pronounced Saint-Saëns "the greatest organist in the world."[1]

A year before writing his First Cello Concerto, Saint-Saëns co-founded the *Société nationale de musique*. France had just suffered a humiliating defeat in the Franco-Prussian War, and nationalistic feelings were running high. Saint-Saëns, Édouard Lalo, Gabriel Fauré, and several other composers felt that concert programs were Beethoven-heavy and did not contain enough French music. The Société aimed "to instruct by study of unknown works, edited or otherwise, by French composers who are part of the Society."[2]

Such musical nationalism did not prevent Saint-Saëns from assimilating German influence in his First Cello Concerto. While French elements abounded, such as prominent parts for the orchestral woodwinds and allusions to Baroque ballet, Saint-Saëns' use of form shows the impact of Robert Schumann's Cello Concerto, Op. 129.

Just as Schumann had done, Saint-Saëns set his concerto in a continuous three-section structure. Because material from the first section reappears in the other sections, we can therefore analyze the First Cello Concerto either

---

[1] Daniel M. Fallon, James Harding, and Sabina Teller Ratner, "Saint-Saëns, (Charles) Camille," *Grove Music Online*, ed. Deane Root, http://oxfordmusiconline.com.
[2] Michel Duchesneau, "Société nationale de musique," dictionary entry at the Bibliothèque Nationale de France website, http://bnf.fr.

as a three-movement cyclical composition or a single large movement in sonata form.³ Another commonality with Schumann's Cello Concerto is the absence of a long orchestral introduction. Whereas Schumann brings the solo cellist in after three orchestral chords, Saint-Saëns provides just one on the downbeat. The soloist "interrupts" the orchestra with an energetic entry on the second beat of the first measure.

After this forceful opening, Saint-Saëns' first theme runs at high speed through scalar patterns in triplets, punctuating itself with syncopated asides in the lower register. A serene second theme leads into the second section of the concerto. Here, an elegant triple meter hints at the *menuet* style of the French Baroque; its accompaniment of muted strings soon gives way to woodwinds. A mini-cadenza in falling arpeggiated patterns gives way to a series of long trills for solo cello over the orchestral accompaniment.

A return to thematic material from the first section connects the second section to the third. Now Saint-Saëns introduces a syncopated theme that recalls a motive from the first section. Graceful at first, the solo cello line evolves into difficult filigree passagework and an ascending string of artificial harmonics ending two octaves above the treble clef. Once the "recapitulation" is complete, Saint-Saëns takes off at a faster tempo for the sparkling final coda in A major.

Reviews of the premiere performance by Auguste Tolbecque described Saint-Saëns's First Cello Concerto as "a beautiful and good work, with an excellent sentiment, perfect cohesion; and the form, as usual, offers great interest."⁴ Saint-Saëns' new approach to timbre and texture provoked the critic Donald Tovey to observe: "Here, for once, is a violoncello concerto in which the solo instrument displays every register throughout its compass without the slightest difficulty in penetrating the orchestral accompaniment."⁵

Writing for the cello appeared to suit Saint-Saëns, since the First Cello Concerto is just one of many solos he wrote for the instrument. Earlier works include the *Romance*, Op. 67 (1866) and the Suite, Op. 16 (1862). After the success of Op. 33, he composed a second concerto (1902), two sonatas (1872 and 1905), *Allegro Appassionato*, Op. 43 (1873), and another *Romance*, Op. 36 (1874). His greatest hit, *Carnival of the Animals* (1887), provided cellists with "The Swan," the most famous Romantic solo in the repertoire.

---

³ Timothy Flynn, *Camille Saint-Saëns: A Guide to Research* (New York: Routledge, 2003), 7.
⁴ *Revue et Gazette Musicale de Paris* (1873), 30.
⁵ Donald Tovey, *Essays in Musical Analysis* (London: Oxford University Press, 1936), 3:192.

Table 4.1.1 Saint-Saëns Concerto in A Minor, analysis

Section	*Allegro ma non troppo*				
Measures	1–15	16–23	24–42	43–58	59–78	79–90
Thematic material	First theme	Transition	First theme	First theme	Second theme	Transition
Key(s)	A minor	Dominant harmony	A minor	E major	F major	G minor

Section	*Allegro ma non troppo* (continued)				
Measures	91–111	111–138	139–166	166–174	174–177	178–190	190–207
Thematic material	Double stops passagework	*Allegro molto* interlude	First theme passagework	Orchestral interlude	Transition to second theme	Second theme	Transition to *Allegretto con moto*
Key(s)	F major	F major	D major to F major	A minor to F major	F major	F major	F major to B♭ major

Section	*Allegretto con moto*				
Measures	209–240	241–270	271–287	287–296	297
Thematic materials	Introduction and *menuet* theme	Cello descant over *menuet* theme	*Menuet* theme continuation	Transition to cadenza	Cadenza (solo)
Key(s)	B♭ major	B♭ major	G minor	G minor to D major	Chromatic sequence

Section	*Allegretto con moto* (continued)				
Measures	298–313	314–338	339–354	354–371	372–411
Thematic materials	Cadenza (accompanied)	*Menuet* theme	Closing section 1	Closing section 2	Return of *Allegro ma non troppo* first theme
Key(s)	B♭ major	B♭ major	B♭ major	B♭ major, modulating	E major

(*continued*)

Table 4.1.1 Continued

Section	Un peu moins vite–Molto allegro						
Measures	412–436	436–440	440–451	452–468	468–480	480–495	496–518
Thematic material	Syncopated theme (derived from Section I first theme)	Orchestral interlude	Modulating scalar passagework	Modulating passagework in string crossings	Modulating passagework in dotted rhythms and octaves	Orchestral interlude	New material
Key(s)	A minor	A minor	B minor, C♯ minor	D major, C major, D minor	D minor to dominant harmony in A minor	Dominant harmony in F major	F major

Section	Un peu moins vite–Molto allegro						
Measures	518–526	526–533	534–551	552–576	576–588	588–612	612–654
Thematic material	Ascending artificial harmonics	Orchestral interlude	Passagework in string crossings (similar material to 452)	Recapitulation of syncopated theme	Più allegro comme le mouvement: orchestral recapitulation of Section I first theme	Molto allegro: orchestral interlude on material derived from Section I first theme	Coda
Key(s)	F major	F major to dominant harmony of A minor	Dominant of A minor	A minor	A minor	A minor	A major

4.2

Édouard Lalo (1823–1892)

Cello Concerto in D Minor (1877)

I. Lento–Allegro maestoso   II. Intermezzo   III. Andante–Allegro vivace

Lalo, the son of a military family from Lille, began his education studying violin and cello at a local conservatory. When he announced plans to become a professional musician, his father was indignant. Lalo defied him and went to Paris, where he built a successful career as a violinist, violist, teacher, and chamber musician.[1]

As a composer, Lalo initially failed to attract much attention, but he persisted even after many setbacks and frustrations. He produced violin pieces, piano trios, a string quartet, an opera, and symphonic music. The efforts of the *Société nationale de musique*, of which he was a founding member, provided a much-needed boost to his career and morale.[2] In his fifties, Lalo finally achieved a major success with the Violin Concerto, Op. 20. The famous violinist Pablo de Sarasate espoused the work and encouraged Lalo to write another. Soon after, Lalo produced the *Symphonie espagnole* for violin and orchestra. Despite the title, this was not a symphony but a violin concerto in a stylized Spanish idiom. Lalo was proud of his own Spanish ancestry,[3] and his association with Sarasate may have inspired him to make it a feature in his compositional vocabulary. The five movements of the *Symphonie espagnole* contain allusions to southern Spanish styles such as the *seguidilla*, a musical and dance form in triple meter, and the *habanera*, a form in duple meter with a lilting rhythmic pattern. Other Spanish elements included long, richly ornamented melodic lines, Phrygian and chromatically altered scalar patterns, compound meters, and two-against-three rhythms.

---

[1] Hugh Macdonald, "Lalo, Edouard(-Victoire-Antoine)," *Grove Music Online*, ed. Deane Root, http://oxfordmusiconline.com.
[2] Macdonald.
[3] Julien Tiersot and Frederick H. Hartens, "Édouard Lalo," *The Musical Quarterly* 11, no. 1 (January 1925): 9–10.

The large orchestra contained snare drums and harps that evoked the timbres of Spanish castanets and guitars.

A few weeks after the well-received premiere of Lalo's *Symphonie espagnole*, another work in an exoticized Spanish style arrived on the Parisian stage. This time it was an opera, Georges Bizet's *Carmen*. In his drama of seduction and violence set in Seville, Bizet juxtaposed French and Spanish musical languages to create contrast and opposition between the two lead characters. The morally compromised protagonist, Don José, typically sings in the more conventional French operatic idiom and the irresistible, treacherous Carmen in the catchy rhythms of Spanish popular music.[4] The audience—then as now—sided with Carmen. After this, the *style espagnol* became wildly popular in Paris.

Lalo may have taken this as encouragement to compose another Spanish-influenced instrumental work. For the Cello Concerto of 1877, he chose a more conventional three-movement plan of sonata-allegro, slow movement, and rondo. The thematic material, however, is as experimental as that in the *Symphonie espagnole*. In choosing 12/8 meter for the first movement, Lalo alludes to the twelve-beat metrical systems of *flamenco* styles.

The opening *Lento* introduces cello and orchestra with operatic grandeur in a recitative-like dialogue. The cello imitates the Spanish vocal style in a long, embellished phrase, punctuated by dramatic chords from the orchestra. Once the main *Allegro maestoso* is underway, Lalo combines chromatic color with complicated rhythmic patterns, often interrupting the cello's melody with an accented orchestral chord on the fourth beat of the measure. In contrast to the Spanish-inflected first theme, a tender second theme resembles the style of French Romantic opera arias. After this dramatic exposition is over, the development section opens with another recitative, now in the dominant key. Once the development proper is underway, Lalo elaborates on material from the second theme, cycling through several keys on the way to the recapitulation. This begins with a forceful return to D minor and the first theme. The movement ends as it began, in vivid and strident character.

The second movement begins in triple meter with an emphasis on the second beat that recalls the Spanish *zarabanda*, or sarabande. A contrasting section in a quick duple meter introduces a repetitive, almost circumlocutory dance theme characterized by hemiolas and other rhythmic interplay. The finale, like the first movement, also begins with an opera-like recitative

---

[4] See Susan McClary, *Georges Bizet: Carmen* (New York: Cambridge University Press, 1992).

before the start of a rousing *Allegro vivace* in rondo form. The cello line races through contrasting melodic sections at exuberant speed, mostly in the brilliant upper registers of the instrument.

The first cellist to perform Lalo's Cello Concerto was the Parisian Adolf Fischer (1847–1891). Over the next decades, it became a staple of the concerto repertoire, especially after Pablo Casals chose it for his Paris and London debuts in 1899.[5] The attractiveness of Lalo's Spanish style, not to mention his idiomatic writing for the cello, makes his Cello Concerto an enduring favorite with audiences and with young players.

---

[5] Robert Anderson, "Casals, Pablo," *Grove Music Online*, ed. Deane Root, http://oxfordmusiconline.com.

Table 4.2.1 Lalo Concerto in D Minor, I. *Lento–Allegro maestoso*, analysis

Section	Introduction		Exposition (23–116)				
Measures	1–7	8–22	23–45	46–58	59–96	97–110	111–116
Thematic material	Orchestral introduction	Cello recitative	First theme	Transition	Second theme	Transition	Closing theme
Key(s)	D minor	D minor	D minor	D minor to F major	F major	A minor	A minor

Section	Development				
Measures	117–124	125–130	131–146	147–156	
Thematic material	Introduction	Cello recitative	Second theme	Transition	
Key(s)	A minor	A minor to E major	E major, modulating	Modulating, ends on dominant of D minor	

Section	Recapitulation				
Measures	157–172	173–196	197–210	211–232	233–240
Thematic material	First theme	Second theme	Transition	Coda	Orchestral conclusion
Key(s)	D minor	D minor	D minor	D major, D minor	D minor

Table 4.2.2 Lalo Concerto, II. Intermezzo, analysis

Section	A			B	A	B
Measures	1–27	28–33		34–85	85–112	113–174
Thematic material	First theme	Transition		Second theme	First theme	Second theme
Key	G minor	G minor to G major		G major	G minor	G major

Table 4.2.3 Lalo Concerto, III. Andante–Allegro vivace, analysis

Section	Introduction	Rondo					
Measures	1–9	10–43	43–64	64–80	81–91	92–104	
Thematic material	Recitative	A	B	A	C	D	
Key(s)	B♭ minor to F major	D major	D minor	D minor	D minor	D major	

Section	Rondo (continued)					
Measures	104–179	179–188	189–204	205–225	225–241	241–289	289–326
Thematic material	E	F	A	B	A	D	A
Key(s)	D major	Modulating	D major	D minor	D major	D major	D major

4.3

Gabriel Fauré (1845–1924)

Élégie for Cello and Piano, Op. 24 (1880)

The compositions of Gabriel Fauré bridge the Romantic language of his onetime teacher Camille Saint-Saëns and the Impressionist explorations of Claude Debussy. Ten years younger than the former and seventeen years older than the latter, Fauré experienced reciprocal influences with both. He also taught many of the next generation of composers, including Maurice Ravel and Nadia Boulanger.

Fauré's education focused on music for the church, especially organ works and sacred polyphony. This led to a career first as an organist and composer, then as professor and ultimately director of the Paris Conservatoire. His most famous sacred composition is his Requiem, Op. 48. Among his secular works, the song *Après un rêve* ("After a Dream"), Op. 7, is a favorite among cellists in the arrangement for cello and piano by Pablo Casals.[1]

Following in the footsteps of Saint-Saëns, Fauré composed several pieces for the cello. After the success of his Piano Quartet No. 1 in C Minor, Op. 15 (1876–79), he became interested in writing a cello sonata. As was his habit, he composed the slow movement first.[2] A successful first performance of this movement in 1880 convinced Fauré that it worked as a standalone piece, so he did not write further movements. Fauré dedicated the movement to his friend, the cellist Jules Loëb (1852–1933), and published it in 1883 with the title *Élégie*.

The definition of an elegy is a poem or piece of music that laments a person who has died. This is not the case for Fauré's *Élégie*. Nor did his Requiem mourn any bereavement of his own. Rather, he seems to have enjoyed composing in an elegiac mood "for the pleasure of it,"[3] and presumably for the pleasure of creating catharsis in performers and audiences.

---

[1] Published in Paris by J. Hamelle, 1900.

[2] Jean-Michel Nectoux, *Gabriel Fauré: A Musical Life*, trans. Roger Nichols (Cambridge: Cambridge University Press, 1991), 88.

[3] Jean-Michel Nectoux, "Fauré, Gabriel (Urbain)," *Grove Music Online*, ed. Deane Root, http://oxfordmusiconline.com.

In this, he was successful. By turns solemn, hushed, graceful, anguished, and ultimately calm, Fauré's *Élégie* carries the listener through powerful and conflicting emotions. Four distinct thematic ideas appear, linked by a motive from the first thematic idea that appears in various guises to connect and accompany other themes. This creates a sense of tight-knit thematic unity even when the characters contrast sharply. The first theme has a sorrowful, descending phrase for the cello to the accompaniment of somber, almost funereal chords for the piano. A second presentation of the theme drops in dynamic from *forte* to *pianissimo* in the cello line, while increasingly chromatic harmony for the piano invites the appearance of a defiant counter-theme. A brief tonicization of the relative major key (E♭ major) departs as swiftly as it arrived, and the first theme appears again, this time in *pianississimo*. The phrase ends on a deceptive cadence, bringing the harmony into A♭ major. The "linking" motive appears as the introduction to a new, syncopated theme for the piano, while the cello continues in an accompanying role. Eventually, cello and piano switch roles. The cello develops the syncopated theme and modulates back to C minor for the beginning of an agitated passage in quick sextuplets. This leads to the climactic section of the piece, a reiteration of the first theme in the cello's soprano register while the piano continues the stormy sextuplet figure. As the turbulence calms down and the harmony stabilizes in A♭ major, Fauré brings back the syncopated theme in a surprise turnaround to C major. This fades gradually back into C minor for a mournful, *pianissimo* ending.

The popularity of Fauré's *Élégie* prompted his publisher, Hamelle, to ask him for a follow-up cello piece. This time, Fauré composed a fast one-movement solo titled *Pièce de violoncelle*, published as *Papillon* ("Butterfly"), Op. 77. Two other salon pieces, the *Romance*, Op. 69 and *Sicilienne*, Op. 78 followed in the 1890s. Fauré's earlier plans for a substantial multi-movement cello-piano work finally came to fruition with the Cello Sonata in D Minor, Op. 109 (1917), and again in 1921 with the Cello Sonata in G Minor, Op. 117. He also made a version of the *Élégie* for cello and orchestra.

Table 4.3.1 Fauré, *Élégie*, analysis

Section	A			
Measures	1	2–5	6–9	10–17	18–22
Thematic ideas	Piano introduction	First theme	First theme variation	Counter-theme	First theme variation
Key(s)	C minor	C minor	C minor	C minor	C minor, deceptive cadence

Section	B		C	
Measures	23–29	30–34	35–38	
Thematic ideas	Second theme (piano) Bassline derived from first theme (cello)	Second theme (cello) Bassline derived from first theme (piano)	Sextuplet theme (cello), bassline derived from first theme (piano)	
Key(s)	A♭ major	A♭ major, tonicizations of F minor and C minor	Dominant harmony of C minor	

Section	A		B	
Measures	39–46	45–46	47–53	
Thematic ideas	First theme in high register (cello) Accompaniment derived from sextuplet theme (piano)	Second theme (piano)	Second theme (cello)	
Key(s)	C minor	C major	C major to C minor	

4.4

Claude Debussy (1862–1918)

Sonata in D Minor (1915)

I. Prologue   II–III. Sérénade et Final

The years of the First World War were a time of anguish for Claude Debussy. He was terminally ill with cancer, and while this did not prevent him from composing and planning new works, he was in no state to contribute to the French war effort. The conflict between France and Germany was not only political, but cultural, and French nationalistic fervor demanded that composers shun anything "German" in music. In his wartime compositions, Debussy reshaped his style in unapologetically patriotic terms. His *Berceuse héroïque* for solo piano (1914) celebrated France's military achievements, and the unfinished cantata *Ode à la France* featured none other than Joan of Arc as its protagonist. In the second movement of the two-piano suite *En blanc et noir* (1915), he allegorized French-German conflict in musical quotations such as a discordant version of the Lutheran chorale *Ein' feste Burg ist unser Gott* ("A Mighty Fortress is Our God") to represent German aggression. Debussy, who was undoubtedly familiar with Heinrich Heine's observation that *Ein' feste Burg* was "the *Marseillaise* of the German Reformation,"[1] ended the movement with a motive of *La Marseillaise*. The symbolism was unmistakable.

Debussy used these same patriotic allusions again in his Sonata for Cello and Piano of the same year, though less explicitly. Moray Welsh, studying Debussy's manuscript at the Stadtbibliothek Winterthur in Switzerland, noticed the *Ein' feste Burg* theme scrawled above the staff in the second movement (see Figure 4.4.1). In an article for *The Strad*, Welsh described it as "plainsong" and speculated that Debussy meant to use it as a "tone row."[2] In response to Welsh's research, the composer Alan Gibbs identified the theme as *Ein' feste Burg* and pointed to places where it appears in the work (see

---

[1] Rebecca Wagner Oettinger, *Music as Propaganda in the German Reformation* (Burlington, VT: Ashgate, 2001), 45.

[2] Moray Welsh, "Un embarras de richesse," *The Strad* 103, no. 1226 (June 1992): 516.

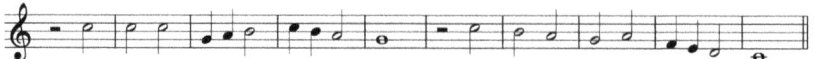

Figure 4.4.1 Debussy's sketch of the *Ein' feste Burg* theme

Figure 4.4.2 Debussy, Sonata in D Minor, *II. Sérénade*, m. 3

Figure 4.4.2).³ *La Marseillaise*, too, makes a heavily disguised appearance in intervallic fragments such as the melodic perfect fourth in measures 3–5 of the *Final*.⁴

Quotations aside, we can find other hints of French-German conflict in Debussy's Cello Sonata. Debussy avoided traditional German concepts of sonata form and tonic-dominant harmony in favor of eighteenth-century movement plans, cyclical structures, and modal, pentatonic, hexatonic, and octatonic scale collections. These allowed him the freedom to create frequent dissonances and shifts to far-flung keys. In rhythm, Debussy looked to the composers of the French Baroque. The triplet, dotted, and dactylic rhythms in the first movement strongly resemble those in *Les fêtes de Polymnie*, a ballet by Jean-Philippe Rameau (1683–1764), a work Debussy had previously edited for the publisher Durand.⁵ In assimilating such characteristics into his wartime idiom, Debussy presented himself as the heir to two hundred years of French musical lineage. He emphasized this in signing himself "Claude Debussy, *musicien français*" on the frontispiece of a projected cycle of six sonatas of which the Cello Sonata was the first. Sadly, he only lived to complete two more.

The first movement, *Prologue*, is in ABA form with an introduction. We may analyze the key center as a quasi-D minor, though the other two movements are hard to analyze as being in any key. Whereas a "Classical" sonata movement

---

³ Alan Gibbs, "Debussy's Lutheran Side," *The Strad* 103, no. 1229 (September 1992): 767.
⁴ See Janelle Ragno, "The Lutheran Hymn 'Ein' feste Burg' in Claude Debussy's Cello Sonata (1915): Motivic Variation and Structure" (DMA diss., University of Texas, 2005).
⁵ Scott Messing, *Neoclassicism in Music: From the Genesis of the Concept through the Schoenberg/Stravinsky Polemic* (Ann Arbor, MI: UMI Research Press, 1988), 45–49.

would likely oppose tonic and dominant harmony (in this case, D minor and A major), Debussy's first tonicization is A♭ major. The subdominant chord, G minor, appears more often than the dominant chord. Debussy uses this chord to facilitate modulation to the secondary key area, C major.

In another nod to eighteenth-century style, the second and third movements, *Sérénade et Final*, are both in rondo form. Both are in a less diatonic idiom than the *Prologue*. Material in the first four measures of the *Sérénade* includes all twelve tones of the chromatic scale, suggesting that Debussy may have pre-empted Arnold Schoenberg in creating dodecaphonic procedures. Other modernistic effects include Debussy's use of then-extended techniques, such as artificial harmonics, *sur la touche* (bowing over the fingerboard), and *sur le chevalet* (bowing by the bridge). In both movements, Debussy uses pizzicato to convey the impression of plucked string instruments such as guitar and mandolin.

The *Sérénade* leads without a break into the *Final*, another rondo. Its two-measure introduction, which Debussy based on a motive from *Ein' feste Burg*, runs without a break into a fragment of *La Marseillaise*. Debussy intersperses pentatonic themes with the cyclic restatement of material from the *Prologue*, ending triumphantly in D minor.

Many program notes to Debussy's Cello Sonata include the subtitle "Pierrot, angry with the moon." (Pierrot, a sad clown, is a stock character of the Italian *commedia dell'arte* pantomimes of the eighteenth century.) There is no evidence that Debussy approved this, however.[6] Rather, the subtitle seems to have been the invention of Louis Rosoor, a cellist of Debussy's acquaintance, who wrote: "Pierrot wakes up with a start and shakes off his stupor. He rushes off to sing a serenade to his beloved [the moon] who, despite his supplications, remains unmoved. To comfort himself in his failure he sings a song of liberty."[7] When Debussy learned of Rosoor's subtitle, he sent an angry letter to his publisher, describing his feelings as "profoundly disturbed." He concluded: "I'm not surprised anymore that my poor music is so often misunderstood."[8] Now that scholars have found evidence of *Ein' feste Burg* and *La Marseillaise* in the Cello Sonata, it is conceivable that they will come to replace the outdated Pierrot story in the imaginations of cellists and pianists interpreting the work.

---

[6] Sunkyung Hwang, "Stylistic Synthesis and Symbolism in Debussy's Sonata for Cello and Piano," *International Journal of Musicology* 3 (2017): 85–101.

[7] François Lesure, "Preface," in Claude Debussy, *Sonate für Violoncello und Klavier* (Munich: G. Henle, 1998), iii.

[8] Lesure, iii.

Table 4.4.1 Debussy, Sonata in D Minor, I. Prologue, analysis

Section	A		B		A			
Measures	1–7	8–15	16–20	21–28	29–34	35–38	39–46	47–51
Thematic materials	First theme (from *Ein' feste Burg*)	Second theme	First theme variant	Second theme variant	First theme	Transition and *quasi cadenza*	Second theme	Coda
Key(s)	D minor; tonicization of A♭ major	D minor	A major	Diminished harmony	C major	Modulating	D minor	D major

Table 4.4.2 Debussy, Sonata in D Minor, II. Sérénade, analysis

Section	A		B	A		C			A
Measures	1–4	5–11	11–18	19–27	28–30	31–34	35–43	44–53	54–64
Thematic material	12-tone theme (derived from *Ein' feste Burg*)	"Guitar" theme	*Sur la touche* theme (cello), *Ein' feste Burg* material (piano)	12-tone theme (developed)	Cadenza	*Vivace* theme	Chromatic triplets theme	Cadential sections	Return to opening material; transition to *Final* on material derived from *Prologue*
Key(s)	Ambiguous	Ambiguous	Chromatic and hexatonic harmony, C major cadence	Ambiguous	Ambiguous	Ambiguous	Chromatic harmony	Quasi-A major	Dominant of D

Table 4.4.3 Debussy, Sonata in D Minor, *III. Final*, analysis

Section	A					B	A		
Measures	1–2	3–5	6–14	15–22		23–36	37–38	39	40–44
Thematic material	Introduction (*Ein' feste Burg* motive)	*Marseillaise* motive	First pentatonic theme	Second pentatonic theme		"Guitar" theme	Material from introduction	*Marseillaise* motive	First pentatonic theme
Key(s)	D minor	A major	A major/A minor	D major		C# major, F# major, cadence in C major	C major	G major	G major/G minor

Section	C		D		E	
Measures	45–48	49–56	57–68		69–78	79–84
Thematic material	First pentatonic theme variant	Material derived from *Prologue* motive (m. 31)	Material derived from *Prologue* 31 motive		New material (triplets)	F-sharp leaps over three octaves
Key(s)	C minor	Diminished harmony	D♭ major		E major	F# major

Section	A				D		A	
Measures	85–86	87–88	91–95	96–103	104–111	112–118	119–123	
Thematic material	Reprise of introduction material	Reprise of *Marseillaise* motive	Reprise of first pentatonic theme	Reprise of second pentatonic theme	Material from *Prologue*	Cyclic restatement of *Prologue* material	Cadential resolution of introduction material	
Key(s)	D minor	A major	A major/A minor	D major	Diminished harmony	D major	D minor	

5
THE GREAT CONCERTOS

5.1

Robert Schumann (1810–1856)

Concerto in A Minor for Cello and Orchestra,
Op. 129 (1850–54)

I. Nicht zu schnell   II. Langsam   III. Sehr lebhaft

Schumann had special affection for the cello, having studied the instrument as a child. After an injury to his right hand ended his career as a pianist, he cheered himself up with thoughts of returning to the cello.[1] Throughout his composing life, he devoted some of his most lyrical solos to the cello in works such as the Piano Quartet, Op. 47 and Piano Quintet, Op. 44 (both from 1842). In a series of miniatures in 1849, he specified the cello as a substitute for the horn in *Adagio and Allegro*, Op. 70 and for the clarinet in the *3 Fantasiestücke*, Op. 73. Later that year, he composed his only surviving work specifically for cello and piano, the *5 Stücke im Volkston*, Op. 102. The success of these charming short pieces may have inspired Schumann to try his hand at a larger-scale work for cello. Though the Cello Concerto is far more ambitious in scope, its thematic material echoes some of the pastoral lyricism of Op. 102. In addition, Schumann kept to the same key centers, A minor and F major, a combination he had previously used in the Piano Concerto in A Minor, Op. 54 (1841–45).

Schumann sketched the Cello Concerto in an intense burst of creativity between October 10 and 16, 1850. Eight days later, the full score was complete. That same day, October 24, marked the first day of his new job as municipal music director in the city of Düsseldorf. The position was not a good fit, however, and this period marked the beginning of Schumann's final decline into mental illness. On February 27, 1854, just days after making his final revisions to the Cello Concerto, he made a dramatic suicide attempt in the Rhine River. Though he survived, he insisted on moving into a mental hospital in Endenich in case he became dangerous to others. Schumann's illness turned out to be incurable, and he died at Endenich in 1856.

---

[1] Michael Thomas Roeder, *A History of the Concerto* (Portland, OR: Amadeus Press, 1994), 256.

Figure 5.1.1 Schumann, Piano Concerto Op. 54, *I. Allegro affettuoso*, mm. 12–15

At the time Schumann composed his Op. 129, no major composer had written a concerto for the cello since Haydn's D major work in 1781[2] (unless we count a lost work by Felix Mendelssohn). There had been plenty of minor concertos by virtuoso performer-composers such as Bernhard Romberg, Johann Justus Friedrich Dotzauer, and Friedrich August Kummer, but none of these made significant innovations to the form. Schumann must have felt that it was time for cello repertoire to go in a new direction. One clue for this is his original title for Op. 129, *Konzertstück* ("Concert Piece"). Schumann used this relatively new name elsewhere, such as his Op. 86 for four horns and orchestra (1849) and Op. 92 for piano and orchestra (1852). Perhaps he saw the *Konzertstück* idea as a new form freed from Classical constraints, one in which the instrumental soloist could introduce thematic material rather than waiting patiently through a long orchestral exposition. His model for this may have been Felix Mendelssohn's Violin Concerto (1845), which brings in the soloist after an introduction of just a measure and a half. The introduction to the Cello Concerto is composed of three chords for orchestral woodwinds before the soloist's first entry.

For his opening thematic material, Schumann inverts the "C–B–A" motive he had previously used in the Piano Concerto (see Figure 5.1.1) into "A–B–C" (prefaced by an anacrusis on E) (see Figure 5.1.2). Many read this as a not-so-veiled reference to the famed pianist-composer Clara Schumann, Robert's wife, in notes that partially spell her name.[3]

The first statement of the Cello Concerto, a rhapsodic *cantilena* for the cello, lasts for 30 measures. With repeated large leaps that land on accented dissonances, the melodic material resembles that in "Einsamkeit" ("Loneliness") from Schumann's *6 Lieder*, Op. 90 (also from 1850). Since there is no human voice, the cellist is now cast in the role of Romantic artist-as-hero.

---

[2] Roeder, 256.
[3] See Carmine Miranda, "Decoding the Schumann Cello Concerto," *The Musical Times* 157 (Spring 2016): 45–66, for an exploration of Schumann's use of musical cryptography.

Figure 5.1.2 Schumann, Cello Concerto Op. 129, *I. Nicht zu schnell*, mm. 5–7

The bittersweet melody of the second movement recalls another song in Op. 90, "Meine Rose" ("My Rose"). Schumann's biographer Judith Chernaik hears the cello's "sighing" motive as another reference to Schumann's great love, writing that "Clara's name appears throughout in the falling figure sounding 'Clara.'"[4] In one of the most heartrending moments in the cello literature, the orchestral principal cellist joins the soloist in a duet marked *mit Ausdruck* ("with expression"). This extended solo for the orchestral cellist recalls the second movement of Clara Schumann's Piano Concerto in A Minor, Op. 7 (1833–35), in which the cellist alone accompanies the pianist. (In the Schumanns' "marriage of true minds," Clara's compositional innovations often preceded and inspired Robert's, so it is plausible that this idea came from her.)

The third movement is the longest and includes a cadenza with orchestral accompaniment. This is another departure from the Classical model, in which an unaccompanied cadenza typically features in the first movement. After this, a fleet-footed coda brings the Cello Concerto to a close in A major.

Schumann's three movements run without a break, with the second and third containing references to thematic material from the first. There are therefore two possibilities for analyzing the overall form of the composition. One is to regard it as a new spin on the traditional three-movement concerto, with a first movement in sonata-allegro form, a second movement in ternary form, and a rondo finale. Alternatively, we could view it as one long movement in three thematically connected sections. In returning to first-movement materials in the second and third movements, Schumann creates a large-scale cyclical structure not unlike those he used in song cycles such as *Frauenliebe und -leben* ("A Woman's Love and Life"), Op. 42 (1840).

---

[4] Judith Chernaik, *Schumann* (New York: Alfred A. Knopf, 2018), 232.

Because of his illness, Schumann did not live to hear the Cello Concerto performed, nor could he supervise its publication. The cellists to whom he showed the manuscript—Robert Bockmühl, Friedrich Wilhelm Forberg, and Christian Reimers—were unenthusiastic.[5] We can see evidence of Schumann's back-and-forth with cellist Bockmühl in the crossings-out and corrections to the manuscript. Bockmühl took issue with Schumann's opening tempo of 144 and persuaded him to make it slower; Schumann seems to have tried 126 and 128, thought better of it, and finally decided on 130. Despite the compromise, most recorded performances of the Cello Concerto begin at a slower tempo. We can attribute this and other performance traditions that deviate from Schumann's specifications to the prevalence of heavily edited nineteenth-century scores, some of which are still in print.[6]

For many years after its publication, Schumann's Cello Concerto was a misunderstood work. Critics judged Schumann's orchestration inadequate because of the "block-like"[7] separation of solo and orchestral parts. No less a composer than Dmitri Shostakovich attempted to improve Schumann's orchestration by adding harp and trumpets, with incongruous results. Later commentators were better able to appreciate Schumann's intentions. "Schumann knew what he was doing," writes the music theorist Peter H. Smith.[8] The musicologist Laura Tunbridge casts Schumann's unusual separation of the solo and orchestral roles not as a deficiency, but as an innovative characteristic of his late compositional language.[9] Clara Schumann would have agreed with this view. Although she destroyed some of Robert's late work because of its supposed unevenness in quality (including, to the dismay of cellists, a set of *Romances* for cello and piano), his Cello Concerto was never under threat. She wrote of it: "The Romantic quality, the flight, the freshness and the humor, and also the highly interesting interweaving of cello and orchestra are, indeed, wholly ravishing, and what euphony and what deep sentiment are all in the melodic passages!"[10]

---

[5] John Worthen, *Robert Schumann: Life and Death of a Musician* (New Haven, CT: Yale University Press, 2007), 315–316.

[6] The most reliable version to date is Robert Schumann, Cello Concerto Op. 129, edited by Josephine Knight (London: Edition Peters, 2021). This scholarly performing edition discards many "traditions" from earlier editions and from the recorded history of the work.

[7] Laura Tunbridge, *Schumann's Late Style* (New York: Cambridge University Press, 2007), 118.

[8] Peter H. Smith, "Schumann's A Minor Mood: Late-Style Dialectics in the First Movement of the Cello Concerto," *Journal of Music Theory* 60, no. 1 (2016): 51.

[9] Tunbridge, 118.

[10] Lawrence Kramer, "A New Self: Schumann at 40," *The Musical Times* 148 (Spring 2007): 14.

Table 5.1.1 Schumann Concerto, Op. 129, I. Nicht zu schnell, analysis

Section	Exposition (1–96)						Development (96–176)				
Measures	1–4	5–34	34–50	50–68	68–96		96–125	125–132	132–153	153–164	165–176
Thematic material	Orchestral introduction	First theme	Orchestral transition	Second theme	Closing theme		Development of closing theme material	Development of first theme	Transition	First theme	Exposition closing theme material
Key(s)	A minor	A minor	A minor	C major	C major		Dominant of A minor, tonicizations of G minor, F major, D major, E major, A minor	C-sharp minor, tonicizations of B♭ minor	C major, G major, A♭ minor	C-sharp minor	F♯ minor, D major, G major

Section	Recapitulation (177–264)					Transition to second movement
Measures	177–205	205–218	218–236	236–264		264–285
Thematic material	First theme	Orchestral transition	Second theme	Closing theme		Transitional material
Key(s)	C major to A minor	A minor	A major	A major		A minor to F major

Table 5.1.2 Schumann Concerto, Op. 129, II. *Langsam*, analysis

Section	A	B	A	Transition to third movement
Measures	286–303	303–311	311–319	320–344
Thematic material	First theme, duet with orchestral principal cello	Second theme, duet with orchestral principal cello	Reprise of first theme	Thematic material derived from first theme of first movement
Key(s)	F major	F major	F major	A minor and F major

Table 5.1.3 Schumann Concerto Op. 129, III. *Sehr lebhaft*, analysis

Section	A	B	A	C	A	D	A	A	Transition
Measures	345–364	365–402	402–409	410–429	430–443	444–464	464–476	476–535	536–549
Thematic material	Rondo theme	Episode 1	Rondo theme	Episode 2	Rondo theme	Episode 3	Rondo theme	Rondo theme	Transitional material
Key(s)	A minor	C major	C major	E major, C major,	D minor	F major to C major	C major	Rapid tonicizations	Modulating to A minor

Section	A	B	A	C	A	A	Cadenza	Coda
Measures	549–569	569–606	606–613	614–633	634–678	678–684	684–732	732–766
Thematic material	Rondo theme	Reprise of episode 1	Rondo theme	Reprise of Episode 2	Rondo theme	Rondo theme, orchestra	Partially accompanied cadenza material	Thematic material from first movement exposition closing theme
Key(s)	A minor	C major to A minor	A major	A major	A major to A minor	A minor	G minor, tonicizations, A major	A major

5.2

Pyotr Ilich Tchaikovsky (1840–1893)

Variations on a Rococo Theme for Cello and Orchestra, Op. 33 (1876–77)

Version A (original)	Version B (ed. Wilhelm Fitzenhagen)
Introduction: *Moderato assai, quasi andante*	Introduction: *Moderato assai, quasi andante*
Thema: *Moderato semplice*	Thema: *Moderato semplice*
Variation 1: *Tempo della Thema*	Variation 1: *Tempo della Thema*
Variation 2: *Tempo della Thema*	Variation 2: *Tempo della Thema*
Variation 3: *Andante*	Variation 3: *Andante sostenuto*
Variation 4: *Allegro vivo*	Variation 4: *Andante grazioso*
Variation 5: *Andante grazioso*	Variation 5: *Allegro moderato*
Variation 6: *Allegro moderato*	Variation 6: *Andante*
Variation 7: *Andante sostenuto*	Variation 7 and Coda: *Allegro vivo*
Variation 8 and Coda: *Allegro moderato con anima*	

Though many of his own compositions exhibit unrestrained Romantic emotion, Pyotr Ilich Tchaikovsky also aspired to the Classical ideals of Mozart. In a letter to the composer Sergei Taneyev, Tchaikovsky raved "My God! how divinely beautiful this music is in its unassuming simplicity!"[1] An entry in his journal elaborates: "It is my profound conviction that Mozart is the highest, the culminating point which beauty has reached in the sphere of music. Nobody has made me cry and thrill with joy, sensing my proximity to something that we call the ideal, in the way that he has … In Mozart I love everything because we love everything in a person whom we truly love."[2]

Tchaikovsky's passion for Classicism found its way into several of his works, including the *Variations on a Rococo Theme* for Cello and Orchestra, Op. 33. This title alludes to the Rococo movement of the eighteenth

---

[1] Pyotr Ilich Tchaikovsky to Sergei Taneyev, April 1883. In *Tchaikovsky Research*, http://en.tchaikovsky-research.net/pages/Wolfgang_Amadeus_Mozart, last modified February 20, 2020.

[2] Pyotr Ilich Tchaikovsky, diary entry for September 20–October 2, 1886. In *Tchaikovsky Research* http://en.tchaikovsky-research.net/pages/Wolfgang_Amadeus_Mozart, last modified February 20, 2020.

century, whose characteristics included lightness, grace, and a playful mood. Musicologists use the term to describe the work of French composers such as François Couperin (1668–1733) and Jean-Philippe Rameau (1683–1764).[3]

The "Rococo theme" of Tchaikovsky's title was not a genuine eighteenth-century melody, but an original theme in a binary structure whose balanced phrases mimic Mozartean period structure. For instrumentation, Tchaikovsky used a Classical orchestra of double winds, two horns, and strings. Variation form was not a typical choice for him but proved useful for writing in a Rococo-inspired style. As the Tchaikovsky scholar David Brown observes, recasting a cello concerto as a set of variations enabled the composer to "avoid the structural complexities and dramatic issues that could not have been skirted, had he attempted to wed his borrowed manners to the concerto principle."[4]

Within the constraints of this chosen form, Tchaikovsky casts his theme in a variety of characters. The waltz variation in C major (Variation 7 in the original Version A, Variation 3 in the more commonly used Version B) resembles the fairytale waltzes in Tchaikovsky's ballets. A cadenza showcases the essentials for a nineteenth-century virtuoso: chromatic double stops, ricochet, and a fearless attitude to high notes. The searching melancholy of a variation in D minor (Variation 3 in Version A, Variation 6 in Version B) creates emotional contrast within an otherwise high-spirited work.

Once Tchaikovsky had finished work on the *Rococo Variations*, he handed over the score to its dedicatee, the German cellist-composer Wilhelm Fitzenhagen (1848–1890). A former student of Friedrich Grützmacher, Fitzenhagen had moved to Russian to take up a professorship at the Moscow Conservatory aged only twenty-two. His assured performance at the premieres of Tchaikovsky's three string quartets dispelled Tchaikovsky's earlier doubts about the suitability of the cello as a solo instrument.[5] It is likely that Tchaikovsky expected Fitzenhagen to suggest some edits to the solo part. He could not, however, have predicted the liberties the cellist would take with the form and structure of his composition.

After performing the *Rococo Variations*, Fitzenhagen decided—without informing Tchaikovsky—to make some extreme edits. He changed the order

---

[3] Daniel Heartz and Bruce Alan Brown, "Rococo," *Grove Music Online*, ed. Deane Root, accessed February 2, 2022, http://oxfordmusiconline.com.
[4] David Brown, *Tchaikovsky: The Crisis Years* (New York: W. W. Norton, 1983), 118–119.
[5] Lev Ginsburg, "Introduction," in *Variations on a Rococo Theme*, Op. 33, comp. Pyotr Ilich Tchaikovsky (Moscow: Muzgiz, 1962), viii.

of the variations, deleted one, and recomposed some sections to compensate. Even by the standards of Fitzenhagen's teacher Grützmacher, whose editions of Boccherini and Bach were notoriously heavy-handed, this was a bold move. When Tchaikovsky learned what Fitzenhagen had done, he was furious. Anatoly Brandukov, a cellist who studied with both Fitzenhagen and Tchaikovsky, found him "very upset, looking as though he was ill. When I asked: 'What's the matter with you?' Pyotr Ilich, pointing to the writing table, said: 'That idiot Fitzenhagen's been here. Look what he's done to my piece—he's altered everything!'"[6] Pyotr Jurgenson, Tchaikovsky's publisher, was similarly furious. "Loathsome Fitzenhagen! He is most insistent on making changes to your cello piece," he told Tchaikovsky, "and he says that you have given him full authority to do so. Heavens! Tchaikovsky *revu et corrigé par* Fitzenhagen!"[7]

Despite this, Tchaikovsky and Jurgenson ended up publishing Fitzenhagen's version of the *Rococo Variations*. ("The devil take it!" Tchaikovsky told Brandukov. "Let it stand!"[8]) They might not have liked the new version, but Fitzenhagen's efforts to promote the *Rococo Variations* abroad at least brought the work some good publicity.[9]

It was not until the publication of a complete Tchaikovsky edition[10] in the mid-twentieth century that cellists could finally access the original version. This required some painstaking detective work from the editor, cellist Victor Kubatsky. With the help of a forensic specialist, he sorted through Fitzenhagen's edits and pasted-over pages to reveal Tchaikovsky's original intentions.[11] Given the easy availability of Kubatsky's edition, it may seem odd that the original version has never superseded Fitzenhagen's version in performances and recordings.[12]

---

[6] Brown, 122.
[7] Pyotr Jurgenson to Tchaikovsky, February 1878, in *Tchaikovsky Research*, http://en.tchaikovsky-research.net/pages/Variations_on_a_Rococo_Theme#cite_note-note9-9, last modified March 27, 2021.
[8] Brown, 122.
[9] Fitzenhagen's connections with the Berlin publisher Luckhardt helped to get the *Rococo Variations* published in Germany. See Sergei Istomin, "The History of Tchaikovsky's *Variations on a Rococo Theme* and the Collaboration with Fitzenhagen," *Music and Practice* 4 (2019), https://www.musicandpractice.org/volume-4/.
[10] See Viktor Kubatsky, "Works for Cello and Orchestra," *Tchaikovsky: The Complete Works* (Moscow: Muzgiz/Muzyka, 1956), 30B:5–46.
[11] Istomin.
[12] A relatively small number of cellists have recorded the original, including Jiří Bárta, Steven Isserlis, Sviatoslav Knushevitsky, Johannes Moser, Alexander Rudin, Daniil Shafran, István Várdai, Raphael Wallfisch, Julian Lloyd Webber, and Pieter Wispelwey.

The power of tradition only partially explains this. While scholars are scathing about Fitzenhagen's "deplorably corrupt"[13] edits, his reasoning was not capricious. When Fitzenhagen performed the *Rococo Variations* at the Wiesbaden Festival in 1879, he reported to Tchaikovsky that the D minor variation (Variation 3 in Version A, Variation 6 in Version B) attracted "stormy applause."[14] On these grounds, Fitzenhagen moved it to a later point in the musical drama, along with the cadenza that prefaces it. With the D minor *Andante* now situated later in the piece, the other *Andante* in C major needed to go in an earlier spot so that the two slower-tempo movements would not appear side by side. This left the new Variation 7 next to Tchaikovsky's original Variation 8, which has a similar character.

Fitzenhagen sincerely believed he had improved the *Rococo Variations*, and even if his actions were arrogant, they made musical sense. Plenty of cellists, past and present, agree with him. According to the cellist and performance practice expert Sergei Istomin, "both versions are legitimate."[15] It is therefore up to cellists to learn and compare both scores on their journeys toward interpretation and performance.

---

[13] Brown, 122.
[14] Brown, 121.
[15] Istomin.

Table 5.2.1 Side-by-side comparison of Tchaikovsky's *Rococo Variations* in the original version and in the edition by Wilhelm Fitzenhagen

Version A (original)		Version B (Wilhelm Fitzenhagen edition)	
1–21	Orchestral introduction: *Moderato assai, quasi andante*	1–21	Orchestral introduction: *Moderato assai, quasi andante*
21–45	*Thema*, A major (38–45: linking section)	21–45	*Thema*, A major (38–45: linking section)
46–69	Variation 1 (*Tempo della Thema*), A major (62–69: linking section)	46–69	Variation 1 (*Tempo della Thema*), A major (62–69: linking section)
70–105	Variation 2 (*Tempo della Thema*), A major	70–102	Variation 2 (*Tempo della Thema*), A major
106	Cadenza leads into D minor variation	N/A	N/A
107–140	Variation 3 (*Andante*), D minor, no linking section	103–172	Version A Variation 7 (*Andante sostenuto*, waltz in C major) becomes Version B Variation 3
141–186	Variation 4 (*Allegro vivo*), A major, no linking section	173–230	Version A Variation 5 (*Andante grazioso*, A major) becomes Version B Variation 4
187–244	Variation 5 (*Andante grazioso— un poco animato*), A major	231–278	Version A Variation 6 (*Allegro moderato*, A major) becomes Version B Variation 5
N/A	N/A	279	Cadenza leads into D minor variation
245–290	Variation 6 (*Allegro moderato*), A major. (258–268: short cadenza; 278–290: linking section)	280–314	Version A Variation 3 (*Andante*, D minor) becomes Version B Variation 6
291–360	Variation 7 (*Andante sostenuto*), waltz in C major	315–390	Version A Variation 4 (*Allegro vivo*, A major) becomes Version B Variation 7 and Coda
361–426	Variation 8 and Coda: *Allegro moderato con anima*	N/A	(Version A Variation 8 is deleted)

5.3

Antonín Dvořák (1841–1904)

Concerto in B Minor for Cello and Orchestra, Op. 104 (1894–95)

I. Allegro   II. Adagio ma non troppo   III. Finale: Allegro moderato

Until late in his career, Antonín Dvořák did not imagine that he might successfully compose a cello concerto. He had previously composed miniatures for cello and piano, including *Klid*[1] and *Rondo*,[2] but ran into troubles when he tried to arrange the piano parts for orchestra. An early attempt at a concerto was so unsuccessful that he did not bother completing the orchestration. He remarked to a student: "The cello . . . is a beautiful instrument, but its place is in the orchestra and in chamber music. As a solo instrument it isn't much good. Its middle register is fine—that's true—but the upper voice squeaks and the lower growls. The finest solo instrument, after all, is—and will remain—the violin."[3]

Dvořák's cellist friends, including his countryman Hanuš Wihan (1855–1920), tried to change his mind. Nothing worked until Dvořák heard the cellist-composer Victor Herbert performing his own Second Cello Concerto in New York. Though Herbert wrote for a large orchestra containing many brass instruments, his skillful use of registral and timbral contrast meant that the accompaniment never covered the soloist. Intrigued, Dvořák attended a second performance and asked Herbert if he could study the score.

When Dvořák began work on Op. 104, he followed Herbert's lead in orchestration and instrumentation. His large orchestra is typical of late Romantic ensembles, containing two each of flutes, oboes, clarinets, and bassoons, four horns, two trumpets, three trombones, tuba, timpani,

---

[1] Also known as *Waldesruhe* and *Silent Woods*, this one-movement work is Dvořák's own arrangement of a movement of *From the Bohemian Forest*, Op. 68. He published versions for cello and piano and for cello and orchestra in 1894 (Berlin: N. Simrock).

[2] Dvořák composed the *Rondo*, Op. 94 for cello and piano in 1891; two years later he arranged it for cello and orchestra. Both were published in 1894 (Berlin: N. Simrock).

[3] Jan Smaczny, *Dvořák: Cello Concerto* (Cambridge: Cambridge University Press, 2004), 2.

triangle, and strings. The solo cello part, like that in the Herbert work, sits mostly in the projecting registers of the instrument. Dvořák, pleased with his progress, wrote to his friend Alois Göbl: "I have actually finished the first movement of a Concerto for violoncello!! Don't be surprised about this, I too am amazed and surprised enough that I was so determined on such work."[4]

The Cello Concerto was one of the last works Dvořák would write in America. Unlike the "New World" Symphony and "American" String Quartet of 1893, it contains no trace of the American folk music or spirituals he had enjoyed during his stay. Instead, as Michael Thomas Roeder observes, it is constantly "looking homeward."[5] Dvořák's nostalgia was not only for his native Bohemia but for his younger self and the memory of a long-ago love affair with the actress Josefína Čermáková. Though Josefína refused to marry Dvořák, they remained close, even when he later married Josefína's sister Anna. While Dvořák was writing the Cello Concerto, he received news from home that Josefína was seriously ill. Stricken, he changed his plan for the second movement by introducing a favorite melody of Josefína's midway through the movement. This was "Kéž duch můj sám" ("Leave Me Alone") from Dvořák's *4 Lieder*, Op. 82 (1888) (see Figure 5.3.1). The text of the song reads "Leave me to walk alone in my dreams / Do not disturb the ecstasy within my heart! / Leave me all the rapture, leave me the pains / That have filled me ever since I saw him!"[6]

The overall design of Dvořák's Cello Concerto corresponds to the Classical three-movement plan. The first movement, *Allegro*, is in sonata-allegro form with a long orchestral exposition that introduces all the main themes. Two clarinets begin the first theme in mournful tones; the horn introduces a pentatonic second theme in D major. Threading the thematic material together is a recurring timpani roll, a motive Roeder describes as "funereal."[7]

By the time the solo cellist enters, Dvořák has transformed the first theme from a subdued B minor into a defiant *risoluto, quasi improvisando* in the parallel major mode. Though the cellist has the heroic leading role, Dvořák creates a large cast of supporting actors in the woodwind and brass sections of the orchestra. The solo cellist often appears in a chamber music-like partnership with the clarinet, flute, oboe, horn, and even—in a technique borrowed from Herbert—a low brass choir.

---

[4] Smaczny, 2.
[5] Michael Thomas Roeder, *A History of the Concerto* (Portland, OR: Amadeus Press, 1994), 280.
[6] Otilie Malybrok-Stieler, "Kéž duch můj sám," text and translation provided by Oxford Lieder, http://oxfordlieder.co.uk, accessed March 6, 2022.
[7] Roeder, 280.

Figure 5.3.1 Dvořák, "Kéž duch můj sám," mm. 10–14

The harmony in the exposition is relatively conservative, with B minor and D major as the principal key centers. The development section, in contrast, travels as far afield as A♭ minor. Dvořák respells this chord enharmonically as G♯ minor soon after the entrance of the soloist. Accompanied by an obbligato flute, the cello line spins material from the first theme into a legato lament. Sequential chromatic passagework becomes the vehicle for modulation back to B minor for the recapitulation.

This section begins with the second theme, now transformed into a triumphant B major. Dvořák quickly adapts all the threads of thematic material into this home key for the conclusion of the movement. Donald Tovey describes this as "[bringing] this great loosely-knit first movement within surprisingly moderate dimensions by 'short-circuiting' its development and recapitulation."[8]

---

[8] Donald Francis Tovey, *Essays in Musical Analysis* (London: Oxford University Press, 1936), 3:150.

The second movement, *Adagio*, is in ternary form. It opens with pastoral calm, but this does not last long after an abrupt key change from G major to G minor brings in more volatile emotions. It is at this point that Dvořák introduces the "Leave Me Alone" theme for the solo cello with the accompaniment of a pair of clarinets whose lines weave closely around the melody (see Figure 5.3.2). As the flute and oboe take over the "Leave Me Alone" material, the texture becomes more and more hectic. The solo cellist performs a syncopated descant melody against chordal *ostinato* patterns in the upper string and wind sections and a "heartbeat" pizzicato pattern for the lower strings. A return to G major signals a return to the peaceful first theme and a short accompanied cadenza. A descant for the solo cello on pentatonic natural harmonics brings the movement to its last cadence.

The third movement, *Allegro moderato*, is in rondo form. Between iterations of the main theme in B minor, Dvořák interpolates three melodic "episodes": the first short, the second more spun-out, and the third in a "Slavic"[9] style featuring the repeated interval of a perfect fourth. In Dvořák's first complete version of this movement, it had a short coda. On the manuscript, the composer wrote: "Thank God! Completed in New York on 9 February 1895 on little Otakar's [his son's] birthday. Saturday morning at 11 ½ hours."[10] Soon afterward, the Dvořáks returned to Bohemia, where they looked forward to settling back into their old life.

Then, on May 27, Josefína died.

Crushed with grief, Dvořák changed his mind about the ending of the Cello Concerto. He went back to the score and replaced the original closing measures with a new, extended coda that re-introduces transformed versions of thematic materials from all three movements. An altered version of "Leave Me Alone," Josefína's theme, appears as a tender violin solo. Finally, a brass choir makes a slow final statement of the main rondo theme before the ecstatic concluding *allegro vivo*. On November 6, 1895, Dvořák added a new note to the manuscript: "I finished the concerto in New York, but when I came back to Bohemia, I changed the ending completely, as it now stands."[11]

The story of the Cello Concerto does not end there. Wihan, happy that Dvořák had finally granted his wish, felt that the Cello Concerto afforded

---

[9] Roeder, 285.
[10] Ondrej Supka, "Concerto for Cello and Orchestra," trans. Karolina Hughes, http://antonin-dvorak.cz/en/concerto-for-cello2, accessed March 5, 2022.
[11] Supka.

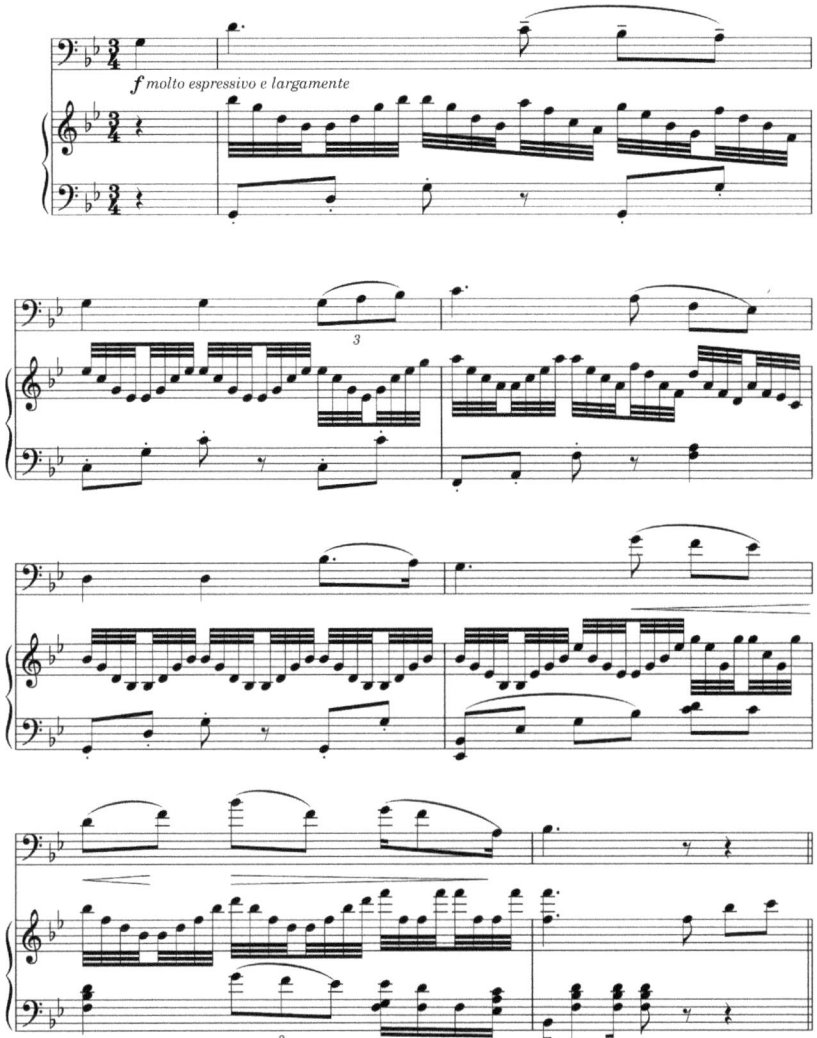

Figure 5.3.2 Dvořák, Cello Concerto Op. 104, *II. Adagio ma non troppo*, mm. 43–49

him insufficient opportunities for technical display. Since Dvořák had allowed him some input in the passagework sections, Wihan took the further liberty of inserting a virtuoso cadenza of his own devising into the score. Dvořák angrily vetoed this plan. "I must insist that my work is published just as I have written it," he wrote to the publisher Fritz Simrock.

I shall only give you the work if you promise that *no one*, including my respected friend Wihan, makes *alterations without my knowledge* and consent... not the cadenza which Wihan has put into the last movement—it must stay in its original form, as I felt and imagined it... The finale closes gradually diminuendo like a sigh—with reminiscences from the first and second movements—the solo dies down to *pp* and then swells again, and the last bars are taken up by the orchestra and it finishes in stormy mood. That was my idea and from it I cannot depart.[12]

It was the right decision, since Dvořák's work needed no decoration. As a sublimation of anguish and yearning, it was one of his most moving works, and as a feat of compositional technique, it opened up new possibilities for the cello-orchestra medium. When the elderly Johannes Brahms heard Robert Hausmann's performance of the work, he exclaimed "Why on earth didn't I know that one could write a violoncello concerto like this? If only I had known, I would have written one long ago!"[13] Brahms died before he could attempt such a work, but for the next generation of composers—Edward Elgar among them—Dvořák's example became the ideal of a large-scale composition for the cello.

---

[12] Smaczny, 90.
[13] Conversation between Robert Hausmann and Donald Tovey, reported by Tovey in *Essays in Musical Analysis*, 3:148.

Table 5.3.1 Dvořák Concerto, *I. Allegro*, analysis

Section	Orchestral exposition			Solo exposition				
Measures	1–56	57–74	75–86	87–109	110–139	140–157	158–191	192–203
Thematic material	First theme	Second theme	Closing theme	First theme	First theme	Second theme	Transition	Closing theme
Key(s)	B minor	D major	D major	B major	B minor	D major	Tonicizations	D major

Section	Development			Recapitulation		
Measures	204–223	224–239	240–266	267–284	285–318	319–354
Thematic material	First theme	First theme	Second theme	Second theme	Reprise of transitional material from the solo exposition	Coda on thematic material from the first theme
Key(s)	Tonicizes D major, C minor, G minor, E♭ minor	A♭ minor, respelled as G♯ minor (228)	Modulates to dominant harmony of B	B major	B major	B major

Table 5.3.2 Dvořák Concerto, II. Adagio ma non troppo, analysis

Section	A				B			
Measures	1–8	9–14	15–21	21–34	39–42	43–57	57–65	65–95
Thematic material	First theme, orchestra	First theme, cello	Second theme	Second theme continuation	Introduction	"Leave Me Alone" theme	Transition	Variation on "Leave Me Alone" theme
Key(s)	G major	G major	G major	Tonicizations, cadence in G major	G minor	G minor. B♭ major, D♭ major	D♭ major, enharmonic modulation, cadence in B minor	Tonicizations of B minor, D major, F major, G major

Section	A			
Measures	95–107	107–129	129–149	149–166
Thematic material	First theme, brass choir version	Quasi cadenza (cello with flute, bassoon, clarinet)	Second theme	Coda
Key(s)	G major	G major	G major	G major

Table 5.3.3 Dvořák Concerto, III. Finale: *Allegro moderato*, analysis

Section	Introduction	Refrain	Episode 1	Refrain	Transition 1	Episode 2	Transition 2	Transition 3
Measures	1–32	33–48	49–72	73–86	87–142	143–176	177–204	204–245
Thematic material	Rondo theme	Rondo theme	Passagework	Rondo theme	Orchestral transition. Cello entry 105	*Poco meno mosso* theme	Cello passagework	Orchestral, similar to transition 1. Cello entry 226.
Key(s)	B minor	B minor	D major to B minor	B minor	B minor to D major	D major	Tonicizations of D major, B♭ major, F major, D major	D major, F♯ major, B minor

Section	Refrain	Transition 4	Episode 3	Transition 5	Episode 3 reprise	Refrain
Measures	246–269	269–280	281–315	315–346	347–381	381–421
Thematic material	Rondo theme	Transitional material		Passagework	Same material as episode 3	Rondo theme
Key(s)	B minor	B minor to G major	G major	G major to B major	B major	B major

Section	Coda						
Measures	421–460	461–467	468–473	477–497	497–508	509–515	
Thematic material	Material from rondo theme	Material from first movement, first theme	Variation on second movement "Leave Me Alone" theme	Material from first movement, first theme	*Andante maestoso*, orchestral *accelerando*	*Allegro vivo* conclusion, rondo theme, orchestra only	
Key(s)	B major	B major	B major	B major	B major	B major	

5.4

Ernest Bloch (1880–1959)

Schelomo: Rhapsodie Hébraïque (1915–16)

The Swiss composer Ernest Bloch's early style absorbed influences from Debussy's modal and non-diatonic scales, the nationalistic fervor of Mussorgsky, and Wagner's ideal of the "music drama."[1] His attempts to combine elements of each in his own work did not impress his composition teacher, Max von Schillings. Hearing one of Bloch's attempts at a symphony, Schillings remarked that it was "German in form, French in rhythm, and nationally unspecific in its melancholic themes."[2]

Many composers of the time, including Bloch's contemporaries Igor Stravinsky and Béla Bartók, sought to feature music from their national or cultural traditions in their work. In correspondence with friends, Bloch began to explore ways in which he might use his own Jewish identity in his composition. Bloch's upbringing had not been particularly religious, but he was intrigued enough to start studying sacred texts in search of ideas. A play by William Trowbridge[3] about the biblical story of Jezebel[4] inspired Bloch to create a new "Hebraic" musical language. Sketches for a planned opera show attempts to convey the dangerous sensuality of the queen of Israel in melodies rich in augmented seconds, tritones, octatonic and Middle East-inspired scalar patterns, melismas resembling the intonations of Jewish liturgical chant, and irregular meters and rhythms.[5]

Bloch did not finish the Jezebel project, but his new "Hebraic" style fueled his creativity. Between 1912 and 1916, he composed a group of religious

---

[1] David Z. Kushner, "Bloch, Ernest," *Grove Music Online*, ed. Deane Root, http://oxfordmusiconline.com.
[2] Klára Móricz, "Sensuous Pagans and Righteous Jews: Changing Concepts of Jewish Identity in Ernest Bloch's *Jézabel* and *Schelomo*," *Journal of the American Musicological Society* 54, no. 3 (Fall 2001): 439.
[3] William Trowbridge, *Jézabel, drame* (Paris: Éditions de la Plume, 1903).
[4] 1 Kings 16:31.
[5] Móricz, 463.

works scholars call the "Jewish Cycle."[6] These include the *Prelude* and *Two Psalms* for soprano and orchestra, *Israel* for vocal soloists and orchestra, *Three Jewish Poems* for orchestra, *Psalm 22* for alto or baritone and orchestra, and *Schelomo* for cello and orchestra.

Bloch initially imagined *Schelomo* as a vocal composition on verses from the Book of Ecclesiastes.[7] Setting the text proved difficult, however, because he did not know Hebrew well enough to use it. The languages he spoke—French, German, and English—were unsuitable for the mood of the music. A chance meeting with a cellist, Alexandre Barjansky, gave him the idea to rewrite it as an instrumental work.

Bloch, depressed after a string of professional disappointments and financial problems, sensed kindred spirits in Barjansky and his sculptor wife, Catherine. During a visit, Alexandre played his cello for Bloch, who reciprocated by performing excerpts from the "Jewish Cycle." As she listened, Catherine Barjansky made sketches for a statuette of King Solomon. This caught Bloch's attention. "My hopes revived," he recalled. "I began to think about writing a work for that marvelous cellist. Why not use my Ecclesiastes material, but instead of a human voice, limited by a text, employ an infinitely grander and more profound voice that could speak all the languages—that of [Barjansky's] violoncello? I took up my sketches, and without plan or program, almost without knowing where I was headed; I worked for days on my rhapsody. As each section was completed, I copied the solo part and Barjansky studied it . . . Mrs. Barjansky worked on the statuette intended as a gift for me . . . We both finished at the same time. In a few weeks my Ecclesiastes was completed, and since the legend attributes this book to King Solomon, I gave it the title *Schelomo*."[8]

Bloch planned *Schelomo* as a rhapsody rather than a concerto, effectively giving himself permission to compose in a concerto-like idiom without the restrictions of a preconceived formal structure. As a genre, rhapsody suggests both "an extravagant effusion of sentiment or feeling" and "a large-scale nationalistic 'epic' for orchestra."[9] This worked well for the story of *Schelomo*, where cellist and orchestra portray the morally conflicted king in opposition to a worldly, depraved crowd.

---

[6] Aaron Klaus, "Ernest Bloch, Richard Wagner, and the Myth of Racial Essentialism," *Studies in Christian-Jewish Relations* 13, no. 1 (2018): 9–10.
[7] Ecclesiastes 1:2–11 (King James Version).
[8] David Z. Kushner, *The Ernest Bloch Companion* (Westport, CT: Greenwood Press, 2002), 35.
[9] John Rink, "Rhapsody," *Grove Music Online*, ed. Deane Root, http://oxfordmusiconline.com.

Though the structure and thematic development are very free, *Schelomo* falls into three distinct parts. There is no specific program, but years after completing the score Bloch described its "psychology" in an essay. "The introduction," he wrote, "which contains the germ of several essential motifs, is the plaint, the lamentation—'Nothing is worth the pain it causes; Vanity of Vanities—all is Vanity'—an emotional, nearly a physiological reaction. The cello cadence then puts this pessimistic philosophy into words—this beginning is a soliloquy."[10]

Three thematic ideas emerge from this first part: an improvisatory, melismatic recitative (hereafter called the "melisma idea"); a flowing melody in compound time and a *siciliano*-like rhythmic pattern (the "*siciliano* idea"); and a cadenza beginning in the cello's bass register ("cadenza idea"). The orchestra introduces an iambic (Scottish snap) idea, a rhythmic device that would become a favorite with Bloch. The cello then introduces another idea characterized by its opening interval of an ascending minor sixth. The orchestra and soloist face off against each other in ever-fluctuating combinations of thematic ideas until a concluding cadenza leads into the second part.

This begins with a new idea in the principal bassoon part, a series of obsessively repeated, speeding-up pitches. The oboe takes over, and soon the rhythm assimilates itself into Bloch's swirling mixture of thematic ideas. "I cannot describe the next episode," Bloch wrote. "It is a motif my father sang in Hebrew; I don't know the meaning of the words."[11] The repeated pitches and perfect intervals recall the sound of a *shofar*, an ancient Jewish ceremonial trumpet made from a ram's horn.[12] Its call summons up a mood of unease. In Bloch's words, "the maddened crowd hurling blasphemies against the Universe? Vanity, Vanity. The tumult is appeased. Schelomo alone meditates, a shudder of sadness—'I have seen it all—wasted effort—the triumph of evil—I too knew hope; it is become barren, sterile ... a gesture of despair."[13]

The third part begins with the return to a slower tempo. There is no new melodic material, but the mood changes as the cellist begins a dreamlike ascending phrase across the full range of the instrument to the eerie plainchant accompaniment of celesta, harp, and three solo violins. The dream

---

[10] Suzanne Bloch and Irene Heskes, *Ernest Bloch: Creative Spirit* (New York: Jewish Music Council of the National Jewish Welfare Board, 1976), 50.
[11] Bloch and Heskes, 51.
[12] Jeremy Montagu, "Shofar," *Grove Music Online*, ed. Deane Root, http://oxfordmusiconline.com.
[13] Bloch and Heskes, 51.

cannot last, and the cellist returns to the lowest range for a deeply pessimistic final solo. Of the ending, Bloch wrote "Even the darkest of my works end with hope. This work alone concludes in complete negation. But the subject demanded it!"[14]

The completion of *Schelomo* marked an end to a difficult period in Bloch's career. Not long afterwards, while on tour in the United States, he received a job offer from the David Mannes Music School in New York. *Schelomo* premiered in Carnegie Hall with Hans Kindler as the soloist. The audience's reaction was effusive. The critic Guido Gatti, wrote, "One finds oneself in the heart of a dream-world, in an Orient of fancy, where men and women of every race and tongue are holding argument, or hurling maledictions; and now and again we hear the mournful accents of the prophetic seer, under the influence of which all bow down and listen reverently."[15]

---

[14] Bloch and Heskes, 51.
[15] Guido M. Gatti and Theodore Baker, "Ernest Bloch," *The Musical Quarterly* 7, no. 1 (January 1921): 31.

Table 5.4.1 Bloch *Schelomo* Part One, analysis

Section	*Lento moderato*	*Più animato*	Cadenza	*Andante moderato*		
Rehearsal number and measure	First 5 measures	R. 1, mm. 1–7	R. 1, m. 8	R. 1, m. 11	R. 2–5	
Thematic material	Melisma idea	*Siciliano* idea	Cadenza idea	Orchestral interlude on iambic idea	Iambic idea and melisma idea	

Section	*Più animato*								*Assai lento*
Rehearsal number and measure	R. 5, m. 7	R. 7	R. 8	R. 9	R. 10	R. 11	R. 12	R. 13–15	R. 15, m. 6
Thematic material	Iambic idea, melisma idea	Melisma idea	Cadenza idea, then combined cadenza, *siciliano*, and iambic ideas	Minor sixth idea	Continuation of minor sixth idea	Cadenza idea	*Siciliano* idea	Orchestral interlude, ending with cadenza idea	Solo cadenza

Table 5.4.2 Bloch *Schelomo* Part Two, analysis

Section	*Allegro moderato*							
Rehearsal number and measure	R. 16–R. 17	R. 18	R. 20	R. 21	R. 22	R. 24	R. 25	R. 27	R. 27, m. 6
Thematic material	*Shofar* idea (bassoon and oboe)	Cadenza idea (cello)	Cello adopts *shofar* idea	Cadenza idea	Melisma idea	Cadenza idea	Orchestral interlude on *shofar* idea	*Siciliano* idea, *shofar* idea	Melisma idea (cello), iambic idea (winds), *shofar* idea (strings)

Section	(*Allegro moderato*)						
Rehearsal number and measure	R. 28	R. 29	R. 30	R. 31	R. 32	R. 33	R. 34
Thematic material	Cadenza idea (cello), *shofar* and iambic ideas (orchestra)	Iambic idea (cello), *shofar* idea (winds), *siciliano* idea (strings)	Orchestral interlude on *siciliano* and cadenza ideas	Orchestral interlude on *siciliano* ideas	Orchestral interlude, melisma idea	*Shofar* idea (cello)	*Shofar* and cadenza ideas (cello)

Section	*Andante moderato*
Rehearsal number and measure	R. 34, m. 7
Thematic material	Transitional

Table 5.4.3 Bloch *Schelomo* Part Three, analysis

Section	*Andante moderato*		*Un poco più lento*	*Tempo del andante*	*Molto moderato*	*Più animato*	*Andante moderato*
Rehearsal number and measure	R. 35	R. 36–37	R. 38, m. 5	R. 42	R. 44	R. 44, m. 7	R. 47
Thematic material	Minor sixth idea (cello)	Variant of minor sixth idea	"Dreamlike" phase	*Siciliano* idea	Variant of *siciliano* idea	Minor sixth idea (orchestra)	Cadenza idea

5.5

Edward Elgar (1857–1934)

Concerto in E Minor for Cello and Orchestra, Op. 85 (1919)

I. Adagio–Moderato   II. Lento–Allegro molto
III. Adagio   IV. Allegro–Moderato–Allegro ma non troppo

1919 was a dark time for the sixty-two-year-old Sir Edward Elgar. The First World War had devastated Europe, and England was in deep mourning for the generation of young men lost on the battlefields. Gone forever was the England Elgar's *Pomp and Circumstance* had once exalted as a "land of hope and glory."

Unlike many of his compatriots, Elgar opposed the war with Germany. He had spent a formative period of his life there and his musical style owed more to Wagner and Brahms than to any English composer. Now that anti-German sentiment was rife in England, Elgar feared that his own German-influenced compositions were becoming irrelevant.

Elgar's Cello Concerto postdates several post-diatonic works for cello such as the Kodály Solo Sonata, but its style belongs firmly to the Romantic era. By looking back to the nineteenth century, Elgar captured the longing of a nation to return to carefree pre-war times. His models in writing for cello and orchestra were Schumann and Dvořák. Like both these predecessors, he used cyclical forms that allowed for "backwards glances" at earlier thematic material. His handling of a large orchestra—double woodwinds, piccolo, four horns, two trumpets, three trombones, tuba, timpani, strings—suggests that he had learned from Dvořák's example now to avoid balance problems between the cello and the orchestra. One aspect of the work that departs from usual Romantic concerto procedures, however, is a movement plan of two pairs of linked movements rather than the usual three movements.

With an opening gesture of four crashing chords for the solo cellist, Elgar's first movement draws the listener immediately into a soundworld of strong emotions. The viola section answers this anguished recitative with the introduction of the main theme of the movement, a meandering melody in

9/8 time. The pastoral tone of this theme made it a favorite of Elgar's; during his final illness, he told a friend "If ever after I am dead you hear someone whistling this tune on the Malvern Hills, don't be alarmed. It's only me."[1] The movement is in ternary form, with a central section in E major giving temporary respite from the sorrowful mood.

The second movement is in ABABA form with an opening recitative and a coda. The first four chords are the same as those that opened the first movement, but here they are pizzicato. Throughout the recitative, these chords alternate with snippets of material (played *arco*) that will become the main theme of the movement. Seventeen measures in, the theme takes off in earnest in a mercurial *moto perpetuo* that resembles material in Elgar's earlier comic work, *Falstaff* (1913). A second, more songful theme appears twice as a break from the *moto perpetuo*, and a coda unifies material from both the themes. In contrast with the distressed character of the first movement, the mood here is exuberant and boisterous.

Elgar's third movement, a yearning *cantilena* in B♭ major, has the most nostalgic character of all. Though the structure is a relatively simple ABA, the modulations (A major, E♭ major, and a return to B♭ major) require some deft chromaticism and enharmonic respellings of pitch classes. The emotion, down to the harmonically ambiguous ending, shows the influence of the second movement of Schumann's Cello Concerto.[2] This open-ended conclusion runs without a break into the fourth movement.

Some commentators analyze this finale as a rondo,[3] others as a freely constructed sonata-allegro.[4] Like the first and second movements, the fourth opens with an introductory recitative. The orchestra first introduces the main theme in B-flat major, but quickly modulates to E minor via a series of diminished harmonic progressions. The majestic cello entry develops and varies material from the main theme. A short, flurried cadenza alludes to the melodic shape from the end of the first movement—the first of many returns to previous material in this movement. Once the exposition is underway, Elgar continues to vary the first theme and introduces a second, more playful theme with dashing downward scales and the ricochet bowstroke.

---

[1] Michael Kennedy, *Portrait of Elgar* (Oxford: Oxford University Press, 1987), 334.
[2] Michael Steinberg, *The Concerto: A Listener's Guide* (New York: Oxford University Press, 1998), 188.
[3] See Michael Thomas Roeder, *A History of the Concerto* (Portland, OR: Amadeus Press, 1994), 31, and Michael Kennedy, *Elgar Orchestral Music* (Seattle: University of Washington Press, 1970), 48.
[4] See Martha McCrory, "A Study of the Elgar Cello Concerto," MMus thesis, University of Rochester, 1944.

The development section of the finale contains a series of variants on the first theme, albeit in many keys and disguises. The recapitulation continues the mostly jovial expression, leading the first-time listener to expect an optimistic conclusion to the concerto. This never comes. In the last few pages of the score, Elgar suddenly changes course into a darker mood. In a coda marked *poco più lento*, he begins a passionate outburst of sorrow that resembles a movement from his *The Dream of Gerontius* (1900): "I can no more; for now it comes again / That sense of ruin, which is worse than pain." Like a vision from the past, the second theme from the third movement returns, lingering on the second inversion of a seventh chord that demands resolution into E minor. This comes with a return to the opening chords of the first movement, but this time Elgar leaves no room for ambiguity, concluding with one last energetic return of the first theme.

The English cellist Felix Salmond premiered the Cello Concerto. Though he played well, lack of rehearsal time and an indifferent conductor caused the orchestra to play poorly.[5] Soon afterwards, Salmond emigrated to America and was unavailable to record the work. Elgar found another sympathetic interpreter in Beatrice Harrison, with whom he recorded it twice. The 1920 recording uses a shortened version of the work because of the constraints of technology, but eight years later they recorded the full concerto. Elgar and Harrison's recordings reveal a highly flexible approach to tempo and expression, and they remain primary documents in performance practice research. By the nineteen-sixties, Elgar's Cello Concerto attained blockbuster status thanks to Jacqueline du Pré's iconic recordings and performances. It remains one of the most beloved concertos in the repertoire.

---

[5] Tully Potter, "A Much Maligned Cellist: The True Story of Felix Salmond and the Elgar Cello Concerto," *The Elgar Society Journal* 19, no. 6 (2016): 7.

Table 5.5.1 Elgar Concerto I. Adagio–Moderato and II. Lento–Allegro molto, analysis

Section	First movement Recitative	First movement A		First movement B		First movement A
Measures	1–8	9–46	47–54	55–74	75–79	80–105
Thematic material	*Adagio* Four chords motive, ascending scalar material	*Moderato* First theme (six repetitions: violas, solo cello, full orchestra, solo cello, orchestra, solo cello)	Bridge theme for woodwinds, solo cello descant	Second theme	Bridge theme	First theme (four repetitions: cello, orchestral accompaniment, orchestra without cello, solo cello) Cadence in E minor, *attacca*
Key(s)	E minor	E minor	E minor to E major	E major	E minor	E minor

Section	Second movement Recitative	Second movement A	Second movement B	Second movement A	Second movement B	Second movement A	Second movement Coda
Measures	1–15	16–39	40–47	47–77	78–85	85–103	104–129
Thematic material	*Lento* Four chords motive in pizzicato. Introduction of motives from first theme.	*Allegro molto* First thematic group	Second thematic group	First thematic group	Second thematic group	First thematic group	Coda with combined material from first and second thematic groups
Key(s)	E minor	G major	E♭ major to G minor	G major	D major to F♯ minor	D major to G major	G major

Table 5.5.2 Elgar Concerto, III. Adagio and IV. Allegro–Moderato–Allegro ma non troppo, analysis

Section	Third movement A		Third movement B		Third movement A	
Measures	1–8		8–52		53–60	
Thematic materials	First theme		Second theme		First theme	
Key(s)	B♭		B♭ major, A major, E♭ major		B♭ major, cadence on dominant harmony, *attacca*	

Section	Fourth movement Recitative			Fourth movement Exposition		
Measures	1–8	9–17	18–19	20–55		56-83
Thematic materials	First theme (orchestral introduction)	First theme (recitative)	Cadenza	First theme		Second theme
Key(s)	B♭ minor	E minor	E minor	E minor		G major to E minor

Section	Fourth movement Development					
Measures	84–125	126–148	149–159	159–166	167–180	181–196
Thematic materials	Variation 1 on material derived from first theme	Variation 2	Variation 3	Variation 4	Variation 5	Variation 6
Key(s)	A♭ major	F minor	A♭ major	C major	B♭ major	F minor

(*continued*)

Table 5.5.2 Continued

Section	Fourth movement Recapitulation			Fourth movement Coda					
Measures	197–231	232–254	255–280	281–302	303–320	321–325	325–331	332–335	336-351
Thematic materials	First theme	Second theme	First theme	Introduction	Material from third movement, second theme	Bridge (chromatic scalar material)	Third movement second theme	Four chords theme from the first movement	First theme
Key(s)	E minor, B minor, E♭ major,	C major, A major, E♭ major, dominant of E minor	E minor to dominant of F♯ minor	Chromatic modulations	F minor, A♭ major, C major		A♭ major to dominant of E minor	E minor	E minor

5.6

Dmitri Dmitriyevich Shostakovich (1906–1975)

Cello Concerto No. 1 in E♭ Major, Op. 107 (1959)

I. Allegretto   II. Moderato   III. Cadenza   IV. Allegro con moto

Shostakovich wrote his First Cello Concerto during a relatively peaceful period in his life. The Soviet dictator Joseph Stalin, whose persecution of artists so traumatized Shostakovich and his contemporaries, had been dead for six years. Shostakovich now had permission to travel abroad more frequently, and to hold important positions such as the presidency of the first Tchaikovsky International Competition.[1]

The First Cello Concerto was Shostakovich's first major work for solo cello since the Sonata in D Minor, Op. 40 (1934). One motivation for composing it was the inspiring artistry of his friend Mstislav Rostropovich, who at thirty-two was already the world's leading cellist and a passionate advocate for new music. Rostropovich's previous association with Sergei Prokofiev had resulted in several major works, including Prokofiev's Symphony-Concerto, Op. 124, and he hoped to convince Shostakovich to compose something on a similar scale. Shostakovich and Prokofiev's relationship might have been contentious,[2] but Shostakovich admired the Symphony-Concerto and Rostropovich knew it. Rostropovich brought the matter up with Nina, Shostakovich's first wife, who advised him not to try the same tactics that had persuaded Prokofiev to compose for the cello. "If you want Dmitri Dmitriyevich to write something for you," she warned, "... never ask him or talk to him about it."[3] Rostropovich had to be patient, but in the end he got

---

[1] Pauline Fairclough and David Fanning, eds., *The Cambridge Companion to Shostakovich* (Cambridge: Cambridge University Press, 2008), xiii.

[2] See Ivana Medić, "Prokofiev and Shostakovich: A Two-Way Influence," in *Rethinking Prokofiev*, ed. Rita McAllister and Christina Guillaumier (New York: Oxford University Press, 2020), 87–106.

[3] Elizabeth Wilson, *Shostakovich: A Life Remembered* (Princeton, NJ: Princeton University Press, 2006), 363–364.

his wish twice, once in 1959 with the First Cello Concerto and again in 1966 with the Second Cello Concerto, Op. 126.

Shostakovich was familiar with the existing repertoire for cello and orchestra,[4] and claimed that his favorite concerto was that of Camille Saint-Saëns.[5] At first glance, this delicate work of French Romanticism might seem an unlikely model for Shostakovich, at least in melody and harmony. In instrumentation and form, its impact is more noticeable. For instrumentation, Shostakovich followed Saint-Saëns' lead in writing for a relatively small ensemble. By confining himself to strings, woodwinds, timpani, celesta, and just one brass instrument, a horn, Shostakovich avoided balance problems between the soloist and the orchestra. In form, Saint-Saëns' use of cyclical thematic return across multiple movements appears to have influenced Shostakovich to try something similar. There is evidence that Shostakovich originally intended to create a three-movement structure like Saint-Saëns',[6] deciding only later to designate the coda as a separate movement.

For the main key center, Shostakovich chose E♭ major—the same key as Beethoven's "Eroica" Symphony and many other works associated with military victories.[7] The distinctive opening gesture, a four-note motive on G, F♭, C♭, and B♭, is a unifying device throughout the concerto. A second unifying device, an anapestic rhythmic motive, punctuates and accompanies repetitions of the first motive. Some commentators liken the first motive to Shostakovich's famous musical monogram, "DSCH" (D, E♭, C, B), which appears in the Tenth Symphony, Eighth String Quartet, and elsewhere.[8] Alexander Ivashkin contradicts this assumption, pointing out that the melodic shape of the first motive resembles the "Death of Heroes" theme in Shostakovich's 1948 score for *The Young Guard*.[9] Given Shostakovich's penchant for quotation and self-quotation, the similarity is more than likely intentional. We can only guess at his reasons for repurposing material from this patriotic film about the courage of Russian soldiers against the Nazis.

The second theme of the first movement contains another allusion, this time to the *Songs and Dances of Death* by the nineteenth-century composer

---

[4] In 1963, Shostakovich made a re-orchestration of Schumann's Cello Concerto, Op. 129.
[5] Wilson, 135.
[6] Alexander Ivashkin, "Shostakovich: First Cello Concerto," *Shostakovich: New Collected Works*, Series III (Moscow: DSCH Editions, 2012), 46:127.
[7] Malcolm MacDonald, "'I Took a Simple Little Tune and Developed it': Shostakovich's String Concertos and Sonatas," in *The Cambridge Companion to Shostakovich*, ed. Pauline Fairclough and David Fanning (Cambridge: Cambridge University Press, 2008), 126.
[8] MacDonald, 128.
[9] Ivashkin, 128.

Modest Mussorgsky. The solo cello line, according to Malcolm MacDonald, quotes a song with the title "Trepak," the name of a Cossack folk dance. The text tells the story of Death visiting a drunken peasant and luring him into a *danse macabre*. In Shostakovich's version, the anapestic rhythms that accompany the second theme also recall the relentless rhythms of the dance.

The forceful character of the first movement contrasts drastically with the stark opening of the second. Here, the main key is A minor, an augmented fourth away from the original key of E♭ major. The cello's opening phrase slightly resembles the melodic shape of the second theme from the first movement, creating a sense of stylistic unity across movements. The character is tragic, even chilling. At the end of the second movement, Shostakovich reprises this melody in artificial harmonics for the cellist, breaking up the line into an ominous back-and-forth between the cello and the orchestral celesta. In using this unusual instrumental timbre, Shostakovich obliquely alludes to a passage for the celesta in Prokofiev's Symphony-Concerto. Here, however, the celesta has a more prominent role, perhaps as an eerie *Doppelgänger* to the cello. Octaves below the cello-celesta dialogue is an accompanying eighth-note motive for muted strings that Michael Steinberg compares to the violin line in "Der Einsame im Herbst" ("The Lonely One in Autumn") from Gustav Mahler's *Das Lied von der Erde*.[10]

The cadenza movement interrupts this otherworldly interlude, bridging the second and fourth movements with an intense acceleration in harmonic rhythm. As the cadenza progresses, so too does the cyclic reintroduction of motives from the first movement. When the orchestra rejoins the cello at the start of the fourth movement, the mood is back in the realms of the *danse macabre*. Also present is a heavily disguised motive from Stalin's favorite Georgian folk song, "Suliko" (Figure 5.6.1). The original has a sweet, naïve melody and an unsettlingly dark text: "I went looking for my sweetheart's grave, I went everywhere. I sobbed, with burning tears, 'Where are you, Suliko?'" Shostakovich's dissonant, violent distortion of the song is darker still (Figure 5.6.2).

The "Suliko" motive eventually merges into other anapestic rhythmic motives, though the menacing feeling continues. The four-note motive from the beginning of the first movement reappears, first in the meter of a quick waltz, then in its original quadruple meter. The concluding coda builds in

---

[10] Michael Steinberg, *The Concerto: A Listener's Guide* (New York: Oxford University Press, 1998), 435.

Figure 5.6.1 Melody of "Suliko," traditional Georgian folk song

Figure 5.6.2 Shostakovich, Cello Concerto No. 1 Op. 107, *IV. Allegro con moto*, mm. 91–96

intensity with the obsessive repetition of the anapest motive across three strings of the cello, ending abruptly on two E♭ major triads.

Shostakovich's First Cello Concerto achieved immediate success at home and abroad. There was enough of the "classical" in its form, melody, and counterpoint to appease the musically conservative Soviet cultural authorities, and its eclectic style also gave it credibility in modernist Western circles. Reviews were enthusiastic: one critic wrote "We have watched [Shostakovich] grappling with his problems, work by work, over the last ten years or so, with excitement and sympathy, for whether his predicament has been personal or political, the inner modesty of the man shines clearly through his music. The Cello Concerto gives the effect of his absolute self-identification with what he has written."[11]

---

[11] Diana McVeagh, "Shostakovich's Concerto," *The Musical Times* 101, no. 1413 (November 1960): 703.

Table 5.6.1 Shostakovich First Cello Concerto, I. *Allegretto*, analysis

Section	Exposition		Development			Recapitulation		Coda
Measures	1–81	82–134	134–157	158–170	170–143	243–259	260–295	296–334
Thematic material	First thematic group (*Young Guards* and anapestic motives)	Second thematic group (*trepak* and anapestic motives)	First thematic group	Second thematic group	First thematic group	First thematic group	Second thematic group	Material from first thematic group
Key(s)	E♭ major	C minor	B minor	B minor, chromatic harmony	B minor, chromatic harmony	E♭ major	C minor	E♭ major

Table 5.6.2 Shostakovich First Cello Concerto, *II. Moderato*, analysis

Section	Exposition						Development	Recapitulation	
Measures	1–15	16–32	33–53	54–69	70–95	95–114	115–148	148–157	158–193
Thematic material	Orchestral introduction, first theme	Cello entry, second theme	Transition	First theme	First theme variant (cello)	Closing theme	Material from exposition closing theme	Orchestral introduction, first theme	Second theme, cello and celesta dialogue
Key(s)	A minor	A minor	A minor to F♯ minor	F♯ minor	F♯ minor	D major	F♯ minor, modulating	F♯ minor	A minor

Table 5.6.3 Shostakovich First Cello Concerto, *III. Cadenza*, analysis

Section	Cadenza						
Measures	1–36	37–51	52–68	69–75	75–99	100–120	121–148
Thematic material	Variant on second movement first theme	Variant on second movement closing theme	Variant on second movement second theme in double stops	Transition, new material	*Allegretto*, new material	*Allegro*, variant on first movement first thematic group	Coda on material derived from first movement thematic material

Table 5.6.4 Shostakovich First Cello Concerto, IV. Allegro con moto, analysis

Section	Exposition				Development			Recapitulation	Coda
Measures	1–9	9–64	65–111	111–131	132–199	199–270	271–304	305–336	337–371
Thematic material	Introductory transition into the first theme	First theme	Second theme, first "Suliko" motive at 91	Variant on first theme	Development theme (waltz-like)	Combination of second theme melodic shape with triple meter from the development theme	Cyclic return of a variant of the first movement Young Guards motive, triple meter	Reprise of first movement first thematic group	Integration of thematic materials from fourth movement first theme, first movement first thematic group, "Suliko" motive (363–365)
Key(s)	Chromatic harmony	G minor	Quasi-C♯ minor	G minor	Quasi-F minor	Quasi-C minor, modulating	E♭ major	E♭ major	E♭ major

6
BEYOND ROMANTICISM
New Directions in the Sonata

# 6.1

Serge Rachmaninoff (1873–1943)

Sonata in G Minor, Op. 19 (1901)

I. Lento–Allegro moderato   II. Allegro scherzando
III. Andante   IV. Allegro mosso

Like so many other composers of cello music, Rachmaninoff began to write for the instrument because of a close friendship with a cellist. In his case, the cellist was Anatoly Brandukov (1856–1930), a friend of Saint-Saëns, Liszt, and Tchaikovsky who inspired the latter's *Pezzo Capriccioso*. In 1892, Brandukov performed the nineteen-year-old Rachmaninoff's earliest works for cello, the first *Trio élégiaque* and the Prelude, Op. 2 for cello and piano.[1] This began a long and fruitful creative association between the composer and the cellist. Nine years later, Rachmaninoff would dedicate the Cello Sonata to Brandukov, and a year after that Brandukov was best man at Rachmaninoff's wedding.

In the intervening years, Rachmaninoff experienced some difficult career challenges, despite his promising start. After studying with Anton Arensky and Sergei Taneyev at the Moscow Conservatory, he graduated with a large portfolio of compositions including a piano concerto and an opera. Soon afterwards, he published the two biggest hits of his early artistic maturity, the C-sharp minor Prelude for piano and an orchestral fantasy, *The Rock*. These early successes encouraged him to start on his most ambitious work so far, the First Symphony of 1895-6. The famous composer Alexander Glazunov was engaged to conduct the first performance but did not prepare well, and the concert was a disaster. "I am amazed how such a highly talented man as Glazunov can conduct so badly," Rachmaninoff fumed. Worse still, the Mighty Five composer and critic César Cui wrote a spiteful review that likened Rachmaninoff's First Symphony to "a program symphony on the 'Seven Plagues of Egypt.'"[2]

---

[1] Geoffrey Norris, *Rakhmaninov* (London: J. M. Dent & Sons, 1976), 14.
[2] Norris, 25.

The failure of the First Symphony sent Rachmaninoff into a three-year depressive episode, during which he could barely compose. A well-meaning friend, Princess Alexandra Liven, thought it might cheer Rachmaninoff up to meet one of his heroes, Leo Tolstoy. She arranged a meeting, telling the great novelist "He has lost faith in his powers. Try to help him."[3] Unfortunately, Tolstoy had exactly the opposite effect on Rachmaninoff. He delivered a lecture on work ethic, scolding "You must work. Do you think that I am pleased with myself? Work. I work every day."[4] Rachmaninoff, unimpressed, continued to languish.

His despairing family eventually decided he needed psychological treatment and sought a therapist. They settled on Dr. Nikolai Dahl, a medical doctor, hypnotherapist, and amateur violist, whose clients included other artists. Seemingly miraculously, Dahl cured Rachmaninoff's ailment in only a few sessions. Dahl's exact methods are a mystery and remain the subject of much conjecture. (The playwright-composer Dave Malloy, for example, wrote a musical called *Preludes* that imagined the dialogue between composer and therapist.)[5] The most likely explanation is that Dahl's ability to converse knowledgably about music helped just as much as hypnotherapy in banishing Rachmaninoff's depression once and for all.[6]

After his recovery, Rachmaninoff's creativity flourished. He began work on one of his most beloved works, the Second Piano Concerto, Op. 18. Dedicated to Dahl, it represents a thanksgiving for Rachmaninoff's return to health. His next work, which he began immediately after, was the Cello Sonata, Op. 19. Echoes of the concerto appear in the sonata, whose piano part is of a similarly titanic difficulty. Such technical demands were no problem for Rachmaninoff, who was also the leading Russian pianist of his time. In demanding concerto-level virtuosity in a cello-piano sonata, he was following the lead of other Romantic pianist-composers such as Chopin, Grieg, and Mendelssohn.

Of these, Chopin's Sonata, Op. 65 seems especially to have influenced Rachmaninoff's Op. 19. Aside from their both being in the key of G minor, they have comparable movement plans: a first movement that ambitiously extends the possibilities of the sonata-allegro concept, a second movement

---

[3] Norris, 29.
[4] Norris, 29–30.
[5] Dave Malloy, *Preludes: A Musical Fantasia Set in the Hypnotized Mind of Sergei Rachmaninoff* (unpublished manuscript, 2015), typescript.
[6] Geoffrey Norris, "Rachmaninoff, Serge," *Grove Music Online*, ed. Deane Root, http://oxfordmusiconline.com.

whose nervous *scherzo* gives way to a songful middle section, an ultra-lyrical third movement, and a finale that concludes the sonata in the parallel major mode. Like Chopin, Rachmaninoff demands few finger-twisting pyrotechnics from the cellist; rather, the difficulty of the cello part lies in sustaining a projecting tone above a massive, texturally complicated piano part. Rachmaninoff's writing for the cello requires the powerful bow-arm and intense vibrato that were hallmarks of the nineteenth-century Russian school of cello playing and at which Brandukov excelled.[7]

The first movement of Op. 19 begins with an introductory section whose ambiguous harmony hints at C minor, the main key of the Second Piano Concerto. The opening motive, an ascending minor second, creates the impression of a melody in search of a key. This searching gesture returns dozens of times throughout the first movement in both ascending and descending motion. Another recurring motive, an anapestic rhythmic cell, ushers in the "real" key of G minor and with it, the first theme. From then on, the sonata-allegro idea is more conventional: Rachmaninoff clearly defines the exposition, development, and recapitulation sections, and the main modulation is to the expected key of D major. Within this Classical structure, he creates luxuriant melodic and harmonic color through borrowed chords from parallel modes, chromatic passing tones, augmented triads, and other uses of dissonance. Syncopated and anapestic rhythms create momentum and an agitated character in the melodic lines, while relentless swirling arpeggios and other pattern-work in the piano part make for a dense, multi-hued texture.

The development section features a rapid chain of modulations that outline the cycle of thirds—a late Romantic use of harmony that stretches diatonicism to its limits. Though the recapitulation follows the Classical sonata-allegro principle in resolving melodic and harmonic materials in G minor, the textures in the piano part remain turbulent. A coda with the marking *leggiero* begins, at last, to release some of the tortured character, resolving and releasing the remaining minor-second and anapestic gestures into a semblance of calm. The movement concludes with a rhythmical gesture for the pianist[8] that some consider Rachmaninoff's musical signature: "*Rach*-ma-ni-noff!"

---

[7] Lev Ginzburg, "Brandukov, Anatoly Andreyevich," *Grove Music Online*, ed. Deane Root, http://oxfordmusiconline.com.

[8] The gesture is composed of a quarter note, two eighth notes, and another quarter note.

Figure 6.1.1 Schubert, *Erlkönig* D. 328, mm. 1–3

Figure 6.1.2 Rachmaninoff, Cello Sonata Op. 19, *II. Allegro scherzando*, mm. 1–4

The second movement, a scherzo, has a relatively straightforward ternary structure. The compound meter and octave-based ostinato patterns suggest the "hoofbeats" motive of Schubert's *Erlkönig*, a *lied* that tells the sinister tale of a child lured from his father's horse into the clutches of an evil elf king. The melodic scalar patterns in *Erlkönig* (see Figure 6.1.1) may equally have inspired another of Rachmaninoff's melodic building blocks, this time the last six pitches of a descending C minor scale (see Figure 6.1.2). Not only does the device provide the seed for melodic material, but it also enables harmonic turnarounds into new keys. A fragment of a scale leads from C minor into E♭ major for a secondary thematic area, for example, and down to A♭ major for the sweeping *cantabile* middle section.

The poignant slow third movement uses another Schubertian device, the fluctuation between parallel major and minor modes. The melodic lines feature one of Rachmaninoff's favorite rhetorical gestures, the syncopated reiteration of a single pitch. The closely arpeggiated texture of the accompanying piano part may owe something to that of another famously heartrending *cantabile*, the slow movement of Beethoven's *Pathétique* Sonata.

For the finale, Rachmaninoff returns to the sonata-allegro principle. Unlike the anguished first movement, the last is in a major key and a jubilant character. A fleeting memory of earlier anxiety reappears in the coda to the finale when a version of the gesture that introduced the first theme of the first movement comes back in a major key. In returning to it in a more optimistic mood, Rachmaninoff at last dispels its melancholy.

Table 6.1.1 Rachmaninoff Sonata, *II. Allegro scherzando*, analysis

Section	A					
Measures	1–32	33–48	49–57	57–68	69–76	77–80
Thematic material	First theme	Second theme	*Tempo primo* bridge to first theme material	First theme	Closing section	First theme material extends the descending scale as a bridge to the B section
Key(s)	C minor	E♭ major	Dominant of C minor	C minor	C minor	C minor to A♭ major

Section	B				
Measures	81–96	97–104	105–116	116–134	135–143
Thematic material	Lyrical theme	Lyrical theme, tonicizations	Reprise of lyrical theme	Cadential section	Bridge to B section
Key(s)	A♭ major	E♭ major, D♭ major	A♭ major	A♭ major	A♭ major to dominant of C minor

Section	A		Coda	
Measures	143–218		219–224	225–233
Thematic material	Written-out *da capo* of 1–76		C minor pedal, arpeggiated patterns	First theme material
Key(s)	C minor		C minor	C minor

6.2

Samuel Barber (1910–1981)

Sonata in C Minor, Op. 6 (1932)

I. Allegro ma non troppo   II. Adagio–Presto—di nuovo Adagio
III. Allegro appassionato

Samuel Barber's Op. 6 is the first American cello-piano sonata to become core repertoire, and until Elliott Carter's contribution in 1948 was the only one. It is an early work, but not a juvenile one, since it was during this period that Barber wrote two of his most famous compositions—*Dover Beach*, Op. 3 for string quartet and baritone (1931) and *Adagio for Strings*, Op. 11 (1936).

Barber came from a younger generation than celebrated modernist composers of the 1930s such as Igor Stravinsky, Béla Bartók, and Arnold Schoenberg, but he chose not to follow their stylistic lead. Barber had plenty of American predecessors, but even in the 1930s there were European musicians, such as the Curtis Institute director Josef Hofmann, who believed that "nothing of worth could be composed by Americans."[1] As one of the first students to attend Curtis, Barber had to contend with such snobbery as he sought his own path in composition. Unlike his contemporary Aaron Copland, Barber did not take inspiration from American folk music; his language has more in common with the chromatic late Romanticism of other older contemporaries such as Richard Strauss, Jean Sibelius, and Serge Rachmaninoff.

Barber's teacher at Curtis, Rosario Scalero, may have had something to do with this. Scalero was a conservative composer whose style looked reverently back to Brahms, and whose lessons emphasized the study of counterpoint.[2] Barber, grateful for Scalero's rigorous training in part-writing and voice-leading, dedicated the Cello Sonata to his teacher.

---

[1] Barbara Heyman, *Samuel Barber: The Composer and His Music* (New York: Oxford University Press, 1992), 118.
[2] Nathan Broder, "The Music of Samuel Barber," *Musical Quarterly* 34, no. 3 (July 1948): 328.

Barber began plans for the work during a European vacation with Gian Carlo Menotti, a fellow composition student who became his partner in life and music. After a long hike through southern Austria and Switzerland, they crossed the border into northern Italy, where they stayed in Menotti's hometown of Cadegliano. In just two weeks, Barber drafted the first movement and what would become the middle section of the second. Scalero's feedback was positive, so he kept going. He even brought in a cellist from La Scala in Milan, some fifty miles away, to try it out.[3] Once he was back in America, Barber sought the collaboration of another Curtis student, the cellist Orlando Cole, whose input is clear in the many additions and pasted-over patches of paper in the manuscript.[4]

The style of Barber's Sonata, Op. 6 is often compared to that of Brahms's two cello sonatas, which Barber knew and had played.[5] Barber's use of sonata-allegro and ternary forms, and of complex rhythmic devices such as hemiolas and cross-rhythms, supports this view. His harmonic language, conversely, owes less to Brahms. Whereas a nineteenth-century sonata usually establishes the key center by beginning with the tones of the tonic triad, Barber's opening measures contain the pitches C, A♭, G♭, and D. Though this is an enharmonic respelling of a French augmented sixth chord, Barber does not use it in the manner of functional harmony, where it would typically precede the dominant chord. Instead, the pitch collection suggests the "weightless" feeling of whole-tone harmony. The French sixth idea becomes a recurring gesture throughout the movement.

The cellist introduces the opening phrase, entering on two tones of the signature chord, a C anacrusis and a downbeat on A♭. During this first A♭, the pianist enters, and the two instruments perform a hocket-like rhythmic back-and-forth across the tones of the French sixth chord until the stormy conclusion of the first four-measure phrase. At last, the two instruments speak together as Barber "resolves" the French sixth chord onto the second inversion of the G♭ minor triad.

The remainder of the first thematic area includes materials derived from the first harmonic and rhythmic ideas. A transition introduces triplets, in both eighth and quarter notes. Finally, Barber releases the harmonic and rhythmic turmoil to introduce a second theme, a tranquil legato in A♭ major. Here the harmony becomes more conventionally diatonic, but when the

---

[3] Heyman, 111.
[4] Heyman, 112, 116–117.
[5] Heyman, 111.

development section arrives, the French sixth idea returns. A twenty-four-measure development explores new keys using fragments of ideas from the first theme. At the recapitulation section, Barber reintroduces the first theme in the cello part, this time in augmented rhythmic values, replacing the "hocket" texture with a harmonic accompaniment of arpeggiated patterns. Barber reaches the dramatic high point of the movement in a climactic cadenza, before attempting to create a resolution to the turbulent mood. By the time the second theme returns, the harmony is in C major, where it remains until the end of the movement. For the last phrase, Barber inverts the cellist's opening phrase so that it is in descending motion, laying the French sixth idea to rest before the concluding C major triad.

The second movement, in ternary form, began life with just the central *Presto* section. Later, perhaps at Cole's suggestion, he placed it between two short *Adagio* sections. This blended the two middle movements of the traditional four-movement plan—*scherzo* and slow movement—into a single movement in ABA form. In the opening slow section, the melodic material is as heartfelt and songful as that in *Dover Beach*. In contrast, the staccato articulations for both instruments in the *Presto* section seem jarring and angular. Barber again creates rhythmic interplay in collections of triplets in both small and large note values, with several measures composed of three sets of triplets in quarter notes against the quadruple meter. The final slow section, while rhythmically related to the first, differs in its harmony and melodic shape.

Barber's last movement is another sonata-allegro. Its key signature is C minor, but Barber departs from this key in non-diatonic ways. The pianist introduces a strident first theme with a sweeping arpeggiated accompaniment in C minor, but by the time the cello enters twelve measures later, the harmony has abruptly changed to F♯ minor. Melodically, the first and second themes are similar in shape. Barber achieves contrast between them in the texture, which switches from arpeggios to spiky block chords. Rhythms appear in increasingly small divisions of the beat. The exposition closes with a fantastical cadenza for the pianist in the form of a B major scale in perfect fourths.

A short development section follows, constructed from variants of the first and second themes. When the recapitulation arrives thirty-seven measures later, it is in F♯ minor. Again, the pianist takes the melodic part. When the cellist enters, it does so in C minor, that is, in reverse order from the exposition. The recapitulation ends just as the exposition did, with a piano cadenza composed of a scale in fourths, this time in E major. Barber takes the E as a pivot, recasting it as the mediant pitch in C major, and starts a coda in this key. He quickly re-establishes C minor, however, and the final twenty-seven measures conclude the sonata in this ostensible home key.

Barber completed his Sonata, Op. 6 in December 1932. In early 1933, he and Cole premiered it first in Philadelphia, then at a League of Composers concert in New York. Thanks to Cole's advocacy of the work, and that of Luigi Silva, Felix Salmond, and Gregor Piatigorsky,[6] it quickly entered the cello canon and has remained there since.

---

[6] Heyman, 115–117.

Table 6.2.1 Barber Sonata, I. Allegro ma non troppo, analysis

Section	Exposition					
Measures	1–15	16–22	23–27	28–38	39–43	44–59
Thematic material	First theme	Transition 1	Variant on first theme, piano cadenza	Transition 2	Introduction to second theme	Second theme
Key(s)	Quasi-C minor, "French sixth" harmony	"French sixth" harmony	C minor, modulating	F minor, B♭ minor, E♭ minor	Modulating to E♭ major	E♭ major

Section	Development		
Measures	60–66	67–81	82–91
Thematic material	Bridge to development	Fragmented variant on first theme	Variant on Transition 1 material
Key(s)	C minor	Quasi-C minor, "French sixth" harmony	B minor, modulating

Section	Recapitulation				
Measures	92–105	106–116	117–121	122–143	144–155
Thematic material	First theme, concluding cello cadenza on material from the piano cadenza at 27	Material from Transition 2	Introduction to second theme	Second theme	
Key(s)	C minor	F♯ minor, D minor, G minor	A major to dominant of C major	C major	F minor, "French sixth" idea, C major

6.3

Sergei Prokofiev (1891–1953)

Sonata for Cello and Piano, Op. 119 (1949)

I. Andante grave   II. Moderato   III. Allegro ma non troppo

Prokofiev's Cello Sonata, Op. 119, his sole contribution to the genre, comes from the last years of his life. It is neo-Classical in conception and differs strongly from the modernist compositions he wrote during an extended period in Europe and America. After decades abroad, Prokofiev made the momentous decision to return to his native Russia in 1936. Doing so compelled him to change his compositional language.

Prokofiev's reasons for returning home were more complicated than the explanations he gave to friends, such as a desire to hear the Russian language and see the Russian winter.[1] Abroad, he was just one of several Russian emigré composers, and never the foremost among them. In Europe, his *Scythian Suite*, Op. 20 (1914–15) was not as successful as Igor Stravinsky's *Rite of Spring*, while in America, conservative audience tastes put him in second place after Serge Rachmaninoff. On visits home, however, his compositions achieved a positive reaction from audiences and critics, and a future in Russia started to look appealing. There was another consideration, which was the fall from grace of Dmitri Shostakovich in January 1936. The younger composer, reeling from the official denunciation of his opera *Lady Macbeth of Mtsensk*, was now lying low. Prokofiev did not take Shostakovich's downfall as a warning; rather, he seems to have assumed that conditions were perfect for his triumphant homecoming.

The Russia he returned to, however, was a very different place from the Russia he had left in 1918. Since that time, the Soviet doctrine of socialist realism had become law for artists of all kinds. At the first All-Union Congress of Soviet Writers in 1934, the cultural commissar Andrei Zhdanov (1896–1948) defined socialist realism as a means to "depict reality in its

---

[1] Dorothea Redepenning, "Prokofiev, Sergey (Sergeyevich)," *Grove Music Online*, ed. Deane Root, http://oxfordmusiconline.com.

revolutionary development... combined with the ideological remolding and education of the toiling people in the spirit of socialism."[2] Problematically for composers, this wording was unspecific in terms of musical language, though most interpreted it as a request for major keys, a positive mood, and the use of a folk-like style.

The opposite of socialist realism in music was "formalism." Though the official definition of this word was just as vague, in practice it described art that gave more emphasis to formal aspects of construction than to subject matter. This included any music that was overly dissonant or atonal: the twelve-tone techniques of Arnold Schoenberg and his circle, for example, were anathema to Soviet cultural authorities. Their "revolutionary" ideals ironically required composers to look back to the styles of the eighteenth and nineteenth centuries.

Prokofiev attempted to reconcile the call for socialist realism in music with his own compositional traits. Though he had previously experimented with modernism, he did not consider such a reconciliation impossible. He sought to integrate socialist realist requirements with style features of his own, including sudden contrasts, distinctive rhythmic ostinato patterns, and surprise harmonic shifts to keys a half-step above or below the "expected" key. The Cello Sonata, Op. 119 seems to embody this shift towards greater musical conservatism.

Like so many cello compositions of the twentieth century, Prokofiev's Cello Sonata was inspired by the artistry of Mstislav Rostropovich. When the two musicians met, Prokofiev was in his late fifties, Rostropovich barely twenty. Hoping to attract the composer's attention, Rostropovich performed Prokofiev's Cello Concerto, Op. 58 (1933–38) with piano accompaniment in a recital at the Moscow Conservatory on December 21, 1947. This work, possibly because of its experimental structure, or its extreme difficulty, had not made it into the standard cello repertoire, but Rostropovich hoped that his persuasive interpretation would change this. His gamble paid off. Prokofiev, intrigued, told Rostropovich that he would revise the work for him. (He would later repurpose themes from Op. 58 into a separate composition, the Symphony-Concerto, Op. 125.)

The Soviet government's resolution against composers on February 10, 1948, interrupted his plans. The cultural commissar Andrei Zhdanov

---

[2] H. D. Scott, ed., *Problems of Soviet Literature: Reports and Speeches at the First Soviet Writers' Congress* (New York: International Publishers, 1935), 21.

harshly censured the leading Soviet composers—Prokofiev, Shostakovich, Aram Khachaturian, and Nikolai Miaskovsky—for "formalistic distortions," "rejection of the principles of classical music," and the "dissemination of atonality."[3] At first, Prokofiev did not take the threat seriously.[4] Six days later, under extreme pressure, he submitted a letter to the Union of Soviet Composers denouncing several of his own compositions. Four days after this humiliation, Prokofiev's foreign-born ex-wife Lina was arrested. Her imprisonment lasted eight years, and Prokofiev never saw her again. The stress of these events sent him into bouts of chronic illness.

Despite this unrest, Rostropovich did not lose hope that Prokofiev might compose some more works for the cello. Later in 1948, he encouraged the ailing composer to attend his premiere performance of a sonata by Miaskovsky. This composition reawakened Prokofiev's interest in the cello, and in the spring of 1949 he began plans for a sonata of his own.[5]

In line with his late-period neo-Classicism, Prokofiev conceived Op. 119 in an outwardly conservative mold. Following the three-movement plan of the Classical sonata, he made the first movement a sonata-allegro, the second a scherzo and trio, and the third a rondo with an extended cyclical coda. The main key is C major, a favorite of Prokofiev's and a resonant one for the cello. The opening measures contain a brief soliloquy for solo cello on its C-string, with the direction *piena voce*—"full voice"—and a heroic mood.

Prokofiev may have been trying his utmost to follow Zhdanov's arbitrary demands, but he could not resist some quirky harmonic digressions. A transitional section between first and second themes veers for a while into the unrelated key of F♯ major before ending up on the dominant, a more conventional starting-point for a second theme. Before the exposition is over, the harmony departs once again for a faraway key—this time C♯ minor. The development section further explores the thematic materials in abruptly changing key centers—F, E♭, C♯ minor, G♯ minor, E major. C major returns for the recapitulation section, but here Prokofiev appends an extended, multi-sectional coda. Another "surprise" key, this time F♯ minor, appears in rapid, bell-like triadic patterns for the cellist, until peace and C major are restored with oscillating patterns on the natural harmonics of the cello.

---

[3] Redepenning.

[4] Simon Morrison, *The People's Artist: Prokofiev's Soviet Years* (Oxford: Oxford University Press, 2009), 299.

[5] Morrison, 343.

The form of the second movement resembles a Beethovenian scherzo and trio with a *da capo*, though in this case the return to the first section is written out in full since it is not an exact repetition. Again, Prokofiev explores un unrelated key with a march-like theme in A♭ major for the pianist, while the cellist swoops up and down arpeggio patterns in the virtuoso *ricochet* stroke. Following the reprise of the first section, a brief coda concludes with a flourish of artificial harmonics for the cellist.

The final movement departs from Classical rondo form in not including a final reprise of the rondo theme. The formal plan is relatively complicated, since Prokofiev intersperses long and multi-thematic sections between iterations of the rondo. Instead of a final iteration, he adds a long and extraordinary coda whose thematic material cyclically returns to the opening theme of the first movement at maximum volume. Now Prokofiev pulls out all the stops, finally releasing unresolved material from the previous movements. His final grand gesture ends where the opening soliloquy began—on the open C-string.

On the first page of his manuscript, Prokofiev subtitled the work with a line from a 1902 play by Maxim Gorky, *The Lower Depths*: "Mankind—that has a proud sound!" At face value, the quote embodies the Soviet ideal of egalitarianism. Simon Morrison points out, however, that Gorky's play is "highly nihilistic, with the characters slowly coming to terms with the idea that the universe is fundamentally indifferent to their plight."[6] Whatever provoked Prokofiev to quote Gorky ultimately did not matter, since the subtitle did not appear in the first published edition by Muzyka.

Prokofiev could not attend the public premiere of Op. 119 on March 1, 1950 because he was in hospital. Together with the pianist Sviatoslav Richter, Rostropovich performed the work to acclaim at the Moscow Conservatory.

---

[6] Morrison, 346.

Table 6.3.1 Prokofiev Sonata, III. Allegro ma non troppo, analysis

Section	Rondo 1		Episode 1					Rondo 2
Measures	1–8	9–17	18–25	26–31	32–47	48–59	59–81	81–101
Thematic material	Rondo theme	Transitional material from rondo theme	March theme 1	Legato theme	March theme 2	Dactylic theme	Lyrical theme	Rondo theme
Key(s)	C major	C major, modulation	E♭ major	E♭ major	D♭ major	D♭ major	G♭ major	A major

Section	Episode 2		Rondo 3	Episode 1 reprise				Coda		
Measures	102–126	126–137	138–153	154–161	162–177	177–193	194–199	199–212	212–221
Thematic material	*Andantino* theme	Variant on *andantino* theme	Rondo theme	March theme 1	March theme 2	Lyrical theme	Transition, scalar material	First movement first theme, scalar material	Cadential section with trills, arpeggiated and scalar material
Key(s)	F major	F major	C major	B♭ major	B♭ major	E♭ minor	Modulating	C major, tonicization of B major	C major

7
SOLOS FROM EASTERN EUROPE

7.1
Zoltán Kodály (1882–1967)
Sonata for Solo Cello, Op. 8 (1915)

I. Allegro maestoso ma appassionato   II. Adagio (con grand' espressione)
III. Allegro molto vivace

Kodály's affinity with the cello began during his collaborations with the Waldbauer Quartet, who premiered his two string quartets and the first four quartets of Béla Bartók. He composed several more pieces for their cellist, Jenő Kerpely (1885–1954), including the Sonatina for Cello and Piano (1909), the Sonata for Cello and Piano, Op. 4 (1909–10), the Duo for Violin and Cello, Op. 7 (1914), a *Capriccio* for Solo Cello (1915), and the Sonata for Solo Cello, Op. 8 (1915).

Aside from the comparatively neglected Suites for Solo Cello, Op. 131c (1915) by Max Reger, Kodály's Solo Sonata is the first canonic concert work for unaccompanied cello since Bach's Cello Suites. Unlike Reger, Kodály chose not to adopt a neo-Bachian approach to composing for solo cello, nor did he imitate the atonality of the Second Viennese School. Here, Kodály's take on modernism fused his formal training in composition with the melodies, harmonies, and rhythms of folk music from his native Hungary.

Kodály's collections of the folk music of his native country have earned him as much fame as his compositions and his contributions to music education. As a young man, he traveled with Béla Bartók around Hungary and Eastern Europe, using the primitive recording technology of the era to preserve folk songs. This fieldwork resulted not only in Kodály's doctoral dissertation, but in the creative impetus for his life's work as a composer.

In an essay on Hungarian music, Kodály described its ethos as "active rather than passive, an expression of will rather than emotion … Hungarian folk music has a rhythm that is sharp, definite and varied. Its melody has buoyancy and freedom of movement, and does not unfold timidly from a pre-meditated harmonic basis. Its form is concise, proportionate, lucid and transparent."[1] This statement equally describes Kodály's Solo Sonata, Op. 8. Though its three large-scale movements correspond with nineteenth-century forms such as the sonata-allegro, its rhythms, melodies, and harmonies owe much to Hungarian folk music. Kodály's borrowings include the speech-like inflections of *parlando rubato* song and the rousing dance rhythms of *verbunkos*, a popular dance style with military origins, and *csárdás*, a couples dance. Kodály does not abandon diatonicism, but builds melodic and harmonic material on modes, pentatonicism, and octatonicism rather than tonic-dominant harmony. He writes for the cello's entire five-octave range, exploiting coloristic effects such as double stops, three- and four-note chords, extensive pizzicato, tremolo, and drones. Another interesting feature of the Solo Sonata, Op. 8 is Kodály's use of *scordatura*—a nod, perhaps, at Bach's Fifth Cello Suite. His retuning of the G- and C-strings to F♯ and B respectively increases resonance in the home key, B minor.

Kodály's first movement, a sonata-allegro, begins with dramatic four-note chords in a *sarabande* rhythm. The melodic material is remarkably economical, with a first theme built on just four tones and a second on a collection of octatonic tetrachords. Kodály treats his austere motives as building blocks, transforming them repeatedly through inversion and sequential repetition.[2]

A dark, wandering second movement in ABA form features the textural device of pairing an *arco* melody with an accompaniment in left-hand pizzicato. Kodály was not the first to use this technique for the cello—it appears in some of David Popper's compositions, for example—but here, through its integration into the two outer sections of the movement, it becomes as much a feature of the form as of the harmony and texture. (The *con fuoco* middle section, while still polyphonic, has a much freer, recitative-like tone, and does not employ left-hand pizzicato.)

The third movement, another sonata-allegro, is wildly and flamboyantly virtuosic. Kodály demands a wide range of tone colors from the cellist in passages that suggest the timbres of Hungarian folk instruments such as hammered dulcimer, bagpipe, reed-pipe, flute, zither, and hurdy-gurdy.[3] This bravura *moto perpetuo* unfolds in long passages of double stops, arpeggios,

---

[1] Zoltán Kodály, "What Is Hungarian in Music?" in *The Selected Writings of Zoltán Kodály*, ed. Ferenc Bonis (London: Boosey & Hawkes, 1964), 32.
[2] Min-Yuan Lin, "The Treatment of the Cello in Kodály's Sonata for Unaccompanied Violoncello, Opus 8" (DMA diss., Boston University, 1995), 5.
[3] Irén Kertész Wilkinson, "Hungary: Instrumental Music," *Grove Music Online*, ed. Deane Root, http://oxfordmusiconline.com.

tremolo, drones, and pizzicato chords, proceeding almost without rest into an extended coda on the earlier thematic materials.

Kodály's Solo Sonata was, in 1915, among the most difficult compositions ever written for the unaccompanied cello. The 1918 premiere by Kerpely did not go well, and Kodály shelved the piece for a few years before eventually publishing it in 1922. He remained proud of his achievement, remarking to the cello professor and former Popper student Adolf Schiffer that "in twenty-five years, no cellist will be accepted into the world of cellists who does not play my piece."[4] His prediction came true as one twentieth-century soloist after another adopted the Solo Sonata, Op. 8 into their repertoire. These included Schiffer's star student, János Starker, whose four recordings remain the gold standard for this work.

---

[4] Joyce Geeting, *Janos Starker "King of Cellists": The Making of an Artist* (Los Angeles: Chamber Music Plus Publishing, 2008), 4.

Table 7.1.1 Kodály Solo Sonata, I. Allegro maestoso ma appassionato, analysis

Exposition

Measures	1–9	10–19	20–25	26–31	32–42	43–79
Thematic material	First theme (sarabande rhythm)	First theme, pentatonic, cadences on dominant	First theme conclusion	Transition, scalar material	Second theme, octatonic	Second theme, polyphonic presentation
Key(s)	B Aeolian	B to F♯ major	B Aeolian to C minor	C minor to B minor	Quasi-E♭ major	E♭ major

Development

Measures	80–99	100–127	128–145
Thematic material	First theme	First theme	Conclusion of development, pentatonic, extended passages of trills
Key(s)	E♭ Aeolian to G♯ Locrian	G♯ Locrian	B minor to C♯ major

Recapitulation

Measures	146–151	152–162	163–197
Thematic material	First theme	Second theme	Second theme, polyphonic presentation
Key(s)	C♯ major-minor	Octatonic, quasi-B major	Cadence in B minor

7.2

György Ligeti (1923–2006)

Sonata for Cello Solo (1948/1953)

I. Dialogo   II. Capriccio

Ligeti's Sonata for Solo Cello comprises two movements composed five years apart. The first dates to Ligeti's student years at the Liszt Academy in Budapest, the second to a period of artistic maturity. At twenty-five, Ligeti was older than the usual college age because of the devastating disruption of the Second World War and the Holocaust. Ligeti, who was Jewish, lost many family members in Auschwitz, and was forced into labor by Hungary's fascist rulers. Once he was free, he resumed his studies, and quickly established himself as a leading composer. His early works show the influence of two giants of Hungarian music, Zoltán Kodály and Béla Bartók.[1]

Ligeti initially envisioned the first movement, *Dialogo*, as a stand-alone piece. It was a gift for a cellist classmate named Annuss Virány, with whom he was hopelessly in love.[2] Too shy to share his feelings, he wrote them into this four-minute movement. Though the title means "dialogue," the conversation was as imaginary as the love affair. A set of variations on a meandering, dreamlike theme, the *Dialogo* falls into two clear sections delineated by tempo. Some variations appear in the lower registers of the cello, others in the higher registers, perhaps in imitation of a male and a female voice conversing. Occasionally, the variations appear in two-part counterpoint. Moments of repose feature three-note pizzicato chords, most of which end in *glissandi* to new chords. (The new pitches are not rearticulated with new pizzicati; they die away quickly with the dying vibration of the cello strings.) Barlines divide the movement into sixteen measures, but there is no time

---

[1] Paul Griffiths, "Ligeti, György," *Grove Music Online*, ed. Deane Root, http://oxfordmusiconline.com.

[2] Steven Paul, "A Tale of Two Movements," liner notes to *Suites and Sonatas for Solo Cello*, Matt Haimovitz, recorded 1991, Deutsche Grammophon 431 813-2, CD, 6.

signature, as Ligeti's barline placement corresponds to the length and shape of the phrases rather than to a meter.

Virány, who did not realize the extent of Ligeti's feelings, thanked him for his composition but never played it. Five years later, at the request of the cellist Vera Dénes, Ligeti turned again to his cello piece.[3] It was then that he decided to add the *Capriccio* to the *Dialogo*. "Because the second movement had the 'ambition' to become a sonata movement," he later explained, "I wrote it in sonata form. It is a virtuoso piece in my later style that is closer to Bartók. I was 30 years old when I wrote it. I loved virtuosity and took the playing to the edge of virtuosity much like Paganini."[4] The title *Capriccio* is an homage to the *24 Caprices* for solo violin by Niccolò Paganini and indicates a work that demands the utmost mastery of instrumental technique. A frequent showpiece at international cello contests, the *Capriccio* requires sufficient agility to play at top speed across the full range of the instrument, often using the most difficult bow techniques.

Between the development and recapitulation of the *Capriccio*, Ligeti suddenly and startlingly interpolates a fragment of the theme from the *Dialogo*. By linking two otherwise unrelated movements in this way, the composer evokes a sudden vision of his past love. The memory fades, and Ligeti returns to *ostinato* patterns that build in intensity, sometimes with the addition of double stops and *bariolage*.[5] Abruptly, the dynamic drops to *pianissimo* for a return to a version of the opening motivic material. A descending chromatic scale marked *quasi glissando* dies away over a long *ricochet* stroke, but it is not the end. After a moment of silence, Ligeti returns to *fortissimo*, building higher and higher in pitch and dynamics before concluding, *tutta la forza*, on a victorious G major triad.

The two movements of Ligeti's Solo Sonata chronicle a composer's artistic development as much as his recovery from disappointed love. In this respect, the Solo Sonata resembles the journey of Bartók's First String Quartet (1909), itself a depiction in music of a failed love affair. The Bartók work, which also opens in a "high art" style and a slow tempo, progresses at increasingly fast speeds and in more folk-like language towards its frenzied conclusion. In

---

[3] Richard Steinitz, *György Ligeti: Music of the Imagination* (Boston, MA: Northeastern University Press, 2003), 51.
[4] Paul, 6.
[5] For an analysis of Ligeti's use of *ostinato*, see Benjamin Dwyer, "Transformational Ostinati in György Ligeti's Sonatas for Solo Cello and Solo Viola," in *György Ligeti: Of Foreign Lands and Strange Sounds*, ed. Louise Duchesneau and Wolfgang Marx (Rochester, NY: Boydell Press, 2011), 19–50.

following Bartók's example, Ligeti found new directions in his cello writing that could, through hectic virtuosity, banish painful memories.

After the Soviet occupation of Hungary, Ligeti and other Hungarian composers had to submit their work to the Composers' Union for approval before performances could take place. Ligeti's Solo Sonata did not pass the test, though Dénes received permission to record it.[6] When Ligeti fled Hungary in 1956, he left many compositions behind. The Solo Sonata manuscript was not among those lost, but it did not receive its premiere performance until the 1980s. In 1990, the German publisher Schott released the first printed edition.

[6] Paul, 6.

Table 7.2.1 Ligeti Solo Sonata, *Dialogo* and *Capriccio*, analysis

Section	*Dialogo* Section 1 (*Adagio, rubato, cantabile*)				
Measures	1–2	3–4	5–6	7	8	9
Thematic material	Pizzicato motive, theme (lower voice)	Pizzicato motive inverted, variation 1 (higher voice)	Partial pizzicato motive, variation 2 (inverted presentation of theme)	Theme	Variation 2 with added double- and triple-stops	Theme with added double- and triple-stops

Section	*Dialogo* Section 2 (*Poco più mosso*)				
Measures	10	11	12	13	14	15	16
Thematic material	Theme in two-part voicing	Variation 3 (wider intervals)	Variation 4 (two-part voicing)	Theme with added continuation	Variation 2 with added continuation	Theme in two-part voicing	Coda (pizzicato motive)

Section	*Capriccio* Exposition			*Capriccio* Development		
Measures	1–40	41–56	57–51	72–85	86–110	111–137	138–142
Thematic material	First theme	Second theme	Second theme variant (tremolo)	Transition	Second theme	Closing theme	*Dialogo* interpolation

Section	*Capriccio* Recapitulation				
Measures	143–190	191–207	208–221	222–247	248–264
Thematic material	First theme (inverted)	Second theme	Transition	Closing theme derived from first theme motives	Coda

7.3

Sofia Gubaidulina (b. 1931)

Ten Preludes for Solo Cello (1974)

I. staccato–legato II. legato–staccato
III. con sordino–senza sordino   IV. ricochet
V. sul ponticello ordinario sul tasto   VI. flagioletti
VII. al taco–da punta d'arco   VIII. arco–pizzicato
IX. pizzicato–arco   X. senza arco

As the descendant of Tatar Muslim and Russian Orthodox Christian forebears, Sofia Gubaidulina's upbringing was divided between two cultures. Her compositions, like her life story, create intersections between seemingly disparate pairings: classical and folk instruments, consonance and dissonance, mathematical objectivity and mystical spirituality. For Gubaidulina, the idea of "crossing" represents the crucifix and is symbolic of her Christian faith. The pairing of opposites is a structural as well as a spiritual feature of her language. For her, the journey "from one type of transition to another . . . creates a two-part form."[1]

The original title of Gubaidulina's *Ten Preludes* was *Ten Etudes*, since she wrote them at the request of a cello professor who sought new pedagogical materials. The professor never played them, however, so Gubaidulina asked another cellist, Vladimir Tonkha, to give the first performance. Tonkha's espousal of Gubaidulina's work led to a decades-long creative collaboration.

When she contemplated the cello, it must have been self-evident to Gubaidulina that the intersection of bow and string creates the shape of a cross. For her, even the different possibilities for bowstrokes carried religious connotations. Years later she reflected "I understand the word 'religion' in its direct meaning, as *re-ligio (re-legato)*, that is, a restoration of *legato* between

---

[1] Julia A. Biber, "Ten Etudes for Solo Cello by Sofia Gubaidulina" (DMA diss., City University of New York, 2016), 29.

me (my soul) and God."[2] It is therefore significant that the title of the first prelude is *staccato–legato*. The transition from the first type of stroke to the second suggests a spiritual journey from human frailty toward divine perfection. The opening three-note cell—an ascending major second followed by a descending minor second—also symbolizes the idea of crossing. It also suggests the religious and superstitious importance of the number three in Russian folklore. This cell returns cyclically in various guises throughout all ten preludes, generating much of the melodic material and unifying the movements.

The second prelude, *legato–staccato*, may represent an opposing journey. Here, *legato* and *staccato* passages appear in alternation, with a texture rich in double stops in contrasting intervals. After this first pair of movements, Gubaidulina switches the opposing parameters to muted vs. unmuted sound in *con sordino–senza sordino*. Since there are no rests, the cellist has to apply and remove the mute with the left hand while bowing on an open string.

The fourth prelude, *ricochet*, hints at Gubaidulina's original pedagogical motivations. Difficulties for the player include bow control over specific note groupings (septuplets, triplets, quintuplets) and oppositional dynamic extremes.

For the fifth prelude, *sul ponticello ordinario sul tasto*, the "crossing" is between three sounding points on the string—another instance of numerical symbolism. Opposing articulations cross between tremolo and legato, culminating in dramatic *glissandi* between widely spaced pitches, contrasting dynamics, and the changing sounding points.

flagioletti, the sixth prelude, also opposes more than one set of parameters. As the title suggests, it opposes artificial and natural harmonics, but other pairings include expressive markings (*giocoso*, *doloroso*) and specific versus semi-improvised notation. By exploiting the infinite overtone series, Gubaidulina further "crosses" the mathematical and religious ideas of infinity.

The seventh prelude, *al taco–da punta d'arco*, features the journey from the frog of the bow to the tip. A bridge-like middle section has the marking *détaché simile* (implying the middle part of the bow) until further directions instruct the cellist to travel little by little toward the tip of the bow and back again.

---

[2] Vera Lukomsky, "The Eucharist in My Fantasy: Interview with Sofia Gubaidulina," *Tempo* no. 206 (September 1998): 33.

Like the first and second preludes, the eighth and ninth, *arco–pizzicato* and *pizzicato–arco*, form another opposing pair. Gubaidulina divides both into clear sections separated by technique. The eighth begins with a long *arco* section that seems to meditate upon the intervallic cell from the beginning of the first prelude. The ninth contains widely spaced, pointillistic pizzicati, often in combination with *glissandi*, before a seamless transition into similar material played with the bow. The ninth prelude alone features twelve-tone serialism,[3] making it a rarity in Gubaidulina's works. (In a biography, Gubaidulina stated that she had gone beyond serialism, which she considered a "historically complete tradition.")[4]

The final prelude, *senza arco*, dispenses with the bow altogether. In the opening section, the cellist strikes the string against the fingerboard with the fingers of the left hand. In interleaved sections, the right thumb performs a *tremolo* motion on the C-string while the nail of the left thumb creates "indefinite" pitches. Gubaidulina's instructions describe the effect as "reminiscent of the tremolo of the snare drum."[5] By necessity, the entire prelude is in a hushed dynamic, with an ending that drifts away into nothingness.

At Vladimir Tonkha's suggestion, Gubaidulina published her work as *Ten Preludes* rather than *Ten Etudes*, though later she regretted this. Even if the movements had not served their intended pedagogical purpose, they were "distinctively my etudes for future pieces."[6] These included *In Croce* ("On the Cross" or "Cross-Wise") for cello and bayan, a type of folk accordion; works for multiple cellos such as *Quaternion* (1996), and works with orchestra such as *Seven Words* (1982) and *Canticle of the Sun* (1997).

---

[3] Biber, 87.

[4] Michael Kurtz, *Sofia Gubaidulina: A Biography*, trans. Christoph K. Lohmann (Bloomington and Indianapolis: Indiana University Press, 2007), 65.

[5] Sofia Gubaidulina, *10 Präludien für Violoncello Solo* (Hamburg: Musikverlag Hans Sikorski, 1979), 15. Translation by the present author.

[6] Biber, 27–28.

Table 7.3.1 Analysis of opposing parameters, Sofia Gubaidulina, *Ten Preludes*

Movement	Oppositional movement titles	Other opposing pairs
I.	*staccato/legato*	Low vs. high *tessitura*
II.	*legato/staccato*	Trills vs. non-trilled
III.	*con sordino–senza sordino*	
IV.	*Ricochet*	Dynamic extremes
V.	*sul ponticello ordinario sul tasto*	Dynamic extremes, *tremolo* vs. *legato*
VI.	*flagioletti*	Natural vs. artificial harmonics, *giocoso* vs. *doloroso*, specific notation vs. semi-improvised
VII.	*al taco–da punta d'arco*	Down-bow vs. up-bow, low vs. high *tessitura*
VIII.	*arco/pizzicato*	Slurred vs. unslurred, high vs. low *tessitura*
IX.	*pizzicato/arco*	
X.	*senza arco*	Left-hand articulation vs. right hand *tremolo*, specific notation vs. semi-improvised

8
HOLY MINIMALISM

8.1

Arvo Pärt (b. 1935)

Spiegel im Spiegel for Cello and Piano (1978)

The Estonian composer Arvo Pärt is a reclusive figure whom journalists often compare to a monk or a mystic. Having begun his career as a member of the Soviet avant-garde, Pärt turned away from modernism after his conversion to Orthodox Christianity in 1972. Studying the plainchant and polyphony of the Notre Dame School led to new directions in his own musical language, one that scholars came to describe as "the new simplicity" or "holy minimalism."[1]

Like other composers from the former Soviet republics, Pärt had his share of run-ins with Communist Party authorities. At first, this was because of his use of post-tonal techniques such as twelve-tone serialism, a style the Estonian Composers' Union pronounced "not suitable for Soviet music."[2] Compositions such as *Nekrolog* for orchestra (1960) and the cello concerto *Pro et Contra* (1966) show evidence of this early dissonance. Pärt's openly religious views also aroused suspicion, atheism being an unofficial state policy in Soviet countries. *Credo*, a 1968 "collage" for solo piano, choir, and orchestra, represents a defiant statement of the composer's faith. With its startling combination of harmonies from Bach's Prelude in C Major from *The Well-Tempered Clavier*, twelve-tone serialism, and total tonal disintegration, *Credo* became an instant success with audiences but a scandal with the authorities. It was hard to know what provoked official disapproval more, Pärt's dissonant style or his religiosity. After the premiere, Soviet authorities banned *Credo* for more than a decade.[3]

Whereas some American minimalist composers sought spiritual enlightenment in the religious practices of Asia, Pärt needed to look no further than his Christian faith—though he claims to have absorbed more influence from the music of Roman Catholicism than from that of the Orthodox

---

[1] Leopold Brauneiss, "Musical Archetypes: The Basic Elements of the Tintinnabuli Style," *The Cambridge Companion to Arvo Pärt*, ed. Andrew Shenton (Cambridge: Cambridge University Press, 2012), 52.

[2] Arvo Pärt Center program notes, https://www.arvopart.ee/en/arvo-part/work/590/.

[3] Paul Hillier, *Arvo Pärt* (Oxford and New York: Oxford University Press, 1997), 55.

church.[4] In a 2010 interview, Pärt remembered that a chance hearing of some Gregorian chant on the radio provoked what would become an obsession with the intertwined aspects of music and religion. "The old music, when it was written, the focus of this music was the Holy Scripture for composers for centuries ... It was the reality for every artist. Through one, you can understand the other."[5]

Pärt's growing interest in medieval sacred music drew him farther from serialism. He explained: "I think if the human has conflict in his soul and with everything, then this system of 12-tone music is exactly good for this ... But if you have no more conflict with people, with the world, with God, then it is not necessary."[6] New directions in his composition included *tintinnabuli*, "little bells," which became his signature technique. Its predominant feature is the triad, a chord whose "natural purity"[7] fascinates Pärt. Since the three tones of the major triad come "pre-formed" from the partials of the overtone series, *tintinnabuli* represents mathematical objectivity as well as religious symbolism. Pärt's first essay in the style was the solo piano composition *Für Alina* (1976).

If the avant-gardism of Pärt's earlier work had led to confrontations with officialdom, the religious connotations of the *tintinnabuli* compositions provoked even more controversy. Eventually, increasing political pressures compelled Pärt and his family to emigrate to the West, first to Vienna, then to Berlin. Pärt's last composition before his departure was *Spiegel im Spiegel* (1978), a chamber work initially conceived for violin and piano.

Along with *Tabula Rasa* and *Fratres*, *Spiegel im Spiegel* is one of Pärt's best-known *tintinnabuli* compositions. The title "mirror in the mirror" describes the infinity of reflections in two opposing parallel plane mirrors. In this work, Pärt brings together an *ostinato* of ascending triads for the piano and a cello melody composed of partial stepwise collections from the F major scale. Though it gives an impression of extreme simplicity, the structure of the piece is a highly controlled set of variations.

Each section of *Spiegel im Spiegel* has a partial scalar melody in long tones for the cello. The first melodic fragment contains just two ascending pitches from the F major scale, immediately followed by a "mirror" version in descending motion. Each successive variation contains one more pitch of the scale than the last, and circles back to end the phrase on an A. The form is ever-expanding, giving the impression that the variations and mirrors could go on forever.

---

[4] Thomas Huizenga, "The Silence and Awe of Arvo Pärt," interview for National Public Radio Classical, June 2, 2014, https://www.npr.org/sections/deceptivecadence/2014/06/02/316322238/the-silence-and-awe-of-arvo-p-rt.

[5] Arthur Lubow, "The Sound of Spirit," *New York Times*, October 15, 2010, https://www.nytimes.com/2010/10/17/magazine/17part-t.html/.

[6] Lubow.

[7] Brauneiss, 55.

The piano part accompanies the long tones with an *ostinato* of arpeggiated triads. Each triad contains the melodic note, or notes close to it. According to the composer, this pairing of scalar melody and arpeggiated harmony is "the whole secret of tintinnabuli ... the two lines. One line is who we are, and the other line is who is holding and takes care of us. Sometimes I say—it is not a joke, but also it is as a joke taken—that the melodic line is our reality, our sins. But the other line is forgiving the sins."[8]

It is tempting to compare *Spiegel im Spiegel* to other compositions on *ostinato* patterns such as Bach's C major Prelude and Beethoven's *Moonlight* Sonata, but Pärt's harmony differs significantly from these predecessors by abandoning the ideas of dominant and tonic, or expectation and fulfillment. *Spiegel im Spiegel* may be diatonic, but its harmony is static and nonfunctional and there is no modulation away from F major. Pärt has pared down every compositional parameter: there is no contrast in timbre and texture, no conflicting emotion, and no sense of *dénouement* or resolution. The F major triad does not appear in root position, even in the final measures. The cello trails away on an A, the median pitch of the triad, while the left hand of the piano part arpeggiates a second-inversion F major triad and the right-hand part concludes on a bell-like high C. It is an ending of perfect equanimity, or—since the patterns could go on infinitely—a non-ending.

At first glance, the score of *Spiegel im Spiegel* appears uncomplicated. The impression of simplicity is misleading, as many an inexperienced player has discovered. Cellist and pianist must possess absolute technical control to adhere to Pärt's slow tempo (quarter note = 100) without inadvertently speeding up. In this respect, *Spiegel im Spiegel* recalls the ultra-slow *Louange à l'éternité de Jésus* from Olivier Messiaen's *Quatuor pour la fin du temps*, in which performers must constantly fight the desire to move forward. Equally challenging is the absence of directions for dynamics or articulations. Pärt gives performers no hint of a desired expression, leaving it to them to settle on an interpretation. Should the cellist use vibrato, or would this disrupt the detached, rational ethos of the piece? Does the pulse demand absolute precision, or is it acceptable to add occasional *rubato*? To such questions, Pärt offers this enigmatic observation: "I have discovered that it is enough to beautifully play this one and only tone."[9] It is an unusual request, and one that requires the "humble overcoming of the personal ego"[10] characteristic of the composer's abstract soundworld.

---

[8] Lubow.
[9] As related to Andreas Peer Kähler: https://www.arvopart.ee/en/arvo-part/article/radiating-from-silence/.
[10] Brauneiss, 52.

Table 8.1.1 Pärt *Spiegel im Spiegel*, analysis

Section	Prelude (piano alone)	Variation 1	Mirror 1	Variation 2	Mirror 2
Measures	1–3	4–7	8–11	12–15	16–21
Number of measures in section	3	4	4	5	5

Section	Variation 3	Mirror 3	Variation 4	Mirror 4
Measures	22–27	28–33	34–40	41–47
Number of measures	6	6	7	7

Section	Variation 5	Mirror 5	Variation 6	Mirror 6
Measures	48–55	56–63	64–72	73–81
Number of measures	8	8	9	9

Section	Variation 7	Mirror 7	Variation 8	Mirror 8	Postlude (piano alone)
Measures	82–91	92–101	102–112	113–123	124–126
Number of measures	10	10	11	11	3

8.2
Sir John Tavener (1944–2013)

The Protecting Veil for Cello and String Orchestra (1988)

*I. Transcendent, with awesome majesty   II. The Birth of the Mother of God
III. Annunciation   IV. Incarnation
V. Lament of the Mother of God at the Cross
VI. Christ is Risen!   VII. The Dormition of the Mother of God
VIII. The Protecting Veil—Like Tears of the Mother of God*

John Tavener's compositional style integrates the radically simple language of the American minimalist movement with the tone system and mysticism of his adopted Orthodox religion. "If an English composer wishes to write music within the Orthodox tradition," Tavener wrote, "he must, like an icon painter, renounce any ideas of his own, and adhere to a strict discipline."[1] In Tavener's case, these disciplined means include economical melodic and harmonic materials, inversions and retrogrades, recurrent refrains, and "block" structures.[2]

Tavener composed *The Protecting Veil* for cello and string orchestra at the urging of the cellist Steven Isserlis, though his previous work was largely in vocal genres.[3] After receiving a commission from the BBC, Tavener worked quickly, finishing in just a few weeks during a stay in Greece. Isserlis premiered *The Protecting Veil* alongside string players from the BBC Symphony at the Proms in 1989, and it became an instant hit.

Tavener's program for the work was the story of the Orthodox Feast of the Protecting Veil, which commemorates a tenth-century vision of the Virgin Mary in Constantinople. During an all-night vigil on the eve of an enemy invasion, Mary appeared above the Christian worshipers, holding a

---

[1] John Tavener, "Christian Values in Music," in *Christian Values*, ed. Edward Stourton and Frances Gumley (London: Hoddern & Stoughton, 1996), 120.
[2] Ivan Moody, "Tavener, Sir John," *Grove Music Online*, ed. Deane Root, http://oxfordmusiconline.com.
[3] Michael Stewart, "A Voice in the Wilderness," *Gramophone* (March 1992): 28–30.

veil in her outstretched hands. "On bended knees the Most Holy Virgin tearfully prayed for Christians for a long time. Then, coming near the Bishop's Throne, she continued her prayer. After completing her prayer she took her veil and spread it over the people praying in church, protecting them from enemies both visible and invisible."[4]

Tavener structures *The Protecting Veil* in eight "blocks." These are sections of varying lengths, connected with interludes on a bell-like motive for the orchestral strings. The first and eighth blocks celebrate the Constantinople vision of the Virgin Mary, and the six between them depict the events of her life from birth until "dormition," the end of mortal life. There is little sense of tonic and dominant harmony, but each block has an implied key. The first and last blocks, which are identical, have the key center of F. In each intervening movement, the key center descends by step. The F major scale therefore determines Tavener's large-scale structure.

The cello enters alone in the highest register of the instrument, at an ultra-slow tempo that creates the impression of timelessness or weightlessness. After the opening statement of F–G–A in the solo cello part, the orchestral strings enter octaves lower, starting with the *divisi* double basses and proceeding upwards through the cello, viola, and violin sections until the ensemble completes an F major triad with an added D.

A new section marked *radiant, flowing* moves the tempo along, but Tavener restricts the range of pitches to a relatively small collection, perhaps in imitation of Byzantine liturgical chanting. A long-held high A for the solo cellist ties over into the first of seven interludes with the direction *like bells*. In each of them, the upper strings oscillate between two chord clusters whose faster tempo and *marcatissimo* articulation contrast starkly with the mostly slow and legato material.

The Birth of the Mother of God introduces new melodic material with wide leaps and ornaments of quarter-tone gestures. A contrasting section marked *lightly, without vibrato, like viols* narrows the range of pitches and hints at the ancient timbres of English Renaissance consort music. Bell sounds take over again, heralding a new block. *The Annunciation* switches to a faster tempo and smaller note values as the cellist moves between notes of a small collection of pitches as if speaking the syllables of plainchant. As the

---

[4] "The Protection of Our Most Holy Lady the Mother of God and Ever-Virgin Mary," Orthodox Church in America, accessed January 2, 2023, https://www.oca.org/saints/lives/2000/10/01/102824-the-protection-of-our-most-holy-lady-the-mother-of-god-and-ever.

blocks and interludes progress, emotions build up to a rapturous frenzy in *The Incarnation*, whose subsequent bell interlude has the cellist alternating measures of bell-like tones with the orchestra.

A short connecting passage for the solo cellist travels from the high to the low register to prepare for *Lament of the Mother of God at the Cross*. This soliloquy is the longest and most despairing section of the work. As the orchestra sits silent, the cellist begins a mournful monologue whose complex ornamentation suggests the sounds of sobbing and weeping. While most of the solo part has so far been in the upper register of the cello, here Tavener writes low pitches to suggest the depths of unhappiness. In the bell interlude that follows, Taverner has replaced the usual fast oscillations with ones at a much slower tempo in the violins' highest register.

Tavener returns to a mood of wild rejoicing in the next block, *Christ is Risen!* The contrast with the darkness of the previous block could not be more pronounced. From here onwards, Tavener progresses towards the resolution and conclusions of the piece. In *The Dormition of the Mother of God*, the earlier meditative stillness returns as the cellist moves back and forth between a small collection of pitches and the orchestra plays a hushed *tremolando*. The last block, *The Protecting Veil*, repeats material from the first twelve measures of the work, but this time Tavener appends a coda section, *Like the Tears of the Mother of God*. Muted and in hushed dynamics, the cellist and orchestra drift into a slow counterpoint of wide *glissandi*. An "evocation of the tears of the Mother of God," the gestures form chiastic shapes in the score. The orchestra fades into silence but the cello remains, lingering alone on an unearthly high pitch until at last that too dies away.

Table 8.2.1 Tavener, The Protecting Veil, analysis

Block	I. Transcendent, with awesome majesty					Bell interlude 1
Measures	1–12	13–18	19–20	21–28	29–42	43–63
Thematic material	A	B	A	C	A	
Key(s)	F	F	F	F	F	

Block	II. The Birth of the Mother of God				Bell interlude 2	III. Annunciation	Bell interlude 3
Measures	64–85	86–95	96–100		101–134	135–161	162–180
Thematic material	A	B	A		(monothematic)	(monothematic)	
Key(s)	E	E	E			D	

Block	IV. Incarnation			Bell interlude 4	V. Lament of the Mother of God at the Cross	Bell interlude 5
Measures	181	182–206	207	208–225	226–228	
Thematic material	A	B	A		(monothematic)	
Key(s)	C	C	C		B♭	

Block	VI. Christ is Risen!	Bell interlude 6	VII. The Dormition of the Mother of God	Bell interlude 7	VIII. The Protecting Veil	Coda: Like Tears of the Mother of God
Measures	248–262	262–287	288–300	301–321	322–332	333–341
Thematic material	Canon		(monothematic)		Same as 1–12	
Key(s)	A		G		F	F

9
THE NEW VIRTUOSITY

9.1
Benjamin Britten (1913–1976)
Suite for Cello No. 1, Op. 72 (1964)

Canto Primo   I. Fuga   II. Lamento Canto Secondo
III. Serenata   IV. Marcia Canto Terzo   V. Bordone
VI. Moto Perpetuo e Canto Quarto

The Cello Suites of Johann Sebastian Bach cast a long shadow over later compositions for unaccompanied cello. Even if the medium was not common in nineteenth-century concert works, the pedagogical literature by cellist-composers such as Johann Justus Friedrich Dotzauer, Friedrich August Kummer, Alfredo Piatti, David Popper, and Louis Feuillard contains many etudes that prepare students for Bach. Well into the twentieth century, when solo cello works became more common, many composers still took Bach as a jumping-off point. The Three Cello Suites (1915) by Max Reger, for example, combine Bachian melodic style with late Romantic textures and *tessiture*, and Ernest Bloch's Three Cello Suites (1956–57) encompass octatonic melody and harmony within neo-Baroque rhythms and phrase shapes. Even present-day works sometimes start with a glance back at Bach, like Adolphus Hailstork's Sonata for Solo Cello (2015).

Benjamin Britten's Three Suites for Cello, Op. 72 (1964), Op. 80 (1967), and Op. 87 (1971–74) are both Bachian and polystylistic, with further elements of Renaissance, Romantic, Impressionist, and twentieth-century styles. Britten's First Cello Suite, with its Baroque movement titles, multi-voiced textures, and imitative counterpoint, is the most Bach-like of the three. Two of Britten's own favorite forms, serenade and march, also make an appearance. Connecting the movements is a recurring theme with the title *Canto*, an Italian word with the literal meaning "I sing." In poetry, a *canto* is a shorter substructure within a larger poem. Two famous examples of this in literature are Dante's *Divine Comedy* and Edmund Spenser's *The Faerie*

Figure 9.1.1 Britten, First Cello Suite Op. 72, *Canto Primo*, mm. 1–2

Queene, which Britten knew well.[1] In Britten's First Cello Suite, the *canto* functions as a framing device for the other movements (see Figure 9.1.1). Britten may have intended it as a modernist take on Baroque *ritornello* form, a rhetorical *idée fixe*, or a "motto theme" like the one that links the movements of Modest Mussorgsky's *Pictures at an Exhibition*.[2]

The opening *Canto Primo*, while not entirely diatonic, implies a key center of D major. The harmony, tenor range, and contemplative character echo the mood of the Sarabande from Bach's Sixth Suite in D Major, though the quadruple meter rules out literal sarabande form. After this introduction, the *Fuga* begins its first subject, a collection of three melodic "cells": the first a pair of eighth notes followed by a triplet in eighth notes, the second an ornamental dotted-eighth note with two thirty-second notes, and the third two sharply accented eighth notes.[3] The first and third cells bear a slight similarity to the subject of the fugue in the Prelude to Bach's Fifth Suite in C Minor, and the second resembles the ornamental gestures common to many Baroque melodies. These three cells generate all the melodic material in the *Fuga*. Further neo-Baroque gestures include a texture of broken chord patterns across multiple strings.

The wide leaps and linear contrapuntal texture in the *Lamento* suggest another movement of Bach's Fifth Suite, this time the tragic Sarabande. Each phrase of the *Lamento* ends in the distinctive mournful refrain of a descending E minor triad. In the second section, Britten inverts the refrain into an ascending triad, and for the concluding section the refrain returns to descending motion. The *Lamento* runs without a break into the *Canto Secondo*, a grave reiteration of the main *Canto* theme in the lower registers of the cello. With a three-voice texture rich in double- and triple-stops, it appears to refer to yet another Bach Sarabande, this time that of the Third Suite in C Major.

For the *Serenata*, Britten temporarily leaves his Bachian mood. Both the title and the whimsical, two-voiced pizzicato writing of this movement recall

---

[1] Peter Evans, *The Music of Benjamin Britten*, 3rd ed. (Oxford: Oxford University Press, 1996), 422.
[2] See Eric Roseberry, "The Solo Chamber Music," in *The Britten Companion*, ed. Christopher Palmer (Cambridge: Cambridge University Press, 1984), 381.
[3] See Mark Alan Taggart, "An Analysis of Suite for Cello, Op. 72, and Second Suite for Cello, Op. 80, by Benjamin Britten" (PhD diss., Cornell University, 1983), 88–93.

the *Sérénade* of Debussy's Cello Sonata (1918). For the next movement, *Marcia*, Britten again departs from the neo-Baroque, though he returns briefly to the *Canto* theme. This march begins with a playful "horn call" figure on the natural harmonics of the cello. Following this is a drum-like theme using the *col legno* technique (where the wood of the bow strikes the strings).

The *Canto Terzo* is the darkest section of Britten's First Suite. In the previous *Canto* sections, the dissonances resolve; here they stand out in relief. Because of this, *Canto Terzo* has no discernable key center and a feeling of tonal ambivalence.

The *Bordone* signals a turn to the neo-Baroque, or perhaps even the neo-Renaissance. The title, an Italian word meaning "drone," refers to *falsobordone*, a fifteenth-century technique for improvising triadic harmonizations over plainchant. In this movement, the cellist must play the open D-string continuously while dipping the bow in and out of the neighboring A- and G-strings. Left-hand pizzicato appears for occasional textural and rhythmic contrast. In the second of two large-scale sections, marked *in tempo tranquillo*, Britten abruptly switches to the key signature of E major while continuing the D-string drone. Julian Lloyd Webber points out a likeness between this section and the "lilting rhythm of the first movement of the Elgar Concerto."[4] Perhaps Britten, who deliberately distanced himself from the English pastoral composers,[5] assimilated this theme into a dissonant context to chase away its influence.

The last movement, *Moto perpetuo e Canto Quarto*, takes selected aspects of the previous movements (including the drone idea from the *Bordone*) and weaves them into a frenetic finale. The main melodic cell of this movement comprises half-step motives, with ubiquitous slurs of two sixteenth notes like those in the Gigue of Bach's Third Suite in C Major. The *Canto Quarto* reappears only briefly, like uncanny memory, before the return of the *moto perpetuo*. Britten intersperses five short returns of the *Canto* between rapid passagework, at last integrating and sublimating the theme. His final measures resemble a heavily disguised Sarabande from Bach's Sixth Suite, albeit in the key and mood of Bach's First Suite in G Major. Though the harmony is now prepared for a cadence in G major, Britten ends on a double stop of G and F♯, a final quirky joke in a work full of humor.

---

[4] Julian Lloyd Webber, "The Cello Music of Benjamin Britten," *The Strad* 86 (September 1975): 387–391.
[5] See Benjamin Britten, "England and the Folk-Art Problem," *Modern Music* 18 (1941): 71–75.

Table 9.1.1 Britten First Cello Suite, I. *Fuga*, analysis

Section	Subject		Episode 1	Subject restatement	Episode 2	Episode 3	Subject restatement	
Measure	1–2	3–5	5–8	9–18	19–22	23–27	28–31	28–31
Thematic material	Three cells (1, 2, and 3)	Continuation of fugue subject	Material from cell 2	Cells 1, 2, and 3	Material from cell 2	Material from cell 1	Material from 11–14	Continuation of fugue subject
Section	Subject restatement		Episode 4	Episode 5	Episode 6	Episode 7	Subject reprise	Coda
Measure	37–64	64–69	70–73	74–76	77–84	84–91	91–107	108–131
Thematic material	Fugue subject	Inverted presentation of fugue subject	Material from cell 2	Material from cell 1	Material from cell 3	Material from cell 1	Material from 37–64	Material from fugue subject, now with natural harmonics

9.2
Coleridge-Taylor Perkinson (1932–2004)
Lamentations: Black/Folk Song Suite (1973)

I. Fuguing Tune   II. Song Form   III. Calvary Ostinato
IV. Perpetual Motion

By naming their son after the Black British composer Samuel Coleridge-Taylor (1875–1912), the parents of Coleridge-Taylor Perkinson foreordained him to become a composer himself. Perkinson grew up immersed in music, attending New York's High School of Music and Art, then New York University and the Manhattan School of Music. He built his career as a conductor, reflecting that he "would rather compose than do anything else . . . [but] I would not want to give up conducting because I find that when I am conducting I am actively composing."[1] Equally fluent in classical and jazz, Perkinson collaborated with leading musicians in both genres.

In 1965, Perkinson became one of eleven co-founders of the Symphony of the New World, the first racially integrated orchestra in the United States. Ronald Lipscomb, a cellist in the orchestra, inspired Perkinson to compose *Lamentations: Black/Folk Song Suite*. This four-movement work contains many religious nuances, from a title that suggests the Biblical Book of Lamentations to the references to spirituals and hymns. Another influence is the melodic and formal language of Johann Sebastian Bach, whose music Perkinson revered. Performing in Bach's *St. Matthew Passion* aged fifteen had convinced him that "music-making could be an overwhelming experience."[2] In *Lamentations*, Perkinson achieves something of Bach's religious intensity: "The common denominator of these tunes," he later explained, "is the reflection and statement of a people's crying out."[3]

---

[1] D. Antoinette Handy, *Black Conductors* (Metuchen, NJ and London: The Scarecrow Press, 1995), 383.

[2] Handy, 380.

[3] Gregory Weinstein, liner notes for *Coleridge-Taylor Perkinson (1932-2004): A Celebration*, Chicago Sinfonietta, cond. Paul Freeman, New Black Music Repertoire Ensemble Quartet, recorded 2005, Cedille Records CDR 90000 087, CD, 6–7.

The title of the first movement, *Fuguing Tune*, plays on the ideas of both Bach's multi-voiced fugues and the "fuging-tunes" of eighteenth-century American hymnody. Though its name suggests a correlation with the fugue, a fuging-tune does not follow the same formal procedure. In fugues, subjects and countersubjects enter separately, whereas in a fuging-tune all the voices enter simultaneously, only later breaking apart into separate entries.[4] Fuging-tunes first appeared in eighteenth-century New England and later became popular in Black churches in the southern states. By changing the spelling to add an extra *u*, Perkinson appears to acknowledge both forms, though the movement does not conform strictly to the principles of either. The opening subject, a syncopated gesture in double- and triple-stops, comes back again and again as a refrain, adding more harmonic and melodic decoration with each statement. Entries of the subject appear in different keys and combinations of double-stops; next, a central climactic section breaks the pattern by plunging into a chain of chromatic scales in double-stops of a minor sixth. The last third of the movement disrupts the double-stopped texture by incorporating single pitches in the linear, yet contrapuntal manner of Bach's writing for solo string instruments.

The short *Song Form* continues in the primarily double-stopped style of the first movement, but in a more lyrical vein, with the directions "plaintive" and "sonorous." The form is AABA, a common plan for twentieth-century American popular songs, and one that also suggests the *da capo* aria form of the eighteenth century. The movement ends with two left-hand pizzicato tones that foreshadow and lead into the entirely pizzicato third movement, *Calvary Ostinato*.

In the Gospels of the New Testament, Calvary (Golgotha) is the "place of a skull" where Jesus is crucified. Perkinson's title also references well-known spiritual, *Calvary*, whose text begins "Every time I think about Jesus / Surely he died on Calvary."[5] The metaphorical meaning of Calvary, an intense feeling of suffering, comes forth in the world-weary sense of despair pervading the movement. The form of this movement is a set of variations over an *ostinato*, a repeating bassline device common in the Baroque era. Perkinson's *ostinato* pattern makes a feature of the open D-, G-, and C-strings of the cello, as well as a stopped low D on the C-string. After the opening

---

[4] Richard Crawford, "Fuging-tune," *Grove Music Online*, ed. Deane Root, http://oxfordmusiconline.com.

[5] Delores Carpenter and Nolan E. Williams Jr., *African American Heritage Hymnal: 575 Hymns, Spirituals, and Gospel Songs* (Chicago, IL: GIA Publications, 2001), 239.

four-note gesture, an eighth rest sets the remaining six notes of the pattern into a syncopated rhythm, creating the impression of pacing footsteps that stumble, then pick up again. After two iterations of the *ostinato*, Perkinson introduces his own version of the *Calvary* theme on higher pitches. The multi-voiced texture requires the cellist to pluck simultaneously using two, three, and sometimes even four fingers. The counterpoint builds in intensity until Perkinson temporarily abandons the *ostinato* pattern for a frantic two-measure cadenza composed of a sixteenth-note run followed by a series of three-note chords. After this outburst the *ostinato* returns, occasionally in an inverted variation. A smaller cadenza section interrupts the *ostinato* once more, but the pattern returns once more as the melodic voices become sparser and eventually die away. The bassline is alone once more, drifting away into nothingness.

The final movement, *Perpetual Motion*, propels itself forward with repeating pedal tones on the open D-, G-, and C-strings, the same pitches Perkinson used in the *ostinato* of the previous movement. The rapid-fire sixteenth-note patterns and oscillating string crossings resemble those in the Prelude to Bach's Sixth Suite, but unlike Bach Perkinson does not allow the cellist any moments of repose. Over five pages of continuous, rest-free music, the momentum becomes more and more relentless in its demands on the player. Just when the feeling of "crying out" reaches overwhelming urgency, Perkinson finishes—just as Bach's Sixth Prelude does—on an ascending arpeggiated tonic chord.

Table 9.2.1 Perkinson, *Lamentations, III. Calvary Ostinato*, analysis

Section	Introduction	Episode 1	Cadenza 1	Episode 2	Cadenza 2	Coda
Measures	1–2	3–8	9–10	11–19	20	21–24
Thematic material	First presentation of *ostinato*	*Calvary* theme, *ostinato* bassline	No bassline. Sixteenth note rhythms, chordal material	Cadential theme, bassline in inverted presentation at 15 and 19	No bassline. Similar three-note chords to those at 10.	*Ostinato* bassline with fragments of the cadential theme, then bassline alone
Key(s)	D minor	D minor	F major with chromatic harmony	D major	Dominant of F major	D minor

9.3
Bright Sheng (b. 1955)

Seven Tunes Heard in China (1995)

I. Seasons II. Guessing Song III. The Little Cabbage
IV. The Drunken Fisherman V. Diu Diu Dong
VI. Pastoral Ballade VII. Tibetan Dance

Bright Sheng was born in Shanghai and grew up studying both Chinese and European music. When the Cultural Revolution began in 1966, the Red Guards confiscated the family piano and put a stop to Sheng's piano lessons. From then on, Sheng could only make music at school.[1] Of this time, Sheng later reflected: "I was one of the millions of Chinese who were the witnesses, victims, and survivors of the Cultural Revolution."[2]

Political upheaval threw China's education systems into disarray. Instead of progressing from high school to university, many students had to go to the provinces for forced "re-education" in peasant communities.[3] From 1971 through 1978, Sheng lived in the mountainous Qinghai province in northwest China, near the border with Tibet. In this remote, ethnically diverse environment, his musical interests expanded. He put his piano-playing skills to use in the Qinghai Song and Dance Troupe, and in his spare time taught himself the principles of Chinese music theory. He then began collecting folk songs from the region—material that would later form part of the fabric of his own compositions.

Once the Cultural Revolution was over, a semblance of normal life could resume. In 1978, Sheng enrolled in the Shanghai Conservatory of Music to study Chinese music, European music theory, and the principles of composition. After his family emigrated to the United States, he followed them there to start graduate study in 1982. In New York City, Sheng's teachers

---

[1] Michelle Harper, "An Interview with Bright Sheng," *The Journal of the International Institute* 7, no. 1 (Fall 1999), http://hdl.handle.net/2027/spo.4750978.0007.103, accessed December 30, 2022.
[2] Bright Sheng, "*H'un (Lacerations): In Memoriam 1966–1976* for Orchestra," *Perspectives of New Music* 33, nos. 1–2 (1995): 560.
[3] Harper.

included George Perle, Wen-Chung Chou, and Leonard Bernstein. Chou, whose music combined elements of Western and Eastern styles, motivated Sheng to do the same. Bernstein, too, was encouraging. He dispelled Sheng's doubts about attempting a fusion of Chinese and European-American styles by telling him "What do you mean, 'impossible'? Everything is a fusion, the works of Brahms, Bartók, Stravinsky, and including my own."[4]

Many years later, when an interviewer asked Sheng if he saw himself as Chinese or American, Sheng replied "I feel 100% Chinese and 100% American."[5] By this, he meant that his music was a "syncretic fusion" of languages.[6] Sheng's model for this was Béla Bartók, a composer he describes as a major influence. "While most composers before [Bartók] used folk materials for various purposes (exoticism, lyricism, nationalism) for their works," he wrote, "Bartók is the contrary . . . In his music, we hear 'unrefined,' 'raw,' peasant songs alongside 'high art' classical music, a coexistent quality obvious even in his most lyrical passages . . . One does not borrow from the other."[7]

In *Seven Tunes Heard in China*, Sheng achieves a tight-knit synthesis of styles that makes it hard for the listener to discern where one starts and another finishes. Explaining the difference in aesthetic between Chinese and Western musics, Sheng asserts "The most important contribution of Western music to humanity is its contrapuntal concept, which emphasizes harmonies and counterpoints. But traditionally, Chinese instruments are solo instruments and therefore Chinese musicians feel themselves each to be solo artists."[8] This statement may be the key to understanding *Seven Tunes*, a work for a solo instrument that contains contrapuntal sections.

The melodies in *Seven Tunes* combine Sheng's folk song collections with newly composed material. Their musical language derives from Chinese five-, six-, and seven-note scalar collections and their associated modes. In the "gong system" modes, the interval between any pair of adjacent notes is either a major second or a minor third—no minor seconds or major thirds are permissible. Hexatonic modes correspond to some of the Western church

---

[4] Su Sun Wong, "An Analysis of Five Vocal Works by Bright Sheng" (DMA diss., The University of Texas at Austin, 1995), 8.

[5] Bright Sheng, "Never Far Away," http://www.brightsheng.com, accessed December 30, 2022.

[6] Peter Chang, "Bright Sheng's Music: An Expression of Cross-Cultural Experience—Illustrated through the Motivic, Contrapuntal and Tonal Treatment of the Chinese Folk Song *The Stream Flows*," *Contemporary Music Review* 26, nos. 5–6 (October–December 2007): 620.

[7] Bright Sheng, "Bartók, the Chinese Composer," htttp://www.brightsheng.com, accessed December 30, 2022.

[8] Harper.

modes, but with a tone omitted. Heptatonic modes correspond to the Dorian, Ionian, and Mixolydian modes.⁹

The first movement, *Seasons*, comes from a Qinhai folk song called *Siji Ge* ("Song of the Four Seasons").¹⁰ It falls into two thematically related sections separated by mode, with one in a quasi-A minor and the other in a mixture of E♭, B♭, and E minor harmonies.¹¹ A coda combines material from both previous sections.

The second movement, *Guessing Song*, comes from a comic "riddles and solutions" song of the Yunnan Province. Over three sections, it displays elements of European tonic-dominant harmony¹² in mostly Mixolydian- and Dorian-mode melodies. Sheng notates much of the double-stopped texture across two staffs.

Little Cabbage, the third and shortest movement, comes from a song of the Hebei region. In contrast to the comical second and fourth movements, it is a tragic tale of a motherless little girl who lives in poverty. Xiao-Qiang Pan's analysis describes the character of the melodic lines as "plaintive," "wailing," and "sobbed."¹³

The unsteady rhythmic and melodic characteristics of the fourth movement, *The Drunken Fisherman*, depict the weaving footsteps and slurred speech of a man under the influence of alcohol. In imitation of the *qin*, a traditional Chinese seven-string zither, the entire movement is pizzicato. Sheng creates extended techniques such as plucking the cello strings close to the bridge with a guitar plectrum or the fingernails.

The fifth movement, *Diu Diu Dong*, is a Taiwanese folk song about a train that goes through a leaking tunnel. In the first of three sections, artificial harmonics imitate the high-pitched screech of a train whistle. In the final section, Sheng extends the artificial harmonics technique by writing double-stopped artificial harmonics in perfect fifths.¹⁴

The sixth movement, *Pastoral Ballade*, comes from a Mongolian song with the title *Muge*, the Chinese word for "herdsman." Harmonically complicated,

---

⁹ Xiao-Qiang Pan, "A Study of *Seven Tunes Heard in China* for Solo Cello by Bright Sheng" (DMA diss., University of Northern Colorado, 2003), 35.
¹⁰ Pan, 39–41.
¹¹ Pan, 79.
¹² Pan, 86.
¹³ Pan, 90.
¹⁴ See Chiao-Hsuan Kang, "Understanding of Authentic Performance Practice in Bright Sheng's *Seven Tunes Heard in China* for Solo Cello" (DMA diss., Louisiana State University, 2016), 44, for a pedagogical explanation of how to execute this technique.

it features long and rhythmically free phrases, and a contrapuntal texture that requires the cellist to leap repeatedly across two to three octaves.

The finale, *Tibetan Dance*, is the longest of the seven and contains the most original material. Imitating the "Lhasa tap dance," a folk dance using wooden boards,[15] Sheng requires the cellist to tap the body of the cello, sometimes at the same time as bowing the string.

Though Sheng's program notes do not specifically state this, the style of *Seven Tunes* expects the cellist to imitate the timbres of Chinese instruments. As well as the *qin*, Sheng's notation implies that another instrument, the *er-hu*, was a sound model. This two-string bowed fiddle has no fingerboard, therefore its note-to-note trajectory typically involves *glissando*. In her discussion of performance practice in *Seven Tunes*, Chiao-Hsuan Kang lists three broad categories of *glissando* ornamentation in Chinese music: narrower than a major third, wider than a major third, and wider than an octave.[16] Sheng notates these techniques in a variety of ways. A *glissando* with a shorter line indicates that the shift to the second pitch begins at the very end of the note value of the first pitch. A *glissando* with a longer line indicates an immediate "departure" from the first pitch. (Yo-Yo Ma's editorial fingerings in the Schirmer edition of *Seven Tunes* facilitate these *glissando* techniques.)

By expecting the performer to assimilate two different musical languages, Sheng combines contrasting materials into a seamless whole. Reflecting on the difficulty of doing so, he writes: "It must come from the deepest roots of both cultures: when two seeming opposites meet at their most original end, a transformation occurs naturally. And the result should enrich both."[17]

---

[15] Pan, 63.
[16] See Kang, 12.
[17] Sheng, "Never Far Away," 1.

Table 9.3.1 Sheng *Seven Tunes Heard in China*, I. *Seasons*, analysis

Section	A	B	Coda
Measures	1–12	13–23	24–27
Thematic material	Three main motives: descending duplets motive, dactylic motive, syncopated motive	Transpositions of descending duplets motive, dactylic motive, and syncopated motive	Synthesis of motivic materials
Implied key(s)	A minor to D minor	E♭ minor to B♭ minor	E minor, F minor, E♭ minor

9.4

Giovanni Sollima (b. 1962)

Alone for Solo Cello (1998)

Yo-Yo Ma describes the Italian cellist-composer Giovanni Sollima as "a supervirtuoso . . . [who] plays like a jazz musician and is part performance artist. He has no fear, and that's unusual in the classical world—we're all terrified of wrong notes."[1] The modern-day counterpart to the virtuoso cellist-composers of the Italian Baroque, Sollima is as well-known for his performances of Boccherini and early music as for his own eclectic compositions.[2] As a composer, his interests encompass minimalism, jazz, rock, and Mediterranean folk music. This polystylism may relate to his Sicilian heritage, which Sollima describes as "the product of Norman, Arab, Greek and Spanish cultures. My name, for example, has Arabic roots. I have lived in many places: Berlin, the United States, Milan. There is a room in my head in which dialects, languages, scales and ancient songs reverberate."[3] The post-minimalist style of Sollima's composition integrates modal melodic material into repetitive *ostinato* patterns and metric modulations.

Sollima has composed prolifically in many genres, including works for cello, multiple cellos, chamber ensembles, and orchestra, as well as operas and ballets. His compositions for the cello often feature unusual extended techniques. *Lamentatio* (2000) requires the cellist to sing Sicilian laments while playing the accompaniment on the cello, creating a polyphonic plainchant effect. *La Folia* (2007), Sollima's exploration of the Renaissance chord progression that inspired Corelli, Scarlatti, and Vivaldi, requires the cellist to

---

[1] "About the Artists," Piatigorsky Festival, accessed March 18, 2023, https://piatigorskyfestival.usc.edu/artists/giovanni.sollima.

[2] Elinor Frey, "We Are All (Baroque) Cellists Now: Baroque and Modern Italian Solo Cello Music in Direct Dialogue" (DMA diss., McGill University, 2012), 8.

[3] James Imam, "Giovanni Sollima to Embrace Intercultural Exchange at the Sounds of the Dolomites," *Bachtrack*, June 10, 2019, https://bachtrack.com/fr_FR/interview-giovanni-sollima-sounds-of-the-dolomites-trentino-italy-2019.

tune the C-string down a perfect fourth to a low G—a modern-day continuation of the Baroque practice of *scordatura*.[4]

Like *La Folia*, Sollima's *Alone* (1998) first appeared as a set work at an international cello competition. It is both technically demanding and inherently idiomatic for the instrument. Sollima displays his intimate knowledge of the cello's capabilities by frequently using the open strings and natural harmonics in double-stopped and drone textures. Sometimes he introduces yet another voice to the polyphony by adding left-hand *pizzicato*. Even if the cellist sits alone on the stage, the melodic lines themselves are never alone.

Alone is a single-movement work in four distinct sections marked *Adagio*, *Allegro*, *Adagio*, and *Allegro*, like the slow-fast-slow-fast sections of early Italian Baroque sonatas. Melodies are modal, often vacillating between major and minor or Dorian and Lydian modes, and a near-constant drone on the open D-strings means that the tonal center never veers far from D major or D minor. The first *Adagio* begins with a slurred modal melody played high on the G-string against the open D-string, with left-hand *pizzicati* on the open strings punctuating the phrases on off-beats. Sollima occasionally transfers this D drone to a stopped D on the G-string to allow for a countermelody on the C-string, which the cellist plays with the thumb.

The second section, *Allegro*, features a rushing sixteenth-note melody in continual double stops against the open D-string or A-string. The sixteenth note value remains constant throughout, but Sollima's different note groupings and occasional accents create metric modulations and an ever-shifting sense of pulse. A *sul ponticello* interlude introduces a trancelike slurred melody in Lydian dominant mode high on the D-string against a drone played with the thumb on the mid-string A harmonic. The sixteenth-note patterns resume briefly before another interlude marked *Tema*. It is not a new theme, but a variation on melodic material from the *Adagio*. After this, the sixteenth-note metric modulation returns, this time building to a dynamic climax and a *fermata*. Now the original *Adagio* returns in an almost note-for-note repeat, changing only in the final four measures with a reversal in order of the plucked A- and D-string pitches. The dynamics also go in reverse, culminating in a dramatic *crescendo* that leads into the final *Allegro* section. Here, Sollima returns to chord progressions from the previous *Allegro*, but speeds up their harmonic rhythm through new metric modulations, hurtling into a final *accelerando* to a *sforzando* on A and D harmonics.

---

[4] Katarina Majcen Pliego, "Performance Guide and Recording of Three Twenty-First-Century Compositions for Solo Cello" (DMA diss., University of Northern Colorado, 2020), 61–78.

Table 9.4.1 Sollima, *Alone*, analysis

Section	Adagio	Allegro			Adagio come l'inizio	Allegro
Measures	1–16	17–69	70–85	86–95	96–110	111–137
Thematic material	M.M. quarter note = 60. Three-voiced texture with slurs. Drones and left-hand pizzicato.	M.M. eighth note = 126/138. Two-voiced texture, separate bowstrokes, metric modulation. Double and triple stops, rapid string crossing	*Tema* interlude. Slurs and drones.	Variant on thematic material from 17–23.	Exact repetition of 1–12, slightly varied cadence 108–110. Drones, left-hand pizzicato.	Reprise of material from 17–69 with increased metric modulation. Double stops, triple stops, rapid string crossings.
Key(s)	D major/D minor	D major/D Lydian	D Mixolydian	Quasi-D Lydian	D major/D minor	D major

10
AMERICAN VOICES

10.1

Dorothy Rudd Moore (1940–2022)

Dirge and Deliverance for Cello and Piano (1971)

I. Dirge   II. Deliverance

Dorothy Rudd Moore was an American composer, pianist, singer, poet, and novelist. Early in her career, after studies with Mark Oakland Fax, Wen-Chung Chou, and Nadia Boulanger, she won several important awards for her compositions. She passionately supported the Civil Rights uprisings of the 1960s, during which time she co-founded the Society of Black Composers.

After her marriage to the American cellist Kermit Moore, the cello became central to Moore's compositions. The two met following a Lincoln Center performance of one of Moore's works and fell quickly in love. A few days afterwards, Moore composed *Baroque Suite* for unaccompanied cello (1964). A modern-day homage to Johann Sebastian Bach, Moore's foremost influence, *Baroque Suite* alludes to the dance rhythms and melodic motives of the Sixth Cello Suite. Just three months later, Moore presented it to her new husband as a wedding gift.

In 1970, Moore composed a longer work featuring the cello, *From the Dark Tower*. This Schubert-influenced song cycle for mezzo-soprano, cello, and piano was Moore's "black power statement."[1] With texts by poets of the Harlem Renaissance, the work emphasizes the "wonder, irony, agony, militancy, and pride characteristic of the Black American experience."[2] A year after that, Moore composed *Dirge and Deliverance* for cello and piano, a work whose musical language strongly resembles that of *From the Dark Tower*.

Many years after she composed *Dirge and Deliverance*, Moore described it as a "cello sonata,"[3] even though its structure does not resemble that of a

---

[1] Helen Walker-Hill, *From Spirituals to Symphonies: African-American Women Composers and Their Music* (Westport, CT: Greenwood Press, 2002), 234.
[2] Walker-Hill, 234.
[3] Bruce Duffie, "Composer Dorothy Rudd Moore: A Conversation with Bruce Duffie," 1990, http://bruceduffie.com/moore.html.

Figure 10.1.1 Moore, *Dirge and Deliverance*, mm. 16–17

traditional three- or four-movement sonata. Instead, as the title implies, *Dirge and Deliverance* features two long, thematically related movements that function as a large-scale antecedent and consequent.[4]

The *Dirge* section begins similarly to *From the Dark Tower*, with an ominous piano *ostinato* on low-pitched octaves and a mood of deep pessimism. The cello introduces the first theme (Figure 10.1.1), which begins with the three-note motive of an ascending minor second followed by a descending major second. Its first appearance on C, D♭, and C♭ sounds strikingly similar to Bach's B–A–C–H motive, and the resemblance was not coincidental. According to Moore, the obsessive reappearance of this intervallic device throughout *Dirge and Deliverance* symbolizes "the imprisonment of the human spirit."[5] In Bach-like fashion, the motive develops organically, generating much of the melodic material throughout both movements on varying pitch classes and rhythmic patterns.

As the *Dirge* unfolds, Moore increases the harmonic rhythm of the accompaniment, pushing the implied key chromatically upwards in faster note values. The movement ends with the exhausted reiteration of the "imprisonment" motive before progressing *attacca* into *Deliverance*. This second movement begins in an aggressive, whirling mini-cadenza for the cello where the "imprisonment" motive appears in sixteenth-note triplets reminiscent of the nightmarish "hoofbeats" motive of Schubert's *Erlkönig*. Cello and piano begin an antagonistic, dissonant counterpoint, building up to a furious

---

[4] Walker-Hill, 230.

[5] Dorothy Rudd Moore, *Dirge and Deliverance*, program note for American Composers Alliance, n.d., http://composers.com/composers/dorothy-rudd-moore/dirge-and-deliverance, accessed March 15, 2023.

outburst before the piano suddenly drops out. Moore then begins a long cadenza for the cello, an anguished meditation on the "imprisonment" motive. Fragmented sections of *pizzicato*, *sul ponticello*, *tremolo*, double-stopping, and *ricochet* appear in turn, each seemingly trying to break free from imprisonment. A new theme in artificial harmonics signals the return of the piano in an agitated dialogue. A return of the opening piano *ostinato* from the *Dirge* reappears before a sudden coda casts aside the "imprisonment" motive once and for all as both instruments travel to their high registers, the cello on frenzied trills and the piano in a rapid succession of block chords. In the composer's words, they "move with great purpose to the spiritual and physical liberation from their shackles."[6]

---

[6] Moore, n.d.

Table 10.1.1 Moore Dirge and Deliverance, analysis

Section	Dirge					
Measures	1–16	16–28	29–60	61–75	76–85	86–92
Thematic material	Piano *ostinato* motive	Cello introduces "imprisonment" motive	Continuation of motivic material	Variation 1 on "imprisonment" motive (legato)	Variation 2 on "imprisonment' motive (*tremolo*)	6/4 Interlude ("A little slower")
Key(s)	F minor	F minor	Ascending chromatic tonicizations			Quasi-C minor

Section	Dirge (continued)					
Measures	93–96	97–115	116–123	124–127	128–152	153–166
Thematic material	Return to *ostinato* motive	Variation 3 on "imprisonment" motive (oscillating tones)	Variation 4 on "imprisonment" motive (double stopping)	Return to *ostinato* motive	3/4 Interlude	Coda, *attacca*
Key(s)	A minor			B♭ minor		Quasi-A minor

Section	Deliverance					
Measures	167–203	204–237	238–249	250–280	281	282–288
Thematic material	*Erlkönig* rhythmic motive with melodic shape of "imprisonment" motive	Cello cadenza	Artificial harmonics theme, piano re-entry	Variation 5 on "imprisonment" motive (agitated, contrapuntal); *ostinato* ends	Last iteration of "imprisonment" motive	Coda: block piano chords, cello trills in the upper register
Key(s)	Quasi-C♯ minor	Quasi-C minor			Ascending chromatic movement	A major

10.2
Mark Summer (b. 1958)

Variations: Lo, How a Rose E'er Blooming (1995)

Mark Summer is one of the first cellist-composers to introduce the idioms, sonorities, and playing techniques of popular music into compositions for the cello. In his childhood, Summer studied cello, jazz piano, and guitar before beginning the traditional classical career path of conservatory studies and orchestral auditions. Summer's professors at the Cleveland Institute of Music helped him win a position in the Winnipeg Symphony but discouraged his practice-room attempts to fuse jazz and classical styles. Summer later described this period of his life as "very unhappy."[1]

When his orchestral career proved unsatisfying, coffee-house gigs with a guitarist colleague provided Summer with the ideal environment for experimentation in jazz, pop, and American fiddling styles. He soon began to meet other string players who shared his vision for a "crossover" string quartet. In 1986, Summer co-founded the Grammy Award-winning Turtle Island Quartet with the violinists Darol Anger and David Balakrishnan and the violist Laurie Moore. The Turtle Island Quartet reinvented classical string playing in a "fusion" with jazz, bluegrass, Indian, and Latin American styles.[2] They emphasized the importance of improvisation, a skill every eighteenth-century string player would have learned, but which died out by the late nineteenth century and was no longer part of standard training on bowed string instruments. By reviving the expectation that modern-day string players should improvise, , Summer and his colleagues increased the accessibility of contemporary non-notated musical genres for classically trained musicians.[3]

This new musical language called for new approaches to playing bowed string instruments. The Turtle Island Quartet pioneered the use of extended

---

[1] Chris White, "Interview with Mark Summer," Internet Cello Society website, 1997, https://www.cellobello.org/cello-blog/artistic-vision/conversation-with-mark-summer-1997/.

[2] George J. Grella, "Turtle Island Quartet (String)," *Grove Music Online*, ed. Deane Root, http://oxfordmusiconline.com.

[3] "Our Story," Turtle Island Quartet, http://turtleislandquartet.com/our-story, accessed March 17, 2023.

string techniques such as the "chop,"[4] "hammer-on," percussive striking of the strings, new types of pizzicato, and other ways of imitating the timbres and idioms of the electric guitar, electric bass, and even drums. Some of these extended techniques appear in Summer's beloved *Julie-O* (1988), one of the first published pieces to make "alternative" cello techniques approachable for intermediate-level players. Summer later published *Julie-O* alongside a more difficult companion piece, *Variations: Lo, How a Rose E'er Blooming* (1995).

Variations is both a study in modern-day cello technique and a revitalization of Baroque improvisation and classical theme-and-variations form. For thematic material, Summer uses the Christmas carol *Lo, How a Rose*, which has its origins in the 1609 chorale setting *Es ist ein Ros' entsprungen* by Michael Praetorius (1571–1621).

The opening theme, "Broad and stately," has a reverent, chorale-like mood. Summer's rhythmic notation has frequent meter changes to reflect the irregular phrase shapes of Praetorius's original. The cello writing is rich in double stops, three- and four-note chords, and florid written-out ornaments like those in Bach's Cello Suites.

Between the final cadence of the theme and the beginning of the first variation, Summer instructs the cellist to set the bow down. Pizzicato articulations include familiar linear and chordal techniques for plucking and strumming. Summer adds an extended technique for the left hand, a guitaristic "hammer-on" in which the fingers strike the fingerboard with a firm enough action to produce a pitched sound. In his notes to the performer, Summer explains that "this permits several notes to be sounded without the awkwardness of trying to pluck them all with the right hand, a technique especially useful with quick tempi."[5]

The second variation also avoids the bow. Here, Summer combines the "hammer-on" technique with pizzicato slurs in which the cellist plucks the first note of the slur with the fingers of the right hand but executes the rest of the notes under the slur with the left hand. Summer also introduces the "thumb strike" technique, in which notes are "sounded by striking the string with the right thumb."[6] These extended techniques create a percussive timbre and the strongly rhythmical pulse of rock or jazz styles.

---

[4] Laura Risk, "The Chop: The Diffusion of an Instrumental Technique across North Atlantic Fiddling Traditions," *Ethnomusicology* 57, no. 3 (Fall 2013): 428–454.

[5] Mark Summer, "Performance Notes," *Julie-O* and *Variations: Lo, How a Rose E'er Blooming* (Ann Arbor, MI: Shar Music Publications, 1997), ii.

[6] Summer.

Arco playing returns in the third variation for repetitive arpeggiations of broken chords that simultaneously recall American fiddling techniques and the *bariolage* bowing of the Prelude to Bach's First Cello Suite. The meter switches restlessly between compound time signatures (6/8, 9/8, 12/8) and irregular meters such as 10/8, creating *hemiola* and other rhythmic patterns.

The final variation concludes the work by looking back to the styles and techniques from the theme and first three variations. A chorale-style opening phrase takes a surprise turn into an ornamental aside for pizzicato and "hammer-on." The Bach-style *bariolage* returns, leading into a final triumphant statement of the chorale theme.

Table 10.2.1 Summer, *Variations on Lo, How a Rose E'er Blooming*, analysis

Section	Theme	Variation 1	Variation 2	Variation 3	Variation 4
Measures	1–10	11–21	22–51	52–92	93–108
Thematic material	Praetorius hymn tune, "Broad and stately." *Arco*, double stops and chords, Baroque ornamentation	Bow down. Pizzicato and hammer-on techniques, strummed "guitar" technique, improvisatory style	Pizzicato, hammer-on, thumb strike, left-hand pizzicato, strummed "guitar" technique, highly rhythmical character	*Arco*, *bariolage* technique, frequent meter change, *hemiola*	Chorale-style section, pizzicato and hammer-on section, *bariolage*, concluding chorale-style section.
Key(s)	G major	G major	G major	G major	G major

10.3
Adolphus Hailstork (b. 1941)

Theme and Variations on "Draw the Sacred Circle Closer" for Solo Cello (2014)

Adolphus Hailstork began his music studies as a violinist, and later took up organ and piano and sang in a cathedral boys' choir. Exposure to the choral works of Shostakovich, Verdi, Kodály, and Bach at Howard University inspired him to compose prolifically in choral genres. Hailstork went on to further studies with Nadia Boulanger in France, and later completed graduate degrees at the Manhattan School of Music and Michigan State University.[1] A longtime professor at Norfolk State University in Virginia, Hailstork has earned many awards, commissions, and performances by leading conductors and ensembles. In a 1999 interview, he described his musical language as a combination of "the two things that interest me a lot, Western (European) choral style and African-American choral writing. Both of them are part of my experience and part of my heritage."[2]

This dual character is especially strong in *Earthrise*, Hailstork's 2006 cantata for double choir and orchestra. A large-scale work with many references to Beethoven's Ninth Symphony, its central themes are love and human rights. In his program note to the score, Hailstork explains, "The Cincinnati May Festival had asked me to write a piece that would join an African-American choir with the festival chorus in a gesture of racial cooperation, a concern in Cincinnati and several American communities. When I asked myself what text addressed issues of joining people together in peace and social healing, the obvious one was the daring one: the Schiller 'Ode to Joy,' which everyone knows in the immortal setting by Beethoven."[3]

---

[1] Gene Brooks, "An Interview with Adolphus Hailstork," *The Choral Journal* 39, no. 7 (February 1999): 29–30.
[2] Brooks, 32.
[3] Adolphus Hailstork, preface to *Earthrise: A Song of Healing* (New York: Carl Fischer, 2006). https://www.carlfischer.com/116-40108-earthrise.html, accessed October 6, 2021.

Hailstork intended the final movement of *Earthrise* as "a hymn of unity as Schiller invokes us to 'Draw the Sacred Circle Closer'. The verses of the hymn increase in intensity, climaxing with the words 'living as one again'. Then those four notes from Beethoven reappear to remind us that when it comes to social harmony and justice, love, and peace, 'it's up...to us.'[4]

Hailstork later repurposed the hymn in his *Theme and Variations* for solo cello. Another influence was the idiom of Bach's solo works for cello. Hailstork explains, "The cello's range and tone evoke the baritone voice, and its facility in contrapuntal playing allows for polyphony in the manner of Bach's cello suites."[5]

Hailstork accordingly transposed the hymn theme from the original D♭ major to G, a key that takes advantage of the sympathetic resonances in the cello's open strings. (He would return to G major a year later in his Sonata for Solo Cello, which contains references to Bach's First Cello Suite in G Major.) The key of G also creates possibilities for harmonic self-accompaniment such as left-hand pizzicato on the open G, D, and C strings. Hailstork does not significantly change the hymn tune, but here the pizzicato accompaniment lends it a quieter, almost folk-like character. In combining aspects of pentatonic and Mixolydian language, the thematic material shares many characteristics with African American spirituals.

Five variations on the theme contain various similarities to Bach's Cello Suites and other landmark cello repertoire. The first, "Sprightly," with its compound meter, slurred passagework, and dashing tempo, hints at the *gigues* that conclude each of Bach's cello suites. Towards the end of the movement, Hailstork develops the material through chromaticism and metric modulation.

The second variation, "Playfully," takes the conversational tone of one of Bach's *courantes* for cello, though unlike the Baroque dance it is not in triple meter. Two distinct voices engage in a bantering back-and-forth, the forceful staccato of one punctuating and interrupting the lyrical slurs of the other. Hailstork switches abruptly to a more serious mood in a recitative-like middle section marked "Dramatic." Playfulness returns, but only temporarily, before another recitative-like section continues without a break into the next variation.

---

[4] Hailstork, preface to *Earthrise*.
[5] Adolphus Hailstork, back cover notes to *Theme and Variations on "Draw the Sacred Circle Closer"* for Solo Cello (Malvern, PA: Theodore Presser Company, 2014).

The third and fourth variations, both slow movements, seem closely related and melancholic in tone. The theme transforms itself into a lonely monologue, with snippets of phrases recalling the cadenza of Shostakovich's First Cello Concerto. Other Shostakovich-inflected touches include collections of octatonic pitches, unexpected tonal shifts, and a sense of unease.

The irrepressible energy of the fifth variation puts an end to this, as Hailstork takes us back to the original key of G Mixolydian, sometimes supplementing tones from the blues scale. The character is syncopated and folk-like. As excitement builds, the melodic line takes the cellist up to the highest registers of the instrument. The final, blues-inflected statement ends the variation in a triumphant character.

Table 10.3.1 Hailstork *Theme and Variations on "Draw the Sacred Circle Closer,"* analysis

Section	Theme	Variation 1	Variation 2	Variation 3	Variation 4	Variation 5
Measures	1–24	25–51	52–93	94–123	124–143	144–173
Thematic material	Syncopated and Scottish snap rhythms, legato bowstrokes with left-hand pizzicato accompaniment	Compound time, *gigue* character	Two-voice contrapuntal texture, *courante* character	Octatonic version of the thematic material	Minor key variation	Animated character with slow interlude, faster coda
Key(s)	G Mixolydian and G pentatonic	G major and G Mixolydian	G major	Octatonic, no clear key center	F♯ minor and D major	G Mixolydian, blues scale

10.4
Reena Esmail (b. 1983)
Varsha (2019)

Reena Esmail wrote *Varsha* (Rain) for the "Seven Last Words Project," a 2019 performance by the period instrument ensemble Juilliard 415. It was one of seven new works commissioned as interludes for the group to play between the movements of Haydn's *Seven Last Words of Our Savior on the Cross*, Op. 51. Esmail's contribution to the occasion connected Sonata V (*Sitio*, "I thirst"), and Sonata VI (*Consummatum Est*, "It is finished").

In a program note, Esmail explains her vision for *Varsha*:

> The combination of Hindustani *raags* used in this piece are from the Malhaar family, which are sung to beckon rain. I imagined an interlude between these two sonatas: Christ thirsts. Rain comes from the distance (*Megh Malhaar*). There is a downpour around him (*Miyan ki Malhaar*), but he grows slowly weaker. His next words make clear that even the rain is not enough: his thirst is of another sort, which cannot be quenched by water. And so, it is finished.[1]

Raag (also known by the Sanskrit word *rāga*) is a term from Indian classical music theory. Neither the Hindi word nor the concept is easily translatable. With multiple meanings including "color," "tone," "passion," and "gamut," a *raag* is a mode or collection of pitches that form the basis for musical improvisation. Every *raag* has rules that determine pitch hierarchy, direction, and ornamentation, and many have connections to nature and religion.[2] Many Hindus believe them powerful enough to launch the monsoon season.

The Juilliard- and Yale-educated Esmail, who also studied Hindustani music in India, finds commonalities between Indian and European classical styles in many of her compositions. The cello writing in *Varsha* recalls the highly ornamented melodic style of Indian stringed instruments such

---

[1] Reena Esmail, program note to *Varsha*, http://reenaesmail.com, accessed August 14, 2022.
[2] Richard Widdess, "Rāga," *Grove Music Online*, ed. Deane Root, http://oxfordmusiconline.com.

as the *sitār*, a fretted lute, and the *tambūrā*, a plucked drone instrument. Harmonically, the cello has a built-in capacity for imitating the drone harmony, since *tambūrā* players often tune in perfect fifths.[3]

In the premiere performance, *Varsha* began *attacca* following the final A major triad of Haydn's Sonata V. The first note of *Varsha* is also a long-held A. From this somber beginning, a melodic line grows gradually in ascending motion. A downward step answers each upward skip, but the ascent ineluctably continues as the tempo and volume increase. Slurred groups of pitches conclude on emphatic *glissandi* that, according to the composer, "should have an implicit *rit.* (which can start a few notes earlier)."[4] The tempo and pulse are *molto rubato*, the rhythmic notation flexible. Esmail's notation of appoggiaturas and acciaccaturas, while precise, gives the impression in performance of an improvisatory style of playing. The mood is prayerful and chant-like.

The most substantial section of the work is the central *Recitativo*, marked "dreamlike." Esmail introduces rapid arpeggiated flourishes across the open strings of the cello, with double and triple stops that seem to imitate the drones of the *tambūrā*. Though there is no key signature, the melody circles around G.

The final section begins with another open-string arpeggiation marked "like a gasp." In these final measures, Esmail reconciles the meditative mood of the first section with the arpeggiations and drones from the *Recitativo*. The rhythm slows and the ambitus of pitches narrows until all that remains is the cellist's open G. (In the original performance context, Haydn's Sonata VI began *attacca* in G minor following the last note of *Varsha*.)

In juxtaposing ideas of the divine from two world religions, *Varsha* creates a spiritual and cultural common ground through music. In Esmail's own words, she "works between the worlds of Indian and Western classical music, and brings communities together through the creation of equitable musical spaces."[5] In her introduction to a video performance of *Varsha*, she reflects on its meaning:

> *Malhaar raags* are supposed to beckon rain, sometimes even beckon floods. I was thinking about what that meant during this time, how everything that we've created and built feels like it's being washed out to sea and

---

[3] Alastair Dick, "Tambūrā," *Grove Music Online*, ed. Deane Root, http://oxfordmusiconline.com.
[4] Reena Esmail, *Varsha* (A Piece of Sky Music, 2019), 1.
[5] Reena Esmail, "Biography," http://reenaesmail.com, accessed August 14, 2022.

there's nothing we can do to stop that from happening. And that might feel like complete despair, but ... rain can also be really cleansing. When everything is gone and nothing remains, maybe we're able to see a new path forward. What I hope is that *Varsha* feels like a prayer for us to be able to find that path forward together.[6]

Table 10.4.1 Esmail, *Varsha*, analysis

Section	First section	*Recitativo*	Final section
Measures	1–13	14–45	46–57
Thematic material	Ascending theme, slurs, *glissando*	"Dreamlike" open-string arpeggios theme, drones	Reconciliation of thematic materials. "Gasp" ornamentation, drones
Key(s)	Quasi-A minor	Quasi-G minor	Quasi-G minor

---

[6] Madeleine Bouïssou, "Varsha वर्षा: Reena Esmail - Madeleine Bouïssou, cello," YouTube video, December 18, 2020, https://www.youtube.com/watch?v=RHftgjttVk8, accessed August 14, 2022.

Bibliography

Domenico Gabrielli, *Ricercar* No. 2 (1689)

Bonta, Stephen. *Studies in Italian Sacred and Instrumental Music in the Seventeenth Century.* Aldershot: Ashgate, 2003.

Bonta, Stephen. "The Use of Instruments in the Ensemble Canzona and Sonata in Italy, 1580–1650." *Recercare* 4 (1992), 23–43.

Caldwell, John. "Ricercare." Grove Music Online. Edited by Deane Root. http://oxfordmusiconline.com.

Dilworth, John. "The Cello: Origins and Evolution." In *The Cambridge Companion to the Cello*, edited by Robin Stowell, 1–27. Cambridge: Cambridge University Press, 1999.

Schnoebelen, Anne. "Performance Practices at San Petronio in the Baroque." *Acta Musicologica* 41 (1969), 37–55.

Suess, John, and Marc Vanscheeuwijk. "Gabrielli, Domenico." *Grove Music Online*. Edited by Deane Root. http://oxfordmusiconline.com.

Johann Sebastian Bach, Suite No. 3 in C Major, BWV 1007

Little, Meredith, and Natalie Jenne. *Dance and the Music of J. S. Bach.* 2nd ed. Bloomington and Indianapolis: Indiana University Press, 2001.

Schenker, Heinrich. "The Sarabande of J. S. Bach's Suite No. 3 for Unaccompanied Violoncello." Translated by Hedi Siegel. *The Music Forum* 2, ed. William J. Mitchell and Felix Salzer, 274–282. New York: Columbia University Press, 1970.

Smith, Mark M. "The Drama of Bach's Life in the Court of Cöthen, as Reflected in His Cello Suites." *Stringendo* 22, no. 1 (2000): 32–35.

Watkin, David. "Corelli's Op. 5 Sonatas: Violino e Violone *e* Cembalo?" *Early Music* 24, no. 4 (November 1996): 645–664.

Antonio Vivaldi, Sonata in B♭ Major, RV 46

Burney, Charles. *The Present State of Music in France and Italy.* London: T. Becket, 1771.

Harris, Ellen T. "Messa di voce." *Grove Music Online.* Edited by Deane Root. http://oxfordmusiconline.com.

Micheletti, André Luis Giovanini, and William Teixeira da Silva. "Cello Development from Gabrielli to Vivaldi." *Revista Música Hodie, Goiânia* 14, no. 2 (2014): 21–30.

Selfridge-Field, Eleanor. "Vivaldi's Cello Sonatas." In *Vivaldi, Vero e Falso*, edited by L. S. Olschki, 127–147. Venice: Istituto Italiano Antonio Vivaldi, 1992.

Jean-Baptiste Barrière, Sonata IV in G Major from *Livre IV*

Corrette, Michel. *Méthode théorique et pratique pour apprendre en peu de tems le violoncelle dans sa perfection.* Paris: Boivin, 1741.

Cyr, Mary. "Barrière, Jean." *Grove Music Online.* Edited by Deane Root. http://oxfordmusiconline.com.

Cyr, Mary. "Berteau [Berthault, Bertaud], Martin." *Grove Music Online.* Edited by Deane Root. http://oxfordmusiconline.com.

Cyr, Mary. *Style and Performance for Bowed String Instruments in French Baroque Music.* Surrey: Ashgate, 2012.

de la Gorce, Jérôme. "L'orchestre de l'Opéra et son évolution de Campra à Ramea." *Revue de Musicologie* 76, no. 1 (1990): 23–43.

Le Blanc, Hubert. *Défense de la basse de viole contre les entreprises du violon et les prétentions du violoncel.* Paris: Pierre Mortier, 1740.

Milliot, Sylvette. *Le violoncelle en France au XVIIIème siècle.* Paris: Champion Slatkin, 1985.

Selfridge-Field, Eleanor. "Vivaldi's Cello Sonatas." In *Vivaldi, Vero e Falso*, edited by L. S. Olschki, 127–147. Venice: Istituto Italiano Antonio Vivaldi, 1992.

Luigi Boccherini, Sonata in A Major, G.4

Baillot, Pierre, Jean-Henri Levasseur, Charles-Simon Catel, and Charles Baudiot, *Méthode de violoncelle.* Paris: Janet et Cotelle, 1805.

de Rothschild, Germaine, and Andreas Mayor. *Luigi Boccherini: His Life and Work.* London: Oxford University Press, 1965.

Heartz, Daniel. "The Young Boccherini: Lucca, Vienna, and the Electoral Courts." *The Journal of Musicology* 13, no. 1 (Winter 1995): 103–116.

Le Guin, Elisabeth. *Boccherini's Body: An Essay in Carnal Musicology.* Berkeley and Los Angeles: University of California Press, 2006.

Micheletti, André Luís Giovanini. "The Role of Luigi Boccherini in the Development of Cello Technique." PhD diss., Indiana University, 2014.

Speck, Christian, and Stanley Sadie. "Boccherini, (Ridolfo) Luigi." *Grove Music Online.* Edited by Deane Root. http://oxfordmusiconline.com.

Speck, Christian. "Boccherini as Cellist and His Music for Cello." *Early Music* 33, no. 2 (2005): 191–210.

Franz Joseph Haydn, Concerto in C Major, Hob. VIIb:1

Anders, Gerhard. Liner notes to *Haydn: Cello Concertos.* Naxos 8.555041, 2001.

Feder, Georg, and James Webster. "Haydn, (Franz) Joseph." *Grove Music Online.* Edited by Deane Root. http://oxfordmusiconline.com.

Furse, Edward Niel. "Perspectives on the Reception of Haydn's Cello Concerto in C, with Particular Reference to Musicological Writings in English on Haydn's Concertos and the Classical Concerto." MMus thesis, University of Birmingham, 2009.

Gerlach, Sonja. Preface to Joseph Haydn, *Konzert in C für Violoncello und Orchester.* Kassel: Bärenreiter, 1988.

Tarling, Judy. *Weapons of Rhetoric: A Guide for Musicians and Audiences.* 2nd ed. Hertfordshire: Corda Music Publications, 2005.

Ludwig van Beethoven, Sonata in A Major, Op. 69

Agmon, Eytan. "The First Movement of Beethoven's Cello Sonata Op. 69: The Opening Solo as a Structural and Motivic Source." *The Journal of Musicology* 16, no. 3 (Summer 1998): 394–409.

Beethoven, Ludwig van. *Grande Sonate pour Pianoforte et Violoncelle*, Op. 69. Leipzig: Breitkopf und Härtel, 1809.

Lockwood, Lewis. *Beethoven: The Music and the Life.* New York: W. W. Norton, 2003.

Lockwood, Lewis. *Beethoven: Studies in the Creative Process.* Cambridge, MA: Harvard University Press, 1992.

Moskovitz, Marc D., and R. Larry Todd. *Beethoven's Cello: Five Revolutionary Sonatas and Their World.* Woodbridge, UK: The Boydell Press, 2017.

Reynolds, Christopher Alan. *Motives for Allusion: Context and Content in Nineteenth-Century Music.* Cambridge, MA: Harvard University Press, 2003.

Fanny Hensel, *Sonata o Fantasia* H-U 238 and *Capriccio* H-U 247

Field, Christopher D. S., E. Eugene Helm, and William Drabkin. "Fantasia." *Grove Music Online.* Edited by Deane Root. http://oxfordmusiconline.com.

Reynolds, Christopher Alan. *Motives for Allusion: Context and Content in Nineteenth-Century Music.* Cambridge, MA: Harvard University Press, 2003.

Schwandt, Erich. "Capriccio." *Grove Music Online*. Edited by Deane Root. http://oxfordmusiconline.com.
Todd, R. Larry. *Fanny Hensel: The Other Mendelssohn*. New York: Oxford University Press, 2010.

Felix Mendelssohn-Bartholdy, Sonata No. 2 in D Major, Op. 58

Horton, John. *Mendelssohn Chamber Music*. Seattle: University of Washington Press, 1972.
Moscheles, Felix, ed. *Letters of Felix Mendelssohn to Ignaz and Charlotte Moscheles*. Boston, MA: Ticknor and Company, 1888.
Niaux, Viviane. "George Onslow: le Beethoven français." *Les sources du romantisme français* (October 2008): 1–18.
Norris, Geoffrey. "Wielhorski, Count Mateusz." *Grove Music Online*. Edited by Deane Root. http://oxfordmusiconline.com.
Sachs, Joel, and Mark Kroll. "Hummel, Johann Nepomuk." *Grove Music Online*. Edited by Deane Root. http://oxfordmusiconline.com.
Seaton, Douglass. "Review of *Sämtliche Werke für Violoncello und Klavier*/Complete Works for Violoncello and Piano, ed. R. Larry Todd." *Nineteenth-Century Music Review* 15, no. 1 (2018): 145–148.
Todd, R. Larry. *Mendelssohn: A Life in Music*. New York: Oxford University Press, 2003.
Aziz, Andrew I. "The Evolution of Chopin's Sonata Forms: Excavating the Second Theme Group." *A Journal of the Society for Music Theory* 21, no. 4 (2015): 1–23.
Franchomme, August. *Partie de violoncelle de la Sonate pour Piano et Violoncelle de Chopin écrite sous sa dictée par moi Franchomme*. Manuscript, 1847. Housed at the Bibliothèque Nationale de France.
Leikin, Anatole. "The Sonatas." In *The Cambridge Companion to Chopin*. Edited by Jim Samson. New York: Cambridge University Press, 1992.
Niecks, Frederick. *Frederick Chopin as Man and Musician*, 160–188. Urbana, IL: Project Gutenberg, 2009..
Samson, Jim. "Chopin, Fryderyk Franciszek." *Grove Music Online*. Edited by Deane Root. http://oxfordmusiconline.com.
Schmalfeldt, Janet. *In the Process of Becoming: Analytical and Philosophical Perspectives on Form in Early Nineteenth-Century Music*. New York: Oxford University Press, 2011.
Sutcliffe, W. Dean. "Chopin's Counterpoint: The *Largo* from the Cello Sonata, Opus 65." *The Musical Quarterly* 83, no. 1 (Spring 1999): 114–133.

Louise Farrenc, Sonata in B♭ Major, Op. 46

Ellis, Katharine. "Female Pianists and their Male Critics in Nineteenth-Century Paris," *Journal of the American Musicological Society* 50, nos. 2–3 (Summer–Autumn 1997): 353–385.
Friedland, Bea. "Farrenc Family." *Grove Music Online*. Edited by Deane Root. http://oxfordmusiconline.com.
Friedland, Bea. "Louise Farrenc (1804–1875): Composer, Performer, Scholar." *Musical Quarterly* 60, no. 2 (April 1974): 257–274.
Friedland, Bea. "Louise Farrenc, 1804-1875: Composer-Performer-Scholar." PhD diss., City University of New York, 1975.
Sensbach, Stephen. *French Cello Sonatas 1871–1939*. Dublin: The Lilliput Press, 2001.

Johannes Brahms, Sonata in E Minor, Op. 38

Altmann, Wilhelm. "Bach-Zitate in der Violoncello-Sonate op. 38 von Brahms." *Die Musik* 12, no. 2 (October 2, 1912): 84–85.
Drinker, Henry S. *The Chamber Music of Johannes Brahms*. Philadelphia, PA: Elkan-Vogel, 1932.
Klenz, William. "Brahms, Opus 38: Piracy, Pillage, Plagiarism, or Parody?" *The Music Review* 34 (1973): 39–50.

Mason, Daniel Gregory. *The Chamber Music of Brahms*. New York: MacMillan, 1933.
Musgrave, Michael. *The Music of Brahms*. London and Boston, MA: Routledge & Kegan Paul, 1985.
Notley, Margaret. "Brahms' Cello Sonata in F Major and Its Genesis: A Study in Half-Step Relations," In *Brahms Studies*, vol. 1. Edited by David Brodbeck, 139–160. Lincoln: University of Nebraska Press, 1994.

Ethel Smyth, Sonata in A Minor, Op. 5

Beecham, Thomas. "Dame Ethel Smyth (1858–1944)." *The Musical Times* 99, no. 1385 (July 1958): 363–365.
Gates, Eugene. "Damned If You Do, Damned If You Don't: Sexual Aesthetics and the Music of Dame Ethel Smyth." *Kapralova Society Journal* 4, no. 1 (Spring 2006): 1–5.
Shaw, George Bernard. *The Bodley Head Shaw: Shaw's Music*. Edited by Dan H. Laurence. London: Max Rheinhardt, 1981.
Smyth, Ethel. Cello Sonata No. 1 in C Minor (1880). Edited by George Kennaway. Leeds: Magellan Publications, 2022.
Smyth, Ethel. *Impressions That Remained: Memoirs by Ethel Smyth*. London: Longmans, Green & Co., 1920.
Zigler, Amy. "Selected Works of Dame Ethel Smyth." PhD diss., University of Florida, 2009.

Camille Saint-Saëns, Concerto No. 1 in A Minor, Op. 33

Duchesneau, Michel. "Société nationale de musique." Dictionary entry. Bibliothèque Nationale de France website. http://bnf.fr, accessed July 2022.
Fallon, Daniel M., James Harding, and Sabina Teller Ratner. "Saint-Saëns, (Charles) Camille." *Grove Music Online*. Edited by Deane Root. http://oxfordmusiconline.com.
Flynn, Timothy. *Camille Saint-Saëns: A Guide to Research*. New York: Routledge, 2003.
Revue et Gazette Musicale de Paris (1873).
Tovey, Donald. *Essays in Musical Analysis*, vol. 3: *The Concertos*. London: Oxford University Press, 1936.

Edouard Lalo, Concerto in D Minor (1877)

Anderson, Robert. "Casals, Pablo." *Grove Music Online*. Edited by Deane Root. http://oxfordmusiconline.com.
Macdonald, Hugh. "Lalo, Edouard (-Victoire-Antoine)." *Grove Music Online*. Edited by Deane Root. http://oxfordmusiconline.com.
McClary, Susan. *Georges Bizet: Carmen*. New York: Cambridge University Press, 1992.
Tiersot, Julien, and Frederick H. Hartens. "Édouard Lalo." *The Musical Quarterly* 11, no. 1 (January 1925): 8–35.

Gabriel Fauré, *Élégie*, Op. 24

Nectoux, Jean-Michel. "Faure, Gabriel (Urbain)." *Grove Music Online*. Edited by Deane Root. http://oxfordmusiconline.com.
Nectoux, Jean-Michel. *Gabriel Fauré: A Musical Life*. Translated by Roger Nichols. Cambridge: Cambridge University Press, 1991.

Claude Debussy, Sonata in D Minor (1915)

Gibbs, Alan. "Debussy's Lutheran Side?" *The Strad* 103, no. 1229 (September 1992): 767.
Hwang, Sunkyung. "Stylistic Synthesis and Symbolism in Debussy's Sonata for Cello and Piano." *International Journal of Musicology* 3 (2017): 85–101.
Messing, Scott. *Neoclassicism in Music: From the Genesis of the Concept through the Schoenberg/Stravinsky Polemic*. Ann Arbor, MI: UMI Research Press, 1988.
Oettinger, Rebecca Wagner. *Music as Propaganda in the German Reformation*. Burlington, VT: Ashgate, 2001.

Ragno, Janelle. "The Lutheran Hymn 'Ein' feste Burg' in Claude Debussy's Cello Sonata (1915): Motivic Variation and Structure." DMA diss., University of Texas, 2005.
Welsh, Moray. "Un embarras de richesse." *The Strad* 103, no. 1226 (June 1992): 516–520.

Robert Schumann, Concerto in A Minor, Op. 129

Chernaik, Judith. *Schumann*. New York: Alfred A. Knopf, 2018.
Kramer, Lawrence. "A New Self: Schumann at 40." *The Musical Times* 148 (Spring 2007): 3–17.
Miranda, Carmine. "Decoding the Schumann Cello Concerto." *The Musical Times* 157 (Spring 2016): 45–66.
Roeder, Michael Thomas. *A History of the Concerto*. Portland, OR: Amadeus Press, 1994.
Smith, Peter H. "Schumann's A Minor Mood: Late-Style Dialectics in the First Movement of the Cello Concerto." *Journal of Music Theory* 60, no. 1 (2016): 51–88.
Tunbridge, Laura. *Schumann's Late Style*. New York: Cambridge University Press, 2007.
Worthen, John. *Robert Schumann: Life and Death of a Musician*. New Haven, CT: Yale University Press, 2007.

Pyotr Ilich Tchaikovsky, *Variations on a Rococo Theme*, Op. 33

Brown, David. *Tchaikovsky: The Crisis Years*. New York: W. W. Norton, 1983.
Ginsburg, Lev. "Introduction." In *Variations on a Rococo Theme*, Op. 33, composed by Pyotr Ilich Tchaikovsky, viii. Moscow: Muzgiz, 1962.
Heartz, Daniel and Bruce Alan Brown. "Rococo." *Grove Music Online*. Edited by Deane Root. http://oxfordmusiconline.com.
Istomin, Sergei. "The History of Tchaikovsky's *Variations on a Rococo Theme* and the Collaboration with Fitzenhagen." *Music and Practice* 4 (2019). https://www.musicandpractice.org/volume-4/.
Jurgenson, Pyotr. Pyotr Jurgenson to Pyotr Ilich Tchaikovsky, February 1878. In *Tchaikovsky Research*. Last modified March 27, 2021. http://en.tchaikovsky-research.net/pages/Variations_on_a_Rococo_Theme. Last modified March 27, 2021.
Kubatsky, Victor. "Works for Cello and Orchestra." In *Tchaikovsky: The Complete Works*, vol. 30B (Moscow: Muzgiz/Muzyka, 1956): 5–46.
Tchaikovsky, Pyotr Ilich. Diary entry, September 20–October 2, 1886. In *Tchaikovsky Research*. http://en.tchaikovsky-research.net/pages/Wolfgang_Amadeus_Mozart. Last modified February 20, 2020.
Tchaikovsky, Pyotr Ilich. Pyotr Ilich Tchaikovsky to Sergei Taneyev, April 1883. In *Tchaikovsky Research*. http://en.tchaikovsky-research.net/pages/Wolfgang_Amadeus_Mozart. Last modified February 20, 2020.

Antonín Dvořák, Concerto in B Minor, Op. 104

Clapham, John. *Antonín Dvořák: Musician and Craftsman*. New York: St. Martin's Press, 1966.
Malybrok-Stieler, Otilie. "Kéž duch můj sám." Text and translation provided by Oxford Lieder, http://oxfordlieder.co.uk. Accessed March 6, 2022.
Roeder, Michael Thomas. *A History of the Concerto*. Portland, OR: Amadeus Press, 1994.
Smaczny, Jan. *Dvořák: Cello Concerto*. Cambridge: Cambridge University Press, 2004.
Supka, Ondrej. "Concerto for Cello and Orchestra." Translated by Karolina Hughes. http://antonin-dvorak.cz/en/concerto-for-cello2. Accessed March 5, 2022.
Tovey, Donald Francis. *Essays in Musical Analysis*, vol. 3: *The Concertos*. London: Oxford University Press, 1936.

Ernest Bloch, *Schelomo: Rhapsodie Hébraïque* (1915–16)

Bloch, Suzanne, and Irene Heskes. *Ernest Bloch: Creative Spirit*. New York: Jewish Music Council of the National Jewish Welfare Board, 1976.
Gatti, Guido M., and Theodore Baker. "Ernest Bloch." *The Musical Quarterly* 7, no. 1 (January 1921): 20–38.

Klaus, Aaron. "Ernest Bloch, Richard Wagner, and the Myth of Racial Essentialism." *Studies in Christian-Jewish Relations* 13, no. 1 (2018): 9–10.
Kushner, David Z. "Bloch, Ernest." *Grove Music Online*. Edited by Deane Root. http://oxford musiconline.com.
Kushner, David Z. *The Ernest Bloch Companion.* Westport, CT: Greenwood Press, 2002.
Móricz, Klára. "Sensuous Pagans and Righteous Jews: Changing Concepts of Jewish Identity in Ernest Bloch's *Jézabel* and *Schelomo*." *Journal of the American Musicological Society* 54, no. 3 (Fall 2001): 439–491.
Montagu, Jeremy. "Shofar." *Grove Music Online*. Edited by Deane Root. http://oxfordmusiconl ine.com.
Rink, John. "Rhapsody." *Grove Music Online*. Edited by Deane Root. http://oxfordmusiconl ine.com.
Trowbridge, William. *Jézabel, drame*. Paris: Éditions de la Plume, 1903.

Edward Elgar, Concerto in E Minor, Op. 85

Kennedy, Michael. *Elgar Orchestral Music.* Seattle: University of Washington Press, 1970.
Kennedy, Michael. *Portrait of Elgar.* Oxford: Oxford University Press, 1987.
McCrory, Martha. "A Study of the Elgar Cello Concerto." MMus thesis, University of Rochester, 1944.
Potter, Tully. "A Much Maligned Cellist: The True Story of Felix Salmond and the Elgar Cello Concerto." *The Elgar Society Journal* 19, no. 6 (2016): 4–18.
Roeder, Michael Thomas. *A History of the Concerto.* Portland, OR: Amadeus Press, 1994.
Steinberg, Michael. *The Concerto: A Listener's Guide.* New York: Oxford University Press, 1998.

Dmitri Shostakovich, Concerto No. 1 in E-flat Major, Op. 107

Fairclough, Pauline, and David Fanning, eds. *The Cambridge Companion to Shostakovich.* Cambridge: Cambridge University Press, 2008.
Ivashkin, Alexander. "Shostakovich: First Cello Concerto." *Shostakovich: New Collected Works.* Series III, vol. 46. Moscow: DSCH Editions, 2012, 122–130.
MacDonald, Malcolm. "'I Took a Simple Little Tune and Developed it': Shostakovich's String Concertos and Sonatas." In *The Cambridge Companion to Shostakovich*, edited by Pauline Fairclough and David Fanning. Cambridge: Cambridge University Press, 2008: 115–143.
McVeagh, Diana. "Shostakovich's Concerto." *The Musical Times* 101, no. 1413 (November 1960): 701–703.
Steinberg, Michael. *The Concerto: A Listener's Guide.* New York: Oxford University Press, 1998.
Wilson, Elizabeth. *Shostakovich: A Life Remembered.* Princeton, NJ: Princeton University Press, 2006.

Serge Rachmaninoff, Sonata in G Minor, Op. 19

Ginzburg, Lev. "Brandukov, Anatoly Andreyevich." *Grove Music Online*. Edited by Deane Root. http://oxfordmusiconline.com.
Malloy, Dave. *Preludes: A Musical Fantasia Set in the Hypnotized Mind of Sergei Rachmaninoff.* Unpublished manuscript, 2015, typescript.
Norris, Geoffrey. "Rachmaninoff, Serge." *Grove Music Online*. Edited by Deane Root. http:// oxfordmusiconline.com.
Norris, Geoffrey. *Rakhmaninov.* London: J. M. Dent & Sons, 1976.

Samuel Barber, Sonata in C Minor, Op. 6

Broder, Nathan. "The Music of Samuel Barber." *Musical Quarterly* 34, no. 3 (July 1948): 325–335.
Heyman, Barbara. *Samuel Barber: The Composer and His Music.* New York: Oxford University Press, 1992.

Sergei Prokofiev, Sonata in C Major, Op. 119

Morrison, Simon. *The People's Artist: Prokofiev's Soviet Years*. Oxford: Oxford University Press, 2009.

Redepenning, Dorothea. "Prokofiev, Sergey (Sergeyevich)." *Grove Music Online*. Edited by Deane Root. http://oxfordmusiconline.com.

Scott, H. D. *Problems of Soviet Literature: Reports and Speeches at the First Soviet Writers' Congress*. New York: International Publishers, 1935.

Zoltán Kodály, Solo Sonata in B Minor, Op. 8

Geeting, Joyce. *Janos Starker "King of Cellists": The Making of an Artist*. Los Angeles: Chamber Music Plus Publishing, 2008.

Kodály, Zoltán. "What Is Hungarian in Music?" In *The Selected Writings of Zoltán Kodály*. Edited by Ferenc Bonis. London: Boosey & Hawkes, 1964, 28–33.

Kertész Wilkinson, Irén, "Hungary: Instrumental Music." *Grove Music Online*. Edited by Deane Root. http://oxfordmusiconline.com.

Lin, Min-Yuan. "The Treatment of the Cello in Kodály's Sonata for Unaccompanied Violoncello, Opus 8." DMA diss., Boston University, 1995.

György Ligeti, Solo Sonata (1948/1953)

Dwyer, Benjamin. "Transformational Ostinati in György Ligeti's Sonatas for Solo Cello and Solo Viola." In *György Ligeti: Of Foreign Lands and Strange Sounds*, edited by Louise Duchesneau and Wolfgang Mark, 19–50. Rochester, New York: Boydell Press, 2011.

Griffiths, Paul. "Ligeti, György." *Grove Music Online*. Edited by Deane Root. http://oxfordmusiconline.com.

Paul, Steven. "A Tale of Two Movements." Liner notes to *Suites and Sonatas for Solo Cello*. Matt Haimovitz. Recorded 1991. Deutsche Grammophon 431 813-2. Compact disc.

Steinitz, Richard. *György Ligeti: Music of the Imagination*. Boston, MA: Northeastern University Press, 2003.

Sofia Gubaidulina, *Ten Preludes* (1974)

Biber, Julia A. "Ten Etudes for Solo Cello by Sofia Gubaidulina." DMA diss., City University of New York, 2016.

Gubaidulina, Sofia. *10 Präludien für Violoncello Solo*. Hamburg: Musikverlag Hans Sikorski, 1979.

Kurtz, Michael. *Sofia Gubaidulina: A Biography*. Translated by Christoph K. Lohmann. Bloomington and Indianapolis: Indiana University Press, 2007.

Lukomsky, Vera. "The Eucharist in My Fantasy: Interview with Sofia Gubaidulina." *Tempo* no. 206 (September 1998): 29–35.

Arvo Pärt, *Spiegel im Spiegel* (1978)

Brauneiss, Leopold. "Musical Archetypes: The Basic Elements of the Tintinnabuli Style." In *The Cambridge Companion to Arvo Pärt*. Edited by Andrew Shenton, 49–75. Cambridge: Cambridge University Press, 2012.

Hillier, Paul. *Arvo Pärt*. Oxford and New York: Oxford University Press, 1997.

Huizenga, Thomas. "The Silence and Awe of Arvo Pärt." Interview for National Public Radio Classical, June 2, 2014. https://www.npr.org/sections/deceptivecadence/2014/06/02/316322238/the-silence-and-awe-of-arvo-p-rt.

Kähler, Andreas. "Radiating From Silence. The Works of Arvo Pärt Seen Through a Musician's Eyes." https://www.arvopart.ee/en/arvo-part/article/radiating-from-silence. Accessed January 2, 2023.

Lubow, Arthur. "The Sound of Spirit." *New York Times*, October 15, 2010. https://www.nytimes.com/2010/10/17/magazine/17part-t.html.

Shenton, Andrew, ed. *The Cambridge Companion to Arvo Pärt*. Cambridge: Cambridge University Press, 2012.

John Tavener, *The Protecting Veil* (1988)

Orthodox Church in America. "The Protection of Our Most Holy Lady the Mother of God and Ever-Virgin Mary." https://www.oca.org/saints/lives/2000/10/01/102824-the-protection-of-our-most-holy-lady-the-mother-of-god-and-ever. Accessed January 2, 2023.

Moody, Ivan. "Tavener, Sir John." *Grove Music Online*. Edited by Deane Root. http://oxfordmusiconline.com.

Stewart, Michael. "A Voice in the Wilderness." *Gramophone* (March 1992): 28–30.

Tavener, John. "Christian Values in Music." In *Christian Values*, edited by Edward Stourton and Frances Gumley, 117–130. London: Hodder & Stoughton, 1996.

Benjamin Britten, Suite No. 1, Op. 72

Britten, Benjamin. "England and the Folk-Art Problem." *Modern Music* 18 (1941): 71–75.

Evans, Peter. *The Music of Benjamin Britten*. 3rd ed. Oxford: Oxford University Press, 1996.

Lloyd Webber, Julian. "The Cello Music of Benjamin Britten." *The Strad* 86 (September 1975): 387–391.

Roseberry, Eric. "The Solo Chamber Music." In *The Britten Companion*, edited by Christopher Palmer, 375–382. Cambridge: Cambridge University Press, 1984.

Taggart, Mark Alan. "An Analysis of Suite for Cello, Op. 72, and Second Suite for Cello, Op. 80, by Benjamin Britten." PhD diss., Cornell University, 1983.

Coleridge-Taylor Perkinson, *Lamentations: Black/Folk Song Suite* (1973)

Carpenter, Delores, and Nolan E. Williams, Jr. *African American Heritage Hymnal: 575 Hymns, Spirituals, and Gospel Songs*. Chicago, IL: GIA Publications, 2001.

Crawford, Richard. "Fuging-tune." *Grove Music Online*. Edited by Deane Root. http://oxfordmusiconline.com.

Handy, D. Antoinette. *Black Conductors*. Metuchen, NJ, and London: The Scarecrow Press, 1995.

Weinstein, Gregory. Liner notes for *Coleridge-Taylor Perkinson (1932–2004: A Celebration*. Chicago Sinfonietta, Paul Freeman, New Black Music Repertoire Ensemble Quartet. Recorded 2005. Cedille Records CDR 90000 087. Compact disc.

Bright Sheng, Seven Tunes Heard in China (1995)

Chang, Peter. "Bright Sheng's Music: An Expression of Cross-Cultural Experience—Illustrated through the Motivic, Contrapuntal and Tonal Treatment of the Chinese Folk Song *The Stream Flows*." *Contemporary Music Review* 26, nos. 5–6 (October–December 2007): 619–633.

Harper, Michelle. "An Interview with Bright Sheng." *The Journal of the International Institute* 7, no. 1 (Fall 1999). http://hdl.handle.net/2027/spo.4750978.0007.103, accessed December 30, 2022.

Kang, Chiao-Hsuan. "Understanding of Authentic Performance Practice in Bright Sheng's *Seven Tunes Heard in China* for Solo Cello." DMA diss., Louisiana State University, 2016.

Pan, Xiao-Qiang. "A Study of *Seven Tunes Heard in China* for Solo Cello by Bright Sheng." DMA diss., University of Northern Colorado, 2003.

Sheng, Bright. "Bartók, the Chinese Composer." http://www.brightsheng.com. Accessed December 30, 2022.

Sheng, Bright. "*H'un (Lacerations): In Memoriam 1966–1976* for Orchestra." *Perspectives of New Music* 33, nos. 1–2 (1995): 560–603.

Sheng, Bright. "Never Far Away." http://www.brightsheng.com. Accessed December 30, 2022.

Wong, Su Sun. "An Analysis of Five Vocal Works by Bright Sheng." DMA diss., The University of Texas at Austin, 1995.

Giovanni Sollima, *Alone* (1998)

Frey, Elinor. "We Are All (Baroque) Cellists Now: Baroque and Modern Italian Solo Cello Music in Direct Dialogue," DMA diss., McGill University, 2012.

Imam, James. "Giovanni Sollima to Embrace Intercultural Exchange at the Sounds of the Dolomites." https://bachtrack.com/fr_FR/interview-giovanni-sollima-sounds-of-the-dolomites-trentino-italy-2019. Last modified June 10, 2019.

Majcen Pliego, Katarina. "Performance Guide and Recording of Three Twenty-First-Century Compositions for Solo Cello." DMA diss., University of Northern Colorado, 2020.

Piatigorsky Festival. "About the Artists." https://piatigorskyfestival.usc.edu/artists/giovanni.sollima. Accessed March 18, 2023.

Dorothy Rudd Moore, *Dirge and Deliverance* (1971)

Duffie, Bruce. "Composer Dorothy Rudd Moore: A Conversation with Bruce Duffie" (1990). http://bruceduffie.com/moore.html.

Moore, Dorothy Rudd. *Dirge and Deliverance*. Program note for American Composers Alliance. http://composers.com/composers/dorothy-rudd-moore/dirge-and-deliverance. Accessed March 15, 2023.

Walker-Hill, Helen. *From Spirituals to Symphonies: African-American Composers and Their Music*. Westport, CT: Greenwood Press, 2002.

Mark Summer, Variations: Lo, How a Rose E'er Blooming (1995)

Grella, George J. "Turtle Island Quartet (String)." *Grove Music Online*. Edited by Deane Root. http://oxfordmusiconline.com.

Risk, Laura. "The Chop: The Diffusion of an Instrumental Technique across North Atlantic Fiddling Traditions." *Ethnomusicology* 57, no. 3 (Fall 2013): 428–454.

Summer, Mark. *Julie-O* and *Lo, How a Rose E'er Blooming*. Ann Arbor, MI: Shar Music Publications, 1997.

Turtle Island Quartet. "Our Story." http://turtleislandquartet.com/our-story. Accessed March 17, 2023.

White, Chris. "Interview with Mark Summer." Internet Cello Society website, 1997. http://cello.org/newsletter/articles/summer.htm.

Adolphus Hailstork, Theme and Variations on "Draw the Sacred Circle Closer" (2014)

Brooks, Gene. "A Conversation with Adolphus Hailstork." *The Choral Journal* 39, no. 7 (February 1999): 29–34.

Hailstork, Adolphus. *Earthrise: A Song of Healing*. New York: Carl Fischer, 2006.

Hailstork, Adolphus. *Theme and Variations on "Draw the Sacred Circle Closer"* for Solo Cello. Malvern, PA: Theodore Presser Company, 2014.

Reena Esmail, *Varsha* (2019)

Bouïssou, Madeleine. "Varsha वर्षा: Reena Esmail - Madeleine Bouïssou, cello." YouTube video, December 18, 2020. https://www.youtube.com/watch?v=RHftgjttVk8. Accessed August 14, 2022.

Dick, Alastair. "Tambūrā." *Grove Music Online*. Edited by Deane Root. http://oxfordmusiconline.com.

Esmail, Reena. "Biography." Accessed August 14, 2022. http://www.reenaesmail.com.

Esmail, Reena. Program Note to *Varsha*. https://www.reenaesmail.com/catalog-item/varsha/?hilite=varsha. Accessed August 14, 2022.

Esmail, Reena. *Varsha*. A Piece of Sky Music, 2019.

Widdess, Richard. "Rāga." *Grove Music Online*. Edited by Deane Root. http://oxfordmusiconline.com.

Index

For the benefit of digital users, indexed terms that span two pages (e.g., 52–53) may, on occasion, appear on only one of those pages

Tables are indicated by an italic *t* following the page number.

Anger, Darol, 197
Arborea, Francesco ("Francischello"), 10, 15–16
Arensky, Anton, 133

Bach, Carl Philipp Emanuel, 34
Bach, Johann Sebastian, 5, 6–9, 39–40, 58, 59, 179, 194, 200
   Art of Fugue, BWV 1080, 59, 60*f*
   Cello Suites, BWV 1007-1012, 5, 6–9, 175, 201
      Suite No. 1, BWV 1007, 177, 199, 201
      Suite No. 3, BWV 1009, 6, 7–9, 9*t*, 176, 177
      Suite No. 5, BWV 1011, 151–52, 176
      Suite No. 6, BWV 1012, 177, 181, 193
   St. John Passion, BWV 245, 33*f*, 33–34, 40–41
   St. Matthew Passion, BWV 244, 179
   Violin Sonatas and Partitas, BWV 1001–1006, 6
   Wedding Cantata, BWV 202 (*Weichet nur betrübte Well-Tempered Clavier* BWV 846–93, 6, 7, 165 Schatten"), 8
Baillot, Pierre, 21
Balakrishnan, David, 197
Barber, Samuel, 139–42
   Adagio for Strings, Op. 11, 139
   Cello Sonata, Op. 6, 139–42, 143*t*
   Dover Beach, Op. 3, 139, 141
Barjansky, Alexandre, 111
Barjansky, Catherine, 111
Barrière, Jean-Baptiste, 14
   Sonatas for cello and basso continuo, *Livres I-IV*, 16
      Sonata IV in G major from *Livre IV*, 16, 17*t*, 17*t*, 18*t*
Bartók, Béla, 110, 139, 151, 155, 156–57, 183–84
   String Quartet No. 1, Sz. 40, 156–57
Basilica di San Marco, Venice, 10

Basilica di San Petronio, Bologna, 3–4
Beethoven, Ludwig van, 32–35, 39–40, 43–44, 49, 53, 55, 59, 69, 200, 201
   Cello Sonata, Op. 5, No. 2, 54–55
   Cello Sonata, Op. 69, 32–35, 34*f*, 36*t*, 41*f*
   Cello Sonata, Op. 102, No. 1, 40–41, 45
   Cello Sonata, Op. 102, No. 2, 45, 58, 59
   Choral Fantasy, Op. 80, 32
   Heiligenstadt Testament, 33–34
   Piano Sonata No. 8, Op. 13 ("Pathétique"), 137
   Piano Sonata No. 14, Op. 27, No. 2 ("Moonlight"), 39–40, 167
   Piano Trios, Op. 70, 32
   String Quartets Op. 59, Nos. 1-3 ("Razumovsky"), 32
   String Quartet Op. 59, No. 1, 35, 40
   Symphony No. 3 in E-flat major, Op. 55 ("Eroica"), 32, 124
   Symphony No. 5 in C minor, Op. 67, 32
   Symphony No. 6 in F major, Op. 68, 32
Berlioz, Hector, 69
Bernstein, Leonard, 183–84
Berteau, Martin, 14, 15–16
Bizet, Georges, 74
   Carmen (1873-4), 74
Bloch, Ernest, 110–13
   Cello Suites (1956-57), 175
   "Jewish Cycle" (*Prelude, Two Psalms, Israel, Three Jewish Poems, Psalm 22, Schelomo*), 110–11
   Jezebel (unfinished), 110–11
   Schelomo (1915-16), 110–13, 114*t*, 115*t*, 116*t*
Boccherini, Leopoldo, 21
Boccherini, Luigi, 21–23
   Cello Sonata in A major, G. 4, 21–23, 24*t*, 24*t*, 24*t*
   "Se d'un amore tiranno," G. 557, 22
Bockmühl, Robert, 92

Boëllmann, Léon, 56
Boismortier, Joseph Bodin de, 15
Bononcini, Antonio Maria, 10
Bononcini, Giovanni, 10
Boulanger, Nadia, 78, 193, 200
Brahms, Johannes, 35, 53–60, 62–63, 106, 117, 139, 183–84
    Cello Sonata No. 1, Op. 38, 58–60, 61*t*, 64
    Cello Sonata No. 2, Op. 99, 60
    Horn Trio, Op. 40, 58
    Piano Quartet No. 1, Op. 25, 58
    Piano Quartet No. 2, Op. 26, 58
    Piano Quintet, Op. 36, 58
    String Sextet No. 1, Op. 18, 58
    String Sextet No. 2, Op. 36, 58
Brandukov, Anatoly, 97–98, 133
Britten, Benjamin, 175–77
    Cello Suite No. 1, Op. 72, 175–77, 176*f*, 178*t*
Brown, David, 97
Burney, Charles, 10

Caldara, Antonio, 10
Carnegie Hall, 113
Casals, Pablo, 75
Cazzati, Maurizio, 3–4
Čermáková, Anna, 102
Čermáková, Josefína, 102, 104
Charpentier, Marc-Antoine, 69
Chernaik, Judith, 91
Chopin, Frédéric, 49–51, 134–35
    Cello Sonata, Op. 65, 49–51, 52*t*, 54–55, 134–35
    Grand Duo Concertant (1832), 49
    Introduction et Polonaise Brillante, Op. 3, 49
Chou, Wen-Chung, 183–84, 193
Cleveland Institute of Music, 197
Cole, Orlando, 140, 142
Coleridge-Taylor, Samuel, 179
Colombi, Giuseppe, 6
Copland, Aaron, 139
Corelli, Arcangelo, 7, 11, 14–15, 16, 188–89
    Trio Sonata Op. 5, No. 3, 7
Corrette, Michel, 15–16
Couperin, François, 14–15, 96–97
Cristiani, Lisa, 43–44
Cui, César, 133
Curtis Institute of Music, 139

Dahl, Nikolai, 134
Debussy, Claude, 78, 81–83, 110
    Berceuse héroïque (1914), 81
    Cello Sonata (1915), 81–83, 84*t*, 84*t*, 85*t*, 176–77
    Allusions to *Ein' feste Burg ist unser Gott*, 81–82, 82*f*, 83
    Allusions to *La Marseillaise*, 81, 82*f*, 83
    En blanc et noir (1915), 81
    Ode à la France (1916–17), 81
Dénes, Vera, 156, 157
Dotzauer, Johann Justus Friedrich, 90, 175
du Pré, Jacqueline, 119
Dvořák, Antonín, 101–6, 117
    Cello Concerto, Op. 104, 101–6, 107*t*, 108*t*, 109*t*
    Klid, Op. 68, 101
    "Leave Me Alone" ("Kéž duch můj sám") from *4 Lieder,* Op. 82, 102, 103*f*, 104
    Rondo, Op. 94, 101
    String Quartet No. 12, Op. 96 ("American"), 102
    Symphony No. 9, Op. 95 ("From the New World"), 102

Elgar, Edward, 62, 106, 117–19
    Cello Concerto, Op. 85, 117–19, 120*t*, 121*t*, 177
    Dream of Gerontius, Op. 38, 119
    Falstaff, Op. 68, 118
    Pomp and Circumstance March No. 1, Op. 39, 117
Ertmann, Baroness Dorothea, 35
Esmail, Reena, 204–6
    Varsha (2019), 204–6, 206*t*

Farrenc, Aristide, 53
Farrenc, Louise, 35, 53–56
    Air russe varié, Op. 17, 53–54
    Cello Sonata, Op. 46, 53, 54–56, 57*t*
    Nonet, Op. 38, 54
Fauré, Gabriel, 69–79
    Après un rêve, Op. 7, 78
    Cello Sonata, Op. 109, 79
    Cello Sonata, Op. 117, 79
    Élégie, Op. 24, 78–79, 80*t*
    Papillon, Op. 77, 79
    Piano Quartet No. 1, Op. 15, 78
    Requiem, Op. 48, 78
    Romance, Op. 69, 79
    Sicilienne, Op. 78, 79
Fax, Mark Oakland,, 193
Feuillard, Louis, 175
Fischer, Adolf, 75
Fitzenhagen, Wilhelm, 97–99
Forberg, Friedrich Wilhelm, 92
Forqueray, Antoine, 14, 15
Franceschini, Petronio, 3–4

Franchomme, Auguste, 49, 51, 54–55
　Co-composition with Chopin of *Grand Duo
　　Concertant* (1832), 49
Frescobaldi, Domenico, 4–5

Gabrielli, Domenico, 3–5, 6, 10
　7 Ricercare for unaccompanied cello, 4–5
　　Ricercar No. 2, 5, 5*t*
　Sonatas for cello and basso continuo, 4–5
Galli, Domenico, 6
Gänsbacher, Josef, 60
Gatti, Guido, 113
Gibbs, Alan, 81–82
Glazunov, Alexander, 133
Göbl, Alois, 102
Gorky, Maxim, 147
Grieg, Edvard, 63, 134
Grützmacher, Friedrich, 97–98
Gubaidulina, Sofia, 159–61
　Canticle of the Sun (1997), 161
　In Croce (1979), 161
　Quaternion (1996), 161
　Seven Words (1982), 161
　Ten Preludes (1974), 159–61, 162*t*

Hailstork, Adolphus, 175, 200–2
　Earthrise (2006), 200, 201
　Solo Cello Sonata (2015), 175, 201
　*Theme and Variations on "Draw the Sacred
　　Circle Closer"* (2014), 201–2, 203*t*
Hallé, Charles, 51
Harlem Renaissance, 193
Harrison, Beatrice, 119
Hausmann, Robert, 60, 106
Haydn, Franz Joseph, 26–28, 32
　Cello Concerto in C Major, Hob. VIIb:1,
　　26–28, 27*f*, 27*f*
　Cello Concerto in D Major, Hob. VIIb:2,
　　26–28, 35, 90
　Destatevi o miei fidi (cantata), Hob. XXIVa:2,
　　26, 27*f*
　Seven Last Words of Our Savior on the Cross,
　　Op. 51, 204, 205
Hensel, Fanny (born Mendelssohn-Bartholdy),
　34, 35, 39–41
　Capriccio, 39, 40–41, 41*f*, 42*t*
　Ostersonate (Easter Sonata), 39
　Sonata o Fantasia, 39–40, 42*t*, 43
Hensel, Wilhelm, 39
Herbert, Victor, 101–2
Herzogenberg, Heinrich von, 62
Hofmann, Josef, 139
Howard University, 200

Hummel, Johann Nepomuk, 43, 53–54

Isserlis, Steven, 169
Istomin, Sergei, 99

Jacchini, Giuseppe, 10
Jaëll, Marie, 56
Juilliard School, 204–5
　Juilliard 415 ensemble, 204
Jurgenson, Pyotr, 98

Kang, Chiao-Hsuan, 186
Kerpely, Jenő, 151
Khachaturian, Aram, 145–46
Klengel, Julius, 63, 64
Kodály, Zoltán, 117, 151–53, 155, 200
　Capriccio (1915), 151
　Cello Sonata, Op. 4, 151, 154*t*
　Cello Sonatina (1909), 151
　Duo, Op. 7, 151
　Solo Cello Sonata, Op. 8, 151–53, 154*t*
Kraft, Antonín, 35
Kraft, Nicolaus, 35
Kubatsky, Victor, 98
Kummer, Friedrich August, 90, 175

Lalo, Édouard, 69, 73–75
　Cello Concerto (1877), 73, 74–75, 76*t*,
　　77*t*, 77*t*
　Symphonie espagnole, Op. 21, 73–74
　Violin Concerto, Op. 20, 73–74
Lanzetti, Salvatore, 14–15, 16
Le Blanc, Hubert, 15
Lebouc, Charles, 55
Leipzig Conservatorium, 62
Ligeti, György, 155–57
　Solo Cello Sonata (1948/1953), 155–57, 158*t*
Lincoln Center, 193
Lipscomb, Ronald, 179
Liszt, Franz, 69, 133
Liven, Princess Alexandra, 134
Lloyd Webber, Julian, 177
Lockwood, Lewis, 32–33
Loëb, Jules, 78
Lully, Jean-Baptiste, 69

Ma, Yo-Yo, 186, 188
MacDonald, Malcolm, 124–25
Mahler, Gustav, 125
　Das Lied von der Erde (1908-9), 125
Malloy, Dave, 134
Manfredi, Filippo, 22
Manhattan School of Music, 200

Mannes School of Music, 113
Marais, Marin, 14
Marcello, Benedetto, 15
Mendelssohn-Bartholdy, Abraham, 39
Mendelssohn-Bartholdy, Felix, 34, 35, 39, 43–45, 134
   Assai tranquillo (1835), 43–44
   Cello Concerto (lost), 43–44, 90
   Cello Sonata No. 1, Op. 45, 43–44, 54–55
   Cello Sonata No. 2, Op. 58, 43–45, 46*t*, 47*t*, 47*t*, 48*t*
   Lied ohne Worte, Op. 109, 43–44
   "Mendelssohn-Merk" variations, 43–44
   Midsummer Night's Dream, Op. 61, 44–45
   Piano Concerto, Op. 40, 45
   Symphony No. 3, Op. 56 ("Scottish"), 44
   Symphony No. 5, Op. 107 ("Reformation"), 45
   Variations Concertantes, Op. 17, 43–44
   Violin Concerto, Op. 64, 90
Mendelssohn-Bartholdy, Paul, 39, 43–44
Menotti, Gian Carlo, 140
Merk, Joseph, 43–44, 49
Merulo, Claudio, 4–5
Messiaen, Olivier, 167
   Louange à L'eternité de Jesus from *Quatuor pour la fin du temps* (1941), 167
Meyerbeer, Giacomo, 49
Miaskovsky, Nikolai, 145–46
Micheletti, André, 11
Michigan State University, 200
Moore, Dorothy Rudd, 193–95
   Baroque Suite (1964), 193
   From the Dark Tower (1970), 193, 194
   Dirge and Deliverance (1971), 193–95, 194*f*, 196*t*
Moore, Kermit, 193
Moore, Laurie, 197
Morrison, Simon, 147
Moscheles, Ignaz, 45
Moscow Conservatory, 145
Moskovitz, Marc D., 35
Mozart, Franz Xaver Wolfgang, 43
Mozart, Wolfgang Amadeus, 32, 34, 96
Müller, Wilhelm, 50
Mussorgsky, Modest, 110, 124–25, 176*f*
   Pictures at an Exhibition (1874), 176*f*
   Songs and Dances of Death (1870s), 124–25

Norfolk State University, 200

Onslow, George, 43
Ospedale della Pietà, Venice, 10

Paganini, Niccolò, 156
Paris Conservatoire, 54, 78
Pärt, Arvo, 165–67
   Credo (1968), 165
   Fratres (1977), 166
   Für Alina (1976), 166
   Nekrolog (1960), 165
   Pro et Contra (1966), 165
   Spiegel im Spiegel (1978), 166–67, 168*t*
   Tabula Rasa (1977)
   Tintinnabuli technique, 166
Pellicia, Clementina, 22
Perkinson, Coleridge-Taylor, 179–81
   Lamentations: Black/Folk Song Suite (1973), 179–81, 182*t*
Perle, George, 183–84
Piatigorsky, Gregor, 142
Piatti, Alfredo, 43–44, 175
Popper, David, 64, 152, 153, 175
   Tarantella, Op. 33, 64
Praetorius, Michael, 198
Prokofiev, Lina, 145–46
Prokofiev, Sergei, 123–24, 144–47
   Cello Concerto, Op. 58, 145
   Cello Sonata, Op. 119, 144, 145–47, 148*t*
   Scythian Suite, Op. 20, 144
   Symphony-Concerto, Op. 125, 123–24, 125
Pulkert, Oldřich, 28

Raag (*rāga*), 204, 205–6
   Malhaar family of *raags*, 204, 205–6
Rachmaninoff, Serge, 133–37, 139, 144
   Cello Sonata, Op. 19, 133, 134–37, 138*t*
   Piano Concerto No. 2, Op. 18, 134
   The Rock, Op. 7, 133
   Symphony No. 1, Op. 13, 133
Rameau, Jean-Philippe, 69, 82, 96–97
   Les fêtes de Polymnie (1745), 82
Ravel, Maurice, 78
Reger, Max, 151, 175
   Cello Suites, Op. 131c, 151, 175
Reicha, Anton, 53
Reimers, Christian, 92
Reinecke, Carl, 62
Reynolds, Christopher Alan, 33–34
Richter, Sviatoslav, 147
Rietz, Julius, 43–44, 45
Roeder, Michael Thomas, 102
Romberg, Bernhard, 54–55, 58, 90
   Cello Sonata, Op. 43, No. 1, 54–55
Röntgen, Julius, 63
Rosoor, Louis, 83
Rostropovich, Mstislav, 123–24, 145, 146, 147

Saint-Saëns, Camille, 56, 69–70, 78, 133
  Allegro Appassionato, Op. 43, 70
  Carnival of the Animals (1886), 70
    "The Swan," 70
  Cello Concerto No. 1, Op. 33, 69–70, 71*t*, 124
  Cello Concerto No. 2, Op. 119, 70
  Cello Sonata No. 1, Op. 32, 70
  Cello Sonata No. 2, Op. 123, 70
  Romance, Op. 36, 70
  Romance, Op. 67, 70
  Suite, Op. 16, 70
Salmond, Felix, 119, 142
Sand, George, 49
Sarasate, Pablo de, 73–74
Scalero, Rosario, 139, 140
Scarlatti, Alessandro, 188–89
Schiffer, Adolf, 153
Schillings, Max von, 110
Schoenberg, Arnold, 83, 139, 145
Schubert, Franz, 39–40, 49, 50, 53–54, 193
  Arpeggione Sonata, D. 821, 63
  Erlkönig, D. 328, 136*f*, 136–37, 194–95
  Fantasie, D. 934, 39–40
  Piano Quintet, D. 667 ("Trout"), 53–54
  Wanderer Fantasy, D. 760, 39–40
  Winterreise, D. 911, 50
Schumann, Clara, 63, 90, 91, 92
  Piano Concerto, Op. 7, 91
Schumann, Robert, 34, 53–54, 59, 117
  Adagio and Allegro, Op. 70, 89
  Cello Concerto, Op. 129, 69–92, 93*t*, 94*t*, 95*t*, 118
  3 Fantasiestücke, Op. 73, 89
  Frauenliebe und -leben, Op. 42, 91
  6 Lieder, Op. 90, 90
  Konzertstück for four horns and orchestra, Op. 86, 90
  Konzertstück for piano and orchestra, Op. 92, 90
  Piano Concerto, Op. 54, 89, 90*f*
  Piano Quartet, Op. 47, 89
  Piano Quintet, Op. 44, 89
  Romances (destroyed), 92
  5 Stücke im Volkston, Op. 102, 89
Seaton, Douglass, 44–45
Selfridge-Field, Eleanor, 10–11
Shanghai Conservatory of Music, 183–84
Shaw, George Bernard, 62–63
Sheng, Bright, 183–86
  Seven Tunes Heard in China (1995), 183, 184–86, 187*t*
Shostakovich, Dmitri, 92, 144, 145–46, 200, 202
  Cello Concerto No. 1, Op. 107, 123–26, 126*f*, 127*t*, 128*t*, 128*t*, 129*t*, 202
    Quotation of "Suliko," 125, 126*f*
  Cello Concerto No. 2, Op. 126, 123–24
  Lady Macbeth of Mtsensk, Op. 29, 144
  String Quartet No. 8, Op. 110
  Symphony No. 10, Op. 93, 124
  Young Guard (film score, 948), 124
Shostakovich, Nina, 123–24
Sibelius, Jean, 139
Silva, Luigi, 142
Simrock, Fritz, 105*f*
Sitār, 204–5
Smith, Peter H., 92
Smyth, Ethel, 62–64
  Cello Sonata No. 1 (1880), 63
  Cello Sonata No. 2, Op. 5, 61*t*, 62, 63–64, 65*t*, 66*t*
  March for the Women (1910), 63
  The Wreckers (1902-04), 63
Société nationale de musique, 69, 73–74
Sollima, Giovanni, 188–89
  Alone (1998), 189, 190*t*
  La Folia (2007), 188–89
  Lamentatio (2000), 188–89
Stalin, Joseph, 123, 125
Starker, János, 153
Steinberg, Michael, 125
Strauss, Richard, 139
Stravinsky, Igor, 110, 139, 144, 183–84
  Rite of Spring, The, 144
Sullivan, Arthur, 63
Summer, Mark, 197–99
  Julie-O (1988), 197–98
  Variations: Lo, How a Rose E'er Blooming (1995), 198–99, 199*t*

Tambūrā, 204–5
Taneyev, Sergei, 96, 133
Tavener, John, 169–71
  The Protecting Veil (1988), 169–71, 172*t*
Tchaikovsky, Pyotr Ilich, 63, 96–99, 100*t*, 133
  Variations on a Rococo Theme, Op. 33, 96–99
Teixeira da Silva, William, 11
Todd, R. Larry, 35
Tolbecque, Auguste, 70
Tolstoy, Leo, 134
Tonkha, Vladimir, 159, 161
Tovey, Donald, 103
Trowbridge, William, 110
Tunbridge, Laura, 92
Turtle Island String Quartet, 197–98

Vandini, Antonio, 10
Verdi, Giuseppe, 200

Viola da gamba, 6, 14, 15–16, 33
Virány, Annuss, 155–56
Vitali, Giovanni Battisti, 3–4
Vivaldi, Antonio, 5, 6, 10–12, 15,
    188–89
  Cello Sonatas Op. 14, 10–11
    Cello Sonata, RV 46 (Op. 14, No. 6),
      11–12, 12*t*, 12*t*, 13*t*, 13*t*

Wagner, Richard, 110, 117
Weigl, Joseph, 26, 28
Welsh, Moray, 81–82
Wihan, Hanuš, 101, 104–5, 106

Yale University, 204–5

Zhdanov, Andrei, 144–45, 146

www.ingramcontent.com/pod-product-compliance
Ingram Content Group UK Ltd.
Pitfield, Milton Keynes, MK11 3LW, UK
UKHW020427170226
468114UK00021B/230